THE LAWS
OF SOFTWARE
PROCESS

A New Model
for the
Production and
Management
of Software

CRC Press
Taylor & Francis Group
Boca Raton London New York

CRC Press is an imprint of the
Taylor & Francis Group, an **informa** business
AN AUERBACH BOOK

THE LAWS OF SOFTWARE PROCESS

A New Model for the Production and Management of Software

CRC Press
Taylor & Francis Group
6000 Broken Sound Parkway NW, Suite 300
Boca Raton, FL 33487-2742

ISBN: 9780849314896 (hbk)

Visit the Taylor & Francis Web site at
http://www.taylorandfrancis.com

and the CRC Press Web site at
http://www.crcpress.com

Library of Congress Cataloging-in-Publication Data

Armour, Philip G.
   The laws of software process : a new model for the production and management of software / Philip G. Armour.
      p. cm.
      ISBN 0-8493-1489-5 (alk. paper)
      1. Software engineering. I. Title.

QA76.758.A75 2003
005.1--dc21

2003052459

Contents

Preface xv

1 **The Nature of Software and the Laws of Software Process** 1
A Brief History of Knowledge 1
The Characteristics of Knowledge-Storage Media 3
The Nature of Software Development 4
The Laws of Software Process 5
The Five Orders of Ignorance 8
The Laws of Software Process 10
The First Law of Software Process 11
The Corollary to the First Law of Software Process 11
Explanation and Observations 11
The Reflexive Creation of Systems and Processes 11
Explanation and Observations 12
The Lemma of Eternal Lateness 12
Explanation and Observations 12
The Second Law of Software Process
(see also The Rule of Process Bifurcation) 13
Explanation and Observations 13
The Rule of Process Bifurcation 13
Explanation and Observations 13
The Dual Hypotheses of Knowledge Discovery 13
Explanation and Observations 14
Armour's Observation on Software Process 14
Explanation and Observations 14
The Third Law of Software Process (also known as the Footwear
Manufacturer's Minor Dependent's Law) 15
Explanation and Observations 15
The Twin Goals of Optimal Termination 15
Explanation and Observations 15
Summary 16

2 **The Purpose of Process** 19
Types of Teams 20
Tactical 20

Problem Solving 21
Creative 22
Learning. 22
Software Teams Are All Types at the Same Time 23
A Range of Unknowns, a Range of Processes 24
Inventing Processes 25
The Purpose of Process 26
The Problems of Process 27
The Usefulness Dilemma 27
The Process Value Paradox. 30
Using Systems to Build Processes 32
Other Problems with Process 33
How Do We Get Process? 33
Who Devises Processes?. 34
Where Do We Put Process?. 35
The Purpose of Process 36
Summary 36

3   **The Meaning of Methodology** **39**
Third Order of Ignorance Processes. 40
The Job of Methodology. 42
A Test System. 43
The Maturity of Testing 48
Summary 48

4   **The Logic of Life Cycles** **51**
The Assembly Line 51
Shooting Down Zeppelins. 57
Shooting Down Jet Planes 60
The True Life Cycle. 62
A More-Complex, Generalized Model 67
Range of Unknown Unknowns. 67
Knowledge Variability with Time 67
Design Dependence of Knowledge 68
Variable Rate of Learning. 69
All Variables. 70
Summary 71

5   **Of Methods and Models and Minds.** **73**
Models of Convention. 73
Models of Numbers. 75
Counting. 77
Chunking. 79
The Physical Nature of Models 85
The Logical Nature of Models 88

Map onto Problem and Solution Space 90
   Requirements 91
   Interfaces. 93
Methods and Models 93
Minds 94
Summary 95

6 The Advent of Agile 97
It Has always Been Agile 97
   Test Phases with Embedded Life Cycles and Test Phases 99
   The "Construct Phases" also Have Feedback. 100
   The Feedback Activities Generate Feedback Activities 101
The Problems of "Big" Process 102
Agile Methods 104
   Change Is Expected 104
   Feedback Is Managed. 104
   Stepwise Development 104
   Human Factors 105
   Customer-Centric. 106
   Agile Is Event Driven 106
Extreme Programming (XP). 109
   The Planning Game 109
   Small Releases 110
   The Use of Metaphor 110
   Simple Design 110
   Refactoring 111
   Testing 112
   Pair Programming. 113
   Collective Ownership. 114
   Continuous Integration 114
   Intentionally Limited Work Week 114
   On-Site Customer 114
   Coding Standards 115
Code Science 115
Crystal Methods 116
   Crystal Clear 117
Scrum 118
   Pre-Sprint 118
   The Sprint 119
   Post-Sprint. 119
Dynamic Systems Development Method (DSDM). 119
   DSDM Occurs in a Collaborative Environment between
   All Stakeholders 120
Feature-Driven Development (FDD) 121

Lean Development 122
Adaptive Software Development (ASD) 123
  Speculate 124
  Collaborate 124
  Learn 125
Why Agile? Why Now? 125
Summary 133

7 Agile and the Orders of Ignorance 135
Agile and the Orders of Ignorance 136
Subdividing the Orders of Ignorance 138
  Zeroth Order Ignorance (0OI): I have 0OI when I (provably)
  know something ... That is, I have the answer 139
    0OI — Fully Factored Knowledge: The Self-Actualized
    Answer. 139
    1/3OI — Applying the Factoring Knowledge: Switch It on.... 140
    2/3OI — Get the Factoring Knowledge: How to Switch It on.. 140
  First Order Ignorance (1OI): I have 1OI when I do not know
  something 140
    1OI: We've Got the Question, Now Get the Answer:
    Just Gimme the Facts. 141
    1.1/3OI: We've Got the Question but How to Get the Answer:
    Who to Ask? 141
    1.2/3OI: We've Kind of Got the Question but Where's the
    Ballpark? 141
  Second Order Ignorance (2OI): I Have 2OI When I Don't Know
  That I Don't Know Something 141
    2OI — General, Unintentional Lack of Awareness:
    Maybe We Don't Know. 142
    2.1/3OI — Nonculpable Lack of Awareness: Blissful
    Ignorance. 142
  Third Order Ignorance: Lack of Process 143
    3OI: General Lack of Process. 143
    3.1/3OI: Unintentional Process Ignorance. 143
    3.2/3OI: Intentional Process Ignorance. 143
  Fourth Order Ignorance: Meta-Ignorance 144
Agile and Zeroth Order Ignorance 145
  Identical Repetition 148
  Minor Variation 148
  Major Variation 149
  Contextual Variation. 149
    Operational Variation 149
Agile and First Order Ignorance 151
Agile and Second Order Ignorance 153

Agile and Third Order Ignorance 153
Agile and the Fourth Order of Ignorance. 157
Summary 159

8   The Future of Software Development 161
The Execution of Knowledge. 162
The Demise of "Software Engineering". 163
The End of Code 166
The Death of CASE, the Death of Method 169
The Incubator of Knowledge Engineering 172
   Model Based 172
   Anthropomorphic Models. 173
   Programmable Interface 174
   Variable Rule Based 176
   Executable. 176
   Translatable 177
   Domain Specific 179
   Object Oriented 180
   Domain Variable 180
   Domain Interdependent. 180
   Model Interdependent 180
   Meta-Models and Meta-Languages. 181
   A Radically Different Project Setup 181
Software Development as an Educational Activity. 187
   How Do We Train People? 189
   Levels of Learning 190
   How Do We Learn Most Efficiently for this System? 191
   Controlled Failure. 193
The Project. 194
   Praveen's Morning 195
   Mayank's Morning 196
   Hafsa's Morning 198
   Maria's Morning 199
   Jill's Morning. 200
   The Meeting 201
Summary 203

Appendix A: The Five Knowledge Storage Media 205
Knowledge 205
A Brief History of Knowledge Storage 208
   DNA 208
   Brains. 210
   Hardware 210
   Books 213
   Software. 213

The Characteristics of the Knowledge Storage Media 215
    DNA. 217
        Persistency 217
        Update Frequency 218
        Intentionality 218
        Self-Modification. 218
        Modify Surroundings 218
    Brain. 219
        Persistency 219
        Update Frequency 219
        Intentionality 219
        Self-Modification. 219
        Modify Surroundings 219
    Hardware Design. 219
        Persistency 219
        Update Frequency 220
        Intentionality 220
        Self-Modification. 220
        Modify Surroundings 220
    Books 220
        Persistency 220
        Update Frequency 220
        Intentionality 221
        Self-Modification. 221
        Modify Surroundings 221
    Software 221
        Persistency 221
        Update Frequency 221
        Intentionality 221
        Self-Modification. 221
        Modify Surroundings 222
    Building on Knowledge. 222
    Brains, Books, and Software 223
    Summary 225

Appendix B: The Five Orders of Ignorance 227
    A Walk in the Woods 232
    A Path Less Traveled 233
    Tracks 233
    Prototyping 234
    The Expectation of Product. 235
    Kinds of Knowledge 235
    The Five Orders of Ignorance 236
        Zeroth Order Ignorance (0OI): Lack of Ignorance 236

First Order Ignorance (1OI): Lack of Knowledge 236
Second Order Ignorance (2OI): Lack of Awareness 236
Third Order Ignorance (3OI): Lack of Process 237
Fourth Order Ignorance (4OI): Meta Ignorance 237
The Five Orders of Ignorance in Systems Development 237
    0OI 238
    1OI 238
    2OI 238
    3OI 238
    4OI 239
The 3OI Cycle 239
The Inability to Measure Knowledge 241
Summary 242

Index **245**

About the Author

Philip Armour is a vice president and senior consultant at Corvus International, Inc., a consulting company that integrates software development and psychology. He has been in the software field for over three decades, and has developed applications in many areas, including steelworks, retail businesses, for a government research laboratory, in telecommunications, and for a major airline. At various times, Mr. Armour has been a programmer, a manager, a database administrator, a process engineer, a consultant, and an educator. As a master instructor at Motorola's Corporate University, as a consultant to many companies, and as external faculty at Lake Forest Graduate School and the University of Notre Dame, he has taught software development principles to tens of thousands of engineers, developers, managers, and executives. Mr. Armour is a contributing editor for the Association for Computing Machinery's flagship periodical *Communications of the ACM,* writing a regular column entitled "The Business of Software." He has a degree in physics and pure mathematics from the University of Sheffield, England, and is a member of IEEE, ACM, and PMI.

Preface

Knowledge, if it does not determine action, is dead...

— *1st Ennead*, Plotinus, 205–270 C.E.

Software is knowledge.

I have spent over 30 years in software — all my professional life. In some ways I have "grown up" with software. From it being an arcane topic known to only a few, this "artifact" has now become one of the driving engines of the modern world. From its isolation in the payroll departments of larger companies, it has become as ubiquitous as electricity. From a subject whose bibliography could be covered in a few pages, it has come to dominate acres of bookstores. From a few thousand professionals, the number of people who can now create software is in the millions. Probably no topic or subject or skill in the history of the world has accelerated in its level of practice at the rate that software has. Within one generation its use has grown from an almost obscure and esoteric subject to one of the principal sources of wealth in the world. And it is growing.

The question is why?

After nearly 20 years as a software developer, with excursions into management, database administration, and software quality and process, in the late 1980s I transitioned into an educational role. Perhaps on the principle that those who cannot do, teach; those who cannot teach, teach software engineering. With a side order of process and design consulting, for a number of years the main course was software engineering training. I have personally taught around 20,000 software engineers, managers, and quality and process staff. I have taught basic software engineering principles and complex theoretical methods.

The body of knowledge of any discipline tends to become the benchmark against which the knowledge itself is judged. As Thomas Kuhn pointed out in *The Structure of Scientific Revolutions*,* scientists spend much of their energy defending what is known, rather than the more-popular view that has them discovering what is not known. So it was with software

* Kuhn, Thomas S., *The Structure of Scientific Revolutions,* University of Chicago Press, Chicago, 1996.

and software process. I grew up with the "structured revolution," which became the accepted wisdom of the age. It, and I, morphed into the "object oriented" view that replaced structured stuff as the accepted wisdom. As I taught each variation of software "truth," I found that most people simply accept it when you are the teacher and they are the students. You are supposed to know, and they are supposed to learn. That is the model. Occasionally, however, some bright young engineer in a class would ask that most difficult of questions: *Why?* Why do we have methods and process? Why do we have life cycles, why do we have different life cycles, and why do they look the way they look? There are pat answers to these questions but underlying each seemed to be a further *"why?"* that was still unanswered. I started to suspect that the accepted-wisdom, certified answers I was giving did not satisfy these occasional questioners. Certainly they did not satisfy me. It is an axiom of teaching that it forces the teacher to look at his or her own level of understanding. I had been doing software things for many years but I felt that something, some key piece of learning, was missing from my understanding of the business.

I found the piece in 1994 while flying between Hong Kong and Los Angeles. I had bought Peter Drucker's *Post Capitalist Society* to read on the plane, and it gave me the answer. Professor Drucker talked about the knowledge economy, the advent of knowledge workers, and the likely changes in society. I started to think, *"Where do we store this knowledge?"* This was the Archimedes moment. It is not that people have not considered this before but it became clear to me in that moment that software is not a product and the software systems we build and sell are not "products" in the classical sense. They are simply containers for knowledge. The true product was not the system; it was the knowledge that went into making the system. Software was just the medium in which this knowledge was ultimately expressed. Many things flowed from this: what the *real* purpose of methods and process are, why we use different languages and which ones are "best," why we continue to have quality problems after we have spent so much energy trying to fix them, why we cannot estimate projects very well, why project management is hard to do, why programs always seem to be "90 percent complete," and many other puzzles of this profession. I started incorporating these ideas in my teaching, and found they clicked with people. Perhaps I could not give explicit answers but often I could show people why they had the questions.

In 2000 I offered the idea to the editorial staff at the Association for Computing Machinery (ACM) flagship magazine, *Communications,* as a possible choice for an article. They counter-offered with a suggestion that I write a regular column. I was, and still am, enormously honored to have such a prestigious and influential magazine regularly find space to allow me to air these ideas, and owe a debt to Diane Crawford and Bob Fox at CACM. Rich O'Hanley at Auerbach Publications was even braver in taking on the idea of publishing these concepts in book form, a task that turned out to be much harder that I thought it would be. Along the way, several people were influential in guiding me, although they may not have known it. Peter Drucker, with whom I exchanged a few letters, has provided the long view of the social and economic concept of knowledge that extends way beyond the narrow but expanding arena of software. Professor Drucker has had many well-deserved accolades heaped on him, and this may be one of the least, but I must acknowledge that pivotal moment on the flight from Hong Kong among all the other insights reading his work has given me. The idea of people at the center of systems development is also not a new idea. I owe an acknowledgment to Jerry Weinberg, whose continuous production of tremendously insightful books is the benchmark. Rich Watts, then-Director of the Worldwide Software Process Initiative at Honeywell, gave me an opportunity to create an unusual program — to teach executives the laws of software. This led to working with the brains at Honeywell's Technology Center in Minneapolis, particularly Tom Edman, Jim Krause, and Jon Krueger, who are some of the smartest people on the planet and have created, in their DOME product, the functional beginnings of the way software will be created in the future. We would not have a software crisis if we could clone a few more of these people.

John Manzo has been a constant friend and support, and, at Geneer and AgileTek, is manfully carrying on one of the best examples of these actual ideas in operation I can imagine. I am indebted to John for the insights into AgileTek's Code Science.

There were many people in the early days of Motorola's corporate University who were enormously instructive, teaching me that having the answer is sometimes less powerful than having the question. Also they were brave enough to let me in a classroom to teach when I was really just a software engineer. In terms of instruction, I learned most from the many software engineers at Motorola, Unisys, Honeywell, and other companies at which I taught. I think I learned more from them than they from me. The ideas in this book have their origins in their healthy and necessary skepticism and their challenging of accepted wisdom.

The major acknowledgment goes to my wife, Susan, and daughter, Gwyneth, who are my life. I sometimes joke that I made a great career move when I married a psychologist, because Susan's insights have been so important in my growth, both professionally and personally. She has been a constant partner in all the ways the word can be used. It was more than a good "career" move; it was the pivotal move of my life. Thank you.

Philip G. Armour
Deer Park, Illinois 2003

Chapter 1
The Nature of Software and the Laws of Software Process

Pardon him, Theodotus: he is a barbarian and thinks that the customs of his tribe and island are the laws of nature.

— **George Bernard Shaw**
Caesar and Cleopatra

Software is not a product.

Behind this simple sentence lies a whole world of behavior, radically changed business models, a fundamentally different economic reality, and a view of development methodology and software process that is quite different from the way we practice the business of software today. Today, most companies view software as a product. But it is not. Software is a medium.

A Brief History of Knowledge

About 2 billion years ago, approximately half the time our planet has been in existence, nature developed a knowledge storage mechanism that allowed species to learn and to store that knowledge in a way that could be passed on to their descendants. Instinctual knowledge is stored and transmitted in strands of deoxyribonucleic acid (DNA). DNA (see Exhibit 1) was the first knowledge-storage medium.

Between 8 and 5 million years ago, it is widely believed, the first recognizable ancestors of the human race evolved. These proto-humans possessed a concentration of nerve cells that was quantifiably different from animals around them. It allowed them to change their behavior and adapt to different situations and environments, to learn and relearn. The brain (Exhibit 2) was the second knowledge-storage medium.

Louis Leakey called early mankind "Homo Habilis" or "tool maker." The primitive tools he discovered in the Olduvai Gorge in Tanzania were made

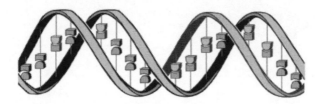

Exhibit 1. DNA: The first knowledge medium.

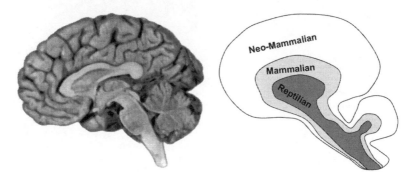

Exhibit 2. The brain: The second knowledge medium. © Wellcome Department of Imaging Neuroscience, University College, London, England. With permission.

of rocks but were more than rocks. Their makers had crafted the rocks by first selecting the types of stone with the properties needed to make cutting instruments (see Exhibit 3). They then flaked them and modified them for the particular task for which they were used. The value of the rock as a tool came mostly from the skill or knowledge of the craftsman creating it. We do not usually think of hardware as being "knowledge storage devices" but it is. The value of any tool is a direct function of the quality and quantity of knowledge that went into its making and its fitness for the use we make of it. Hardware was the third knowledge-storage medium.

The first recognizable books appeared around 3500 B.C.E. in the Middle East and were created using clay tablets. Around 2500 B.C.E., people in Western Asia wrote on animal skins and Egyptians started using papyrus to record their thoughts, instructions, transactions, and laws. But it was not until about 600 years ago with the invention of moveable type that books really started to be used in society to record, store, transmit, and reuse knowledge. Books were the fourth knowledge-storage medium.

After World War II, a number of scientists collaborated to create the earliest computers. John von Neumann is generally credited with the first statement of the concept of the stored program in 1945. The knowledge

Exhibit 3. Hand axes: Hardware, the third knowledge medium.

Exhibit 4. Comparison of properties of knowledge media.

Storage medium	Persistency in medium	Update frequency	Intentionality	Ability to self-modify	Ability to modify the outside world
DNA	Very persistent	Very slow	Low	Moderate	Quite limited
Brain	Very volatile	Very fast	High	High	Quite limited
Hardware design	Very persistent	Slow	High	Low	Limited to specific design
Books	Quite persistent	Quite slow	High	None	None
Software	Quite persistent	Fast	Quite high	High	Relatively unlimited

that goes into a computer program has the distinct characteristic that it has been made executable. Software is the fifth knowledge-storage medium.

The Characteristics of Knowledge-Storage Media

If we look at the characteristics of knowledge stored in each of the media shown in Exhibit 4 and Exhibit 5, we can see why software is becoming so universal.

From these charts we can see that knowledge stored in software has a wider range of useful characteristics than knowledge stored in other media. It is more intentional in its knowledge storage than DNA, has a

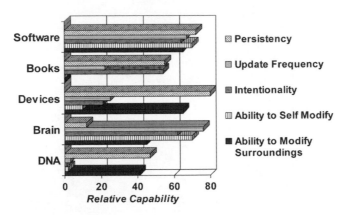

Exhibit 5. Relative capabilities of knowledge media.

greater capacity to modify itself or be modified than knowledge stored in hardware, is more persistent than knowledge stored in brains, and is infinitely more able to interact with its surroundings than knowledge in books. It is for these reasons that all of human knowledge is currently being transcribed into software.

If software is not a product, then what product do we create when we build software systems? The answer is simple — the product is not the software, it is the knowledge contained in the software.

The Nature of Software Development

If software is not a product, then software development is not a product producing activity — it cannot be. If the true product is not the software but the knowledge contained in the software, then software development can only be a knowledge acquisition activity. True, we may consider some of the software development function to be a transcription of knowledge into the executable form. This is what coding is. However, coding is only one small part of the software development activity, and it is getting smaller. We can also reasonably assert that if we already have the knowledge, then transcribing it does not require much effort. The real work occurs when we try to transcribe our knowledge and find it is incomplete. The activity then quickly changes into a search for the correct knowledge.

But software development is not usually viewed or managed as a knowledge acquisition activity. Most of our processes and our expectations in the software business are centered on the creation of a product (the delivered system). This is a quite logical view but it is also quite wrong. The creation of a functional system is not the product of the true activity of software development; it is the by-product of the activity of learning.

This can be seen using a negative example: it is quite easy to deliver a system to the customer. The challenge is not to create a system but to create the correct system. If we know exactly what it is we have to do, we can create systems as fast as our fingers can type. The real challenge is finding out what the system should do, and how we can construct a system that does it. Once we have acquired this knowledge, the creation of the system is usually quite straightforward. Of course, once we (think we) have acquired the appropriate knowledge, and go ahead and build and test the system, we invariably find out there are things we did not know. This, of course, requires further knowledge acquisition.

We can see this very clearly in the activity of testing systems. Testing of systems usually takes very little time — if we do not find out anything new. It is only in the uncovering of new knowledge that we take time. The purpose of testing is only partially to prove what we know. In reality, most of our time is spent finding out things we did not know.

The Laws of Software Process

In the 1980s, I participated in two separate "process definition" activities at the major airline where I was then employed. For the first endeavor about a dozen of us were locked up in the company's training center, chartered with the task of attempting to define just how the computer department would create software. After several months of diligent labor, we proudly unveiled our process definition.

It was very big.

Occupying three large ring-binders, it described, sometimes in exquisite detail, exactly all the steps we thought necessary to create functional software.

The binders were duly shipped to the designated recipients — every manager and team leader in the installation. They promptly and strategically positioned the unopened binders on their bookshelves where they sat gathering dust, until a couple of years later when I participated in another process definition exercise. The first process was generally not used because it was felt it was too heavy, too cumbersome, too restrictive, and too "big." Our mandate for the second attempt was to "cut it down" — to provide more a set of guidelines than a restrictive recipe, to give a framework rather than a prescription, to direct rather than constrain but mainly to make it smaller. This much-faster exercise resulted in a slim volume being produced just a few weeks later. It was mailed out to the designated recipients, only to suffer the same fate as the first edition. This time the criticism was that the guidelines were "too vague," and that the process did not really add anything that was not already known, that it did not have enough "meat."

5

In some circles, software process is considered to be *the* issue that needs to be resolved to fix "the software crisis." Improving process has become an article of faith in some corners, while avoiding organizationally imposed process has assumed the status of guerilla warfare in others. Process models and methodologies duel with each other across message boards, magazines, and bookshelves. People are assessed and undergo extensive certification to allow them in turn to assess and certify others in process frameworks, while others espouse rapid "get-it-done-now" approaches as well as process so lightweight it barely exists.

Why is this? Why have some companies, institutions, and individuals allocated such significant resources to defining a process for the construction of software, while all too often the supposed users of the process, the developers themselves, pay lip service to it, severely modify parts of it, or simply shun it altogether? Are the processes badly defined? Is the process we use to define the process flawed? Should we not attempt to define process at all, and let the developers make it up as they go along? Or should we try to define process to greater levels of precision?

Maybe the answer is both. But first, perhaps, we should take a look at the purpose of process — what do we expect process to do for us? Where is the value added by applying process? It might be that our problem is not process, it is what we are asking process to do, and when, where, and how we apply it.

Software is knowledge made active. The difficult and time-consuming activity in creating software is not one of transcribing our already-available knowledge into the active form; it is in effectively acquiring this knowledge in the first place. Even more specifically, it is in finding the essential knowledge necessary to make the system work that we do not know we are missing.

By "effectively acquiring" I mean obtaining all the necessary knowledge and then structuring it so that it is consistent, complete, and usable. "Consistent" means that the knowledge does not "contradict" itself (including being consistent with the transcription activity and language, of course). "Complete" means that all the necessary knowledge required for correct executability is obtained, and "usable" means that the knowledge is rendered into a form that we can easily process to create the system.

Software is a knowledge-storage medium and the development of software is a knowledge-acquiring activity. But most companies do not manage the creation of software as a knowledge-acquisition activity. The lack of focus on knowledge acquisition and management is the root cause of many of the problems we perennially experience in the creation of software. To take the argument a step further we can, in fact, make a case that our basic business model for the production of software is simply wrong.

Starting from these premises:

- Software is a knowledge medium.
- The "product" is the knowledge contained in the software.
- The activity of developing software is the activity of acquiring specific types of knowledge and translating that knowledge into a specific language form known as "code."

First, we have to look at the source: what kinds and quantities of knowledge need to be gained? These will vary enormously from project to project, environment to environment, and system to system. There is knowledge of what the customer requires, usually known as "requirements." There is knowledge of which system and module designs would work best to deliver the functionality to the customer; and there is knowledge of how to transcribe the knowledge into executable form ("coding" knowledge). Of course, there are many, many finer distinctions of these knowledge forms: the format of the customer interface, the persistent data storage needs of the system, data security, operational states, and error recovery. The list goes on and on.

However, even without pausing to categorize the knowledge needed, we can abstract characteristics of all knowledge into the degrees of "unknownness" that I call the "Five Orders of Ignorance":

- *Zeroth Order Ignorance (0OI):* Lack of ignorance. I have 0OI when I provably know something.
- *First Order Ignorance (1OI):* Lack of knowledge. I have 1OI when I do not know something.
- *Second Order Ignorance (2OI):* Lack of awareness. I have 2OI when I do not know that I do not know something (see Exhibit 6).
- *Third Order Ignorance (3OI):* Lack of Process. I have 3OI when I do not know of a suitably efficient way to find out that I do not know that I do not know something.
- *Fourth Order Ignorance (4OI):* Meta ignorance. I have 4OI when I do not know about the Five Orders of Ignorance.

Each of the Orders of Ignorance requires a different type of process. Zeroth Order Ignorance (0OI), the application of already-known information, requires a stable, detailed, and highly repeatable process — basically a streamlined version of the same process that was used when the knowledge was first successfully implemented after being obtained. On the other hand, Third Order Ignorance (3OI) requires a very different kind of process. With 3OI, not only do we not have the necessary knowledge, we do not know exactly what it is that we need to find out, and we are wrestling with defining and implementing a process of any sort that will help us find out what we need to know.

Exhibit 6. The effects of 2OI.

Inaccurate Estimates

When projects are started, an estimation of effort, schedule, and cost that is used to define the project expectations and commitment is usually prepared. Experienced developers know that their best efforts at estimating the effort are always less than the task turns out to require. Why? Because of Second Order of Ignorance, we can only estimate based on what we know plus what we know we need to know (0OI and 1OI). It is not possible to estimate based on what we do not know we do not know any more than a scientist can design an experiment for something for which she is not looking. The usual coping mechanism for this is to add "contingency." This is often a simple percentage — for example, 35 percent — that is added to the calculated effort or schedule. The contingency shows for the things that we do not know we do not know. Note that we typically assign a much-higher contingency for really new projects than we would for projects that are routine and we have successfully completed before. This is tacitly acknowledging that such projects are higher in 2OI. In fact, it is reasonable to assert that almost all of the effort on a project is the result of 2OI (with some 3OI).

Our usual compensating mechanism for 2OI is the addition of contingency resources and time for those things that we know will go wrong but which we cannot actually identify.

The 90-Percent-Complete Syndrome

This occurs when a programmer (or tester or whomever) maintains, sometimes for months, that despite diligent effort he remains at "90-percent complete." Basically, the programmer does not actually know how complete he is. Why? Second order ignorance is always high when we are engaged in a discovery activity. The 90 percent complete syndrome occurs when we believe we are performing a product-production activity. The "completeness" question is actually misplaced because it cannot be assessed realistically beyond a finite degree of accuracy. The question should be, of course, "how much have we learned that is valuable?"

The Five Orders of Ignorance

Because the nature of these "levels of ignorance" is quite different, we need to establish different process criteria for each Order of Ignorance:

- *0OI:* I have the answer. Developing a system is simply a matter of transcribing what I already know, into the appropriate programming instructions. Note that this is not possible unless I know the appropriate coding medium — that is, I know how to program. Of course, not knowing the language, not knowing how to program, is actually a form of ignorance, which I would presumably know about. If that were the case, I would classify it as a form of 1OI to be dealt with below.

- *1OI:* I have the question, and I either know how to get the answer to it (I have 0OI about the activity of answer acquisition) or I do not know how to get the answer (I have 1OI about answer acquisition).

In the first case, I simply go and get the answer. In the second case, I have two questions: how do I get the answer? And then what is the answer? In the event that there is no way to get the answer, I may have to ask a different question and look for a different answer, such as "what do I do when I cannot get an answer?" Both the question and the answers can have levels of "granularity." We can classify very high-level, open questions (such as, "What are the requirements for this system?") as being type-questions. They are the typical questions posed by meta processes (such as a process defined as Gather Requirements). They are generic, vague, context-free, and domain nonspecific — they could apply to any domain or a wide range of domains. They may also not be very useful in some situations because they will often generate vague (context-free) answers. Type-questions occur when the question knowledge content is non-specific and is simply of a type of knowledge. For instance, I could ask the question, "What are the requirements for this system?" I know that all systems have some requirements; it is simply a type of knowledge I need to get. The format of the question is very nonspecific and could generate a wide range of responses. I might get generalized function information ("this system must process credit card transactions") or I might get detailed implementation information ("This system must be written in Z8000 assembly language"). While such questions are helpful when I do not have a context to ask specific questions, they do not usually produce usable engineering answers. The most useful output from a type-question is often another more-specific question. If I find I am using many type-questions, it usually indicates that I have significant amounts of 2OI.

- *2OI:* I do not have the question. I do not know enough to frame a question that is contextual enough to elicit a definitive answer. I may fall back on type-questions or some other mechanism. This fall-back mechanism is a "Third Order Ignorance Process." I will argue that most, if not all, software methods are 3OI processes. Some types of systems are predominantly 0OI and 1OI heavy and others have large amounts of 2OI. A research project, for example, is often heavy in 2OI problems. Tactical systems development, such as porting, which has been successfully completed before, tends to emphasize 0OI and 1OI — the issues and questions are quite well known and answers are readily forthcoming. But in any systems development there is always some measure of 2OI, and we must deal with this in a different way than 1OI. This means we have to adopt a different process for each kind of unknown and different processes for 0OI/1OI and 2OI/3OI.

- *3OI:* 3OI is the process level. As there are levels of granularity of questions at the 1OI level, there are levels of granularity of processes at 3OI. Detailed, granular processes are the most useful, although they are usually only useful across restricted problem spaces. The reason they are useful is that the processes contain the context of the problem. I call high-level, general processes that do not contain the context meta processes. They are usually not very useful in obtaining definitive answers and instead tend to generate more questions. The highest level of a waterfall life cycle model is an example with its phases of: Requirements, Design, Code, and Test. While undoubtedly "correct," this tends not to be a very useful process. We have to get requirements for every system; ditto design and code and test. The process at the life cycle level does not tell us exactly what to do, and when and where to do it. It does not tell us what kind of requirements to get and from whom. This is because generically we do not know what to do that would be effective; because we do not know what questions we are trying to answer, until we start operating on this system. This limitation is inherent to all processes.

- *4OI:* 4OI is the understanding that software development is a knowledge-acquisition activity. The global application of the same methodology regardless of what is known or not known of the problem, or what kind of problem it is, could be viewed as 4OI in operation. The squandering of hard-won knowledge assets is another example of this level of ignorance in operation.

There seem to be some basic "laws" or conventions operating in the software area and in the software business that can help us to understand the nature of this activity.

The Laws of Software Process

A few years ago, I was asked to be a keynote address speaker at the end of a five-day conference on software process. The conference organizers had scheduled this address as the final activity of the conference to fill a 4-hour time slot(!). Because I and my presentation would be the only things keeping the attendees from returning home to their loved ones, the occasion called for some humor and audience participation if I did not want to see people sneaking out of the conference as I was speaking. For the occasion, I formulated a set of "laws" for software process and engaged people in working with them interactively.

The presentation was intentionally light and humorous, although with an underlying vein of seriousness. At one level, these "Laws of Software Process" are intended to be "catchy" — humor can be a useful mnemonic device. However, their point and their humor lies in the fact that they are actually very true, and the humor just allows us to appreciate the sometimes-incongruous nature of what we do. The laws are not intended to be rigorous as, for example, a physical law but are more on the lines of "Murphy's Law."

They are accompanied by a collection of related observations on software process.

The First Law of Software Process

Process only allows us to do things we already know how to do.

The Corollary to the First Law of Software Process

You cannot have a process for something you have never done nor do not know how to do.

Explanation and Observations

The First Law is saying is that we can only define processes to the extent that we know what to define. Topics that are extremely well defined — that is, about which we know a great deal — can have extremely well-defined processes. Topics that are vague or even unknown cannot have well-defined processes. In Orders of Ignorance terms, we can only define really detailed processes for 0OI and 1OI. Therefore, detailed processes are useful only in known situations, and the applicability of processes for 2OI must be limited because, by definition, we do not know what the 2OI knowledge is.

A further inference of the First Law is that in general we cannot have well-defined processes for things we have never done. Because every software development must have some components (or combinations of components) we have never created before, we have an immediate restriction on the applicability of any process to software development. Of course, this restriction can be modified in several ways:

- Even the most radically new elements of most development activities tend to be similar to development activities in other projects. We may be able to apply analogistic and metaphoric processes (this is like that) to allow us to move forward.
- The activity of learning may have attributes that are more a function of the action of learning than what is being learned.
- We can "bootstrap" processes from the known to the unknown elements, in a way analogous to a student answering the well-known questions on an exam paper before tackling the unknowns, although this approach has its perils.

The Reflexive Creation of Systems and Processes

1. The only way that effective systems can be created is through the application of effective processes.
2. The only way that effective processes can be created is through the construction of effective systems.

Explanation and Observations

These two statements are so self-referential that they can be neither separated nor disputed. As well as being mutually self-referential (between statements 1 and 2), they are also internally self-referential (within statements 1 and 2). The only logical definition of an "effective" process is that it is able to effectively create systems (although there may be other "effective" attributes). If an effective system is created, then the process used must have been effective, at least to some extent. Underlying the surface paradoxes, which always accompany self-referential statements, is a core truth. Systems development processes cannot be created independently of their purpose, which is to create systems, any more than the activity of reading can be separated from something being read. Having said that, there have been many cases in the history of software development where software development processes have been developed without acknowledgment of the actual necessities of creating systems in the real world. And I have personally participated in the development of systems where it would be hard to point to anything that we could really qualify as a "process." One of the tenets of the "Agile Methods" is most of them have been created by practitioners, rather than theoreticians, practicing their craft.

The general view of software process is that the process is created to allow the development of systems. This is true, and we should not create processes that do not do that. However, a legitimate use of systems development is to create processes that facilitate later development. This is an underlying principle of most process control methodologies: learn from your process to build your product; learn from building your product to improve your process.

The Lemma of Eternal Lateness

The only processes we can use on the current project were defined on previous projects, which were different from this one.

Explanation and Observations

We develop our processes at least one project behind, sometimes on systems that are not quite like the current system. Therefore, always to some extent, the processes will not quite apply. The extent to which the previous processes do not fit the existing situation is determined by the degree of difference between the previous projects and the current one. The degree of 2OI is also determined by the differences between the projects — in fact it usually is the difference. The fact that both govern the applicability of the process is not a coincidence.

The Second Law of Software Process
(see also The Rule of Process Bifurcation)

We can only define software processes at two levels: too vague or too confining.

Explanation and Observations

This is a direct consequence of having to deal with both 0OI/1OI and 2OI/3OI at the same time. The anecdote I related concerning creating process for my airline employer illustrates this exactly: the first process definition activity for the airline fell into the "too confining" category. Learning from that, our second effort was promptly deemed "too vague."

Processes always tend to be too vague for those things we know exactly how to do. In fact, not only should the process tell us exactly what to do, ideally it should do it for us. Highly detailed, specific processes are useless or dangerous for those things that the process does not fit. The things that do not fit are usually the 2OI problems we have not encountered before — which is, of course, why they are 2OI problems.

The Rule of Process Bifurcation

Software process rules are often stated in terms of two levels: a general statement of the rule, and a specific detailed example (e.g., The Second Law of Software Process).

Explanation and Observations

This is actually a good approach to use to explain many problems: describe the theory and then give a good example. The theory deals with the high-level conceptualization or general rule, and the example with the low-level implementation or application of the rule. Engineers, in particular, tend to be more comfortable with concrete examples than with general rules. However, in systems development the structure of the systems is usually defined in the general rules from which the exceptions and examples flow. Also, engineers tend to be solution oriented rather than problem oriented. So for engineers, it is a good idea to back up the general rule statement with an example that explains the use of the rule. As an example for the Rule of Bifurcation, engineers might not know how to use the Rule of Bifurcation unless I included this sentence as an example.

The Dual Hypotheses of Knowledge Discovery

- Hypothesis One: We can only "discover" knowledge in an environment that contains that knowledge.
- Hypothesis Two: The only way to assert the validity of any knowledge is to compare it to another source of knowledge.

Explanation and Observations

In some ways, these are a pivot point around which opinions of knowledge rotate. Debating these points has occupied the attention of some of the best thinkers the human race has ever known. From a purely practical point of view, however, they appear to be reasonable working hypotheses. We cannot obtain requirements from a customer who does not know what he or she wants (Hypothesis One). We cannot test a system unless we have a set of test data and expected results against which to measure the system's performance (Hypothesis Two). These hypotheses have some significant practical use in designing projects. For instance, there is no point in engaging in a long and detailed analytical process to derive requirements if no one can be specific about them. What we must do is move the project into an environment where the necessary knowledge will be exposed. We see this, for instance, in the testing of large and popular operating systems. There is no analytical process that Microsoft could use to perform complete environmental testing of its Windows™ operating system. The knowledge of all the different ways people might choose to run Windows™, and all the applications and hardware configurations that people might decide to run it with, simply do not exist in Redmond, Washington. To expose what might happen when Windows™ is run with these various configurations, we have to place Windows in the only environment that contains that knowledge. Specifically, we have to run it in the "real world," because that is the only place the knowledge actually exists.

Armour's Observation on Software Process

What all software developers really want is a rigorous, iron-clad, hidebound, concrete, universal, absolute, total, definitive, and complete set of process rules that they can break.

Explanation and Observations

This is a wry description of the need for both rigor and flexibility. For those things that are or can be well defined (0OI and 1OI) we need and can obtain a precise (rigorous, iron-clad, etc.) process definition. Following such a process will duplicate our earlier successful effort and give us the result we are looking for. However, precise definition for those Second and Third Order Ignorance things that the process does not fit is usually very ineffective, the process does not work, and has to be modified (they can break). The challenge for process definition is that it is intrinsically very difficult and perhaps impossible to clean both sides of the street at the same time — to define a single process at a single level of abstraction that will be both sufficiently rigorous for the known quantities and sufficiently flexible for the unknown quantities.

The Third Law of Software Process (also known as the Footwear Manufacturer's Minor Dependent's Law)

The very last type of knowledge to be considered as a candidate for implementation into an executable software system is the knowledge of how to implement knowledge into an executable software system.

Explanation and Observations

The Third Law targets the software development process. We could plausibly argue that the job of the software developer is to take knowledge from the brain and book media (talk with the customer, read the specification) and convert it into an executable form. For several reasons, which I will discuss later, most process initiatives seem to target the book form of knowledge as the final location in which to deposit an organization's software development knowledge. Additionally, most project managers attempt to hire experienced developers. These developers presumably have some quantity of effective process knowledge stored in their brain medium. This knowledge was deposited by the activity of completing software development projects both successfully and sometimes unsuccessfully. To say the least, it is a little ironic that the target media of software process efforts is usually brains or books, when our job is to make knowledge executable.

The Twin Goals of Optimal Termination

1. The only natural goal of a software process group should be to put itself out of business as soon as possible.
2. The end result of the continuous development and application of an effective process will be that nobody actually has to use it.

Explanation and Observations

It is an axiom of the quality movement in particular and process improvement in general that a quality group should fold the results of its efforts back into the manufacturing line. Done effectively, this should result in a high-quality process that does not actually need a separate quality group. In exactly the same way, a "process group" should encapsulate both the known process and the mechanisms for changing the process into the development activity in a way that does not actually require a separate process group. For the unknowns (2OI and 3OI), of course, rigid process cannot be well defined, so most of these processes will reference 0OI and 1OI. The logical result of efforts in this area is to create a highly flexible learning organization that is attuned to the process of learning and discovery.

The second part of the Twin Goals alludes to the fact that, because process can only be defined for well-understood activities, such process can and should be made so automated and mechanical that it does not actually need the intervention of developers. This frees up the developers to work on the things that we do not know how to do — the Second and Third Order Ignorance activities — for which we cannot have an explicit process. This is exactly the service that most software developers want from process — that the process automatically and effortlessly takes care of the mundane, repetitive, and well-defined activities from which little can be learned, while the developer takes care of the inventive, creative, and new knowl-edge-discovery activities for which rigorous process cannot be defined or will not be effective.

Summary

The development and application of process as it is generally defined and understood is constrained by some of the realities of the business of creating software. The key to this is that the development of executable knowledge is first and foremost a discovery activity. However, it is associ-ated with certain well-defined translation activities and a certain amount of routine and repetitive work.

We can, and should, rigorously define process for those aspects of our work that we can define rigorously. However, we cannot rigorously define process for those aspects of work that are discovery based. While we can have processes of a general kind for learning and discovery activities, they differ enormously from the repetitive and mechanical actions necessary for true application of the well-known knowledge.

There are several problems we have experienced as an industry in defin-ing process, including:

- Attempting to define a "one-size-fits-all" process or process frame-work for different kinds of systems where knowledge content and knowledge availability is quite different
- Failing to differentiate between knowledge discovery and knowledge application in process definition
- Attempting to define a single level of abstraction for all process types
- Depositing our process knowledge in book form or leaving it in brain form rather than developing automated systems that assist the knowledge acquisition and application process
- Not properly allowing for the nature of the learning activity in setting up processes, particularly the nature of cognition and problem understanding

The application of the Laws of Software Process and the associated observations should lead us to adopt the following approaches to process:

- Separate activities in software development into known (0OI, 1OI) and unknown (2OI, 3OI) elements, and define different types and granularity of processes for each.

- Stop trying to define monolithic processes.
- Develop processes only from within the context of real systems development to provably solve real problems.
- Recognize the limitations of historically defined processes, and learn from them.
- For processes dealing with 2OI, develop "creative spaces" within the real projects where solutions can be explored.
- On top of the creative spaces, build "process labs" to explore different process options.
- Have term limits and terminating charters for process groups.
- Develop and apply value-added metrics for processes to ensure that following the process actually results in gains over the cost of defining and implementing the processes.
- Build systems that capture knowledge as it is gained, store it in both executable and understandable forms, and make it available to others in a usable form.
- Automate! Automate! Automate! Take as a goal of development the automation, not only of the target system but all varieties of knowledge that are gained as the development progresses.

Chapter 2
The Purpose of Process

Yet I doubt not through the ages
One increasing purpose runs,
And the thoughts of men are widen'd
With the process of the suns.

— Alfred Lord Tennyson
Locksley Hall

Why do we have software process? For perhaps half of the time that has elapsed since software was first produced, practitioners seemed to get along without anything that could be reasonably called "process." A whole new generation of software developers has moved into the workforce since serious and concerted efforts have been made to codify the process for creating software. Yet still there is little consensus as to the degree of process we should use. There is a similar lack of agreement on the type of process, its sequencing, the work products and deliverables it produces, the languages, patterns, thought processes, and even organizational structures required to successfully create software.

On the occasions when processes (sequencing, work products, etc.) are explicitly defined, they are all too often strongly resisted by the people who are expected to use them. Certainly, process is less than optimally implemented in many organizations. There are improvements that could be made to our approach to software process and the processes our approach produces. But is all the inattention, hesitancy, reservations, resistance, and outright rebellion simply the work of recidivists? Is it just stepping on the cowboy programmers' god-given right to program whatever and however the heck they please? What is it they object to? *"Your (sic) process is stifling my creativity!"* is the cry. Do they have a point?

The cornerstone of the software process faith is that process engenders repeatability. "Repeatable" is even the name of the first level above bare existence in the SEI model. But what is "repeatability?" And is it valuable?

From working with a variety of software and other technical groups (see Exhibit 1), it became evident that the nature of process for a creative group producing something for the first time was and should be different than for a product group producing the fifth in a series of system upgrades. It turns

Exhibit 1. Telecomm Advanced Products Group.

"What's the name of SEI Level 2?" Jim asked, as aggressively as ever. "Repeatable? Repeatable? Let me tell you about repeatability."

This scenario occurred several years ago, during the facilitation of a management workshop for a systems engineering group. In the room were the group's VP and 14 senior managers. These managers were, in their engineering youth, the people responsible for making the first cellular telephone systems work. They were a very "can-do" group. With the exception of one person, they were utterly "un-process" oriented. Their idea of process was *"Just do it!"* Collectively, they had both the right approach and the right personalities to break new ground, to build products that could not be built. But they were not believers in process.

I was giving a pitch on the Software Engineering Institute's Capability Maturity Model[SM] (SEI/CMM[SM]) of software process and organization. It received a predictable response. Jim was one of the more challenging of a challenging group.

"SEI Level 2 is 'repeatable', right? Well, look at our title." Challenging accepted wisdom was as natural to Jim as breathing. "We're the Advanced Products Group, right? Advanced. New. Everything we build is new and different. We don't *want* to repeat anything! Repeatability is of no use to us."

He had a point. But I had a counterpoint. The implementation of the SEI model (and in fact any process) must support the business practice and goal. This group's business practice and goal was to be creative and innovative. Their purpose in attaining SEI Level 2 should be to become repeatably creative and innovative. That kept them quiet for a while, although it did not turn them into converts to process.

out that the type, degree, and purpose of process varies with the type of team defining and using it.

Types of Teams

There are four general types of project teams, and each of them has specific needs and goals. Because each team is trying to do something different, it is reasonable to presume that the nature of their processes must be different if each is to be successful. In process, one size probably does not fit all. The four types of teams are:

1. *Tactical:* The job is to *do* something.
2. *Problem solving:* The job is to *fix* something.
3. *Creative:* The job is to *build* something.
4. *Learning:* The job is to *learn* something.

We can map these on to the Five Orders of Ignorance (see Exhibit 2).

Tactical

A tactical team working to execute a plan requires, above all else, well-defined roles and processes for the team members. The reason is that the

Exhibit 2. Mapping of process to the Five Orders of Ignorance.

Type of team	Purpose	Key issue	Key need	Orders of ignorance covered			
				0OI	1OI	2OI	3OI
Tactical	Do something	Follow a plan	Well-defined roles and processes	X			
Problem solving	Fix something	Solve a problem	Defined roles and trust	X	X		
Creative	Build something	Build something new	Freedom from restrictions		X	X	
Learning	Learn something	Construct a model of understanding	Consistent, shared models			X	X

Note: X = primary ignorance area(s) worked by this type of team.

team is mostly dealing with known quantities to produce known or expected results. For a very highly tactical project or team there are no unknowns. In the software world, well-defined and repetitive projects such as porting operations tend to fall into this area. Well-understood and refined project activities such as configuration management within more creative projects also tend to be highly tactical. For these kinds of processes, the issue is not one of discovering new knowledge, but of repetitively and flawlessly applying old knowledge. There is a pressing need or advantage *not* to do things in a different way. Such activities comprise almost 100 percent Zeroth Order Ignorance (0OI) and deal only with answers that are already available. Outside of the software arena, a good example of a tactical team is the flight deck operations on an aircraft carrier. Encouraging creativity in the midst of launching and landing planes would be positively dangerous. Once a good system is devised, there is no sense in doing things in a different way, and in fact these operations are almost choreographed to perfection.

Problem Solving

A problem-solving team also uses 0OI, but tends to work somewhat more in the area of First Order Ignorance (1OI). If the team does not have the answer, then it does generally have the question. The job then becomes one of finding and implementing the answer. Perhaps some of the work of a problem-solving team will tend to be slightly creative (such as in how they get the questions answered), but mostly it will be data collection and application. The problem-solving team shares with the tactical team a need for role definition, but it is not as strong and requires a certain amount of flexibility in the application of roles and process. The reason for this is that the answers to the questions might well change these roles and processes — so too-rigid process definition might be harmful. These teams also need an

21

Exhibit 3. The IBM PC team and freedom.

One of the definitive creative teams in the computer world was the team that created the original IBM PC. Their need for freedom from IBM's corporate culture (and process) led their project leader, Don Estridge, to relocate the team as far away from Armonk as he could. The team moved to Boca Raton, Florida. This "isolation" gave them the freedom they needed to develop something that, if not "new," was certainly new to the IBM corporate culture. Estridge and his technical planning manager, Larry Rojas, kept a very careful interface between head office and the team, and IBM personnel were actually refused "visiting rights" in order to keep the highly effective team functioning without corrupting influences.*

element of trust, particularly that each team member will solve the problem assigned to him. A software project tracking down and debugging network problems is a good example of this kind of team. Outside the software arena, the function of the Centers for Disease Control (CDC) in tracking down the sources of epidemics largely operates as a problem-solving team.

Creative

The creative team may actually require an explicit *lack* of process, or at least a much-less-restrictive one. Highly defined process always enables known activities (that is its purpose), but usually restricts or compromises unknown activities or activities that are different this time around. For truly creative activities, i.e., activities that are creating something that has *never* been created before, we honestly cannot have a "process" as it is generally viewed. This is not that there is not a process for creation, but such a process cannot be rigidly defined without predicating the answer. Certainly, whatever process we do impose must allow some freedom in application. That the software processes we apply often do not allow a "creative space" is one of the major and most justified criticisms of process as it is usually implemented (see Exhibit 3).

Even in the most prosaic software development, there is always some element of creativity that requires this freedom. The most creative of knowledge acquisition always addresses Second Order Ignorance (2OI) for it is in resolving 2OI that we find out things that we did not know that we did not know, and genuinely innovative.

Learning

The learning team is a research group. Its "output" is some intellectual model of whatever has been, is being, could be, or must be learned. The key need for this is the construction of shared mental models between the team members. Constructing these models has some strong elements of

---

* Larson, C.E. and LaFasco, F.M., *Teamwork: What Must Go Right/What Can Go Wrong,* Sage, Newbury Park, CA, 1989.

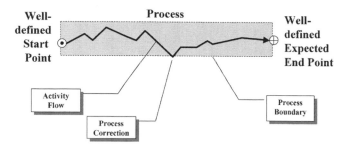

Exhibit 4. Conformed process flow.

creativity, but does not necessarily produce a tangible "product." The output is often simply a better idea of what *might* work. For true research groups, most of the effort is spent in finding approaches or processes that will or might unveil what is not currently known. This kind of team focuses on the 2Ol-3Ol levels.

Software Teams Are All Types at the Same Time

The challenge for most software teams is that *all* types of processing are necessary. Usually a software team is not just one or even two of these types. It may be a learning team in gathering requirements, experimenting with different ways of interacting with the customer or environment. It may become a creative team when figuring out how to design the system, then tactical in implementing it, and problem solving in debugging it. This is why defining software processes is so hard, and why rigid processes do not work very well. This variability operates at quite detailed task levels: we might be creative in developing a piece of code, and highly tactical in logging it with the configuration management system. Then we might operate in a learning mode as we figure out how to test it in a new environment, but shift into problem solving as we hit the inevitable snags the learning presents to us.

One of the skills a software team must learn is the ability to reinvent and restructure itself, sometimes on a week-by-week basis, sometimes even task-by-task.

The approach to defining process must take these issues into account. The peril of not doing so is that the process will force us to come up with the "wrong" answer. Rigidly defined process is only effective when the variables are few and, most importantly, *we know in detail what we want to achieve.* The extent to which we do not know what the target is, or the extent to which our job is to determine the target, is the same extent to which we will find a rigidly defined process will not work.

The job of process is to keep the activity within a defined range, so that the expected result will be obtained (see Exhibit 4). One of the main compliance

23

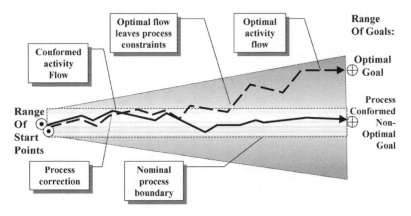

Exhibit 5. Modified process flow.

activities within most processes is to assure that the defined process is actually being followed. If it is not, then some correction in the errant process is enforced. There are several situations where this does not tend to work well:

- When the "correct" or optimal end result is not known in advance, as mentioned earlier
- When the result is heavily dependent on the process used
- Where there is a significant time dependency of the target result *and* the process is time consuming

Working toward a defined and expected goal is fine, if that is what is needed, but it is harmful if the results are not known in advance or are not optimal because of something we did not know. Generally, the further away from the prescribed process an activity gets, the more pressure will be applied to it to conform. However, when the optimal answer lies far outside the boundaries of what is allowed by the defined process, strict adherence to this process will force a suboptimal answer.

Difficulties occur when the end goal is not well defined, there are a number of potential end goals, or the way to achieve the end goal is unknown. In this case, an explicit process will tend to work against the resolution of the problem, and may even result in achieving the wrong goal (Exhibit 5).

A Range of Unknowns, a Range of Processes

In reality, projects consist of a range of known and unknown factors. Some of the effort on a project involves factoring known or highly predictable unknowns. Some of the project involves discovering unknowns, and some of the project requires the discovery of processes that will allow the discovery of unknowns (see Exhibit 6).

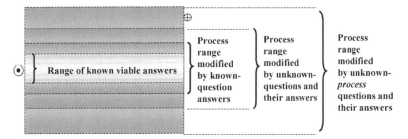

Exhibit 6. Layers of process flow.

Inventing Processes

There is a point that should be addressed here, relating to "new processes." One could argue that we always use the "same" process for discovery, and that we do not actually invent new processes. Testing might be put up as a good example. We *always* test a system. In fact, we may have documented testing processes and "well-defined" testing methods. However, until they have been applied to *this* system, they have not been proven, and the testing process cannot tell us exactly what we will find. Invariably, in applying the process and method to the system at hand, we are inventing the testing process and *learning* how to test this particular system. This activity always results in us discovering other facts about the system:

- We validate that some of what we assumed about the system is, in fact, true.
- We are forced to codify and assign values to the variables we know exist in the system.
- The act of creating test plans or test processes often results in discovery of unknowns in the system.
- We discover factors that operate in the executable environment simply by trying to create an executable test environment.
- We find that the testing activity must be modified to be most effective.

These realizations represent the application of existing knowledge and the discovery of new knowledge as predicted by the Five Orders of Ignorance.

Nested within one of the Orders of Ignorance are the other Orders of Ignorance (see Exhibit 7), and exploring one level almost always results in discovery at another level; we learn what code to write and we learn better how to write code at the same time as we are learning what "better code" is.

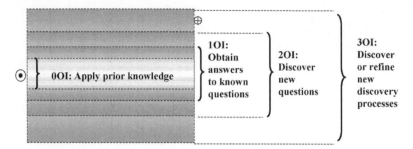

Exhibit 7. Process layers and the 5OI.

The Purpose of Process

Putting this all together:

- We can only have a process for those (0OI and 1OI) things that are well defined and we have done before.
- We cannot have a process for things (2OI and 3OI) we have not done before and do not know how to do.
- Defined process only supports tactical and problem-solving activities.
- All software teams have elements of creativity and learning that may be hampered by restrictive process and tactical application of existing knowledge that is strongly supported by explicit process.
- Nonrestrictive processes (guidelines) are necessarily generic and vague and are therefore not much use in specific instances.
- The ideal process is wholly predictable and can even be completely automated.

Therefore we can state what the purpose of process really is:

The true purpose of process is to liberate us from the mundane.

The purpose of process is to take those things that we already know how to do successfully and to package them so that they are entirely predictable and invariably successful. The process serves to free up our energies so that we do not have to reprocess those things that really do not need to be processed again.

What does this leave us doing?

The freeing of the brain cycles from the repetition of the more-predictable and mechanistic activities of our projects gives us the bandwidth to work on the unknown aspects of building systems. These are the unstructured, unpredictable, undefined, variable, and creative activities for which we cannot have a rigidly defined process. In Orders of Ignorance terms, the job of process is to take care of 0OI and 1OI. The job of the human developers is to take care of 2OI and 3OI.

This, incidentally, is exactly what engineers and developers want process to do. The fact that they often view process as preventing them from being creative (read: learning new things) is a legitimate criticism of process as it is often done.

The Problems of Process

The logic chain we have been pursuing follows like this:

1. Software is a knowledge storage medium.
2. Therefore, software itself is not a product.
3. The real product is the knowledge contained within the software (and the work products necessary to deposit the knowledge effectively in the software).
4. Therefore, software "development" is really a knowledge-acquisition activity.
5. We can reuse knowledge we already have (0OI), assuming it is available and packaged correctly.
6. But we will need to acquire the knowledge we do not have already.
7. This involves getting answers to the questions we already have (1OI).
8. And discovering knowledge we did not know we needed (2OI).
9. We know the knowledge we have (0OI), we have a good idea of the 1OI knowledge we do not have, but we have little idea of the 2OI knowledge we do not have.
10. The most valuable knowledge to acquire is knowledge that no one has, which is almost always 2OI.
11. The most difficult knowledge to acquire is 2OI knowledge.
12. Therefore, we spend most of our time acquiring 2OI knowledge.
13. Process is most applicable and useful in well-defined situations, but less useful in unknown situations.
14. Therefore, 2OI is the kind of knowledge for which process is *least* applicable.

The Usefulness Dilemma

This, rather disturbingly, leads us to the assertion that where we need the most help is the place where process provides the least. This means we can craft an extension to the First Law of Software Process:

> *Software process is only really useful for things that we do not want to do anyway.*

This extension I call *the usefulness dilemma*. The rationale is as follows: if software development is really a knowledge-acquisition activity, then we are only really concerned with the things we do not know, because we should not need to acquire knowledge that we already have. The things we do already know, we should simply be able to reuse. A process to do this can be extremely well defined and possibly even automated. Of all the things we do not know, some are things we know we do not know (1OI) and some are things we do not know we do not know (2OI). For 0OI and 1OI, process can be useful and well defined. Because the answer or the question is known, the essential parameters of how to factor the knowledge, what kind of question to ask, who to ask, when to ask, etc., can usually be explicitly laid out. It is true that for 1OI, the answer is not known, but at least the question is. From there it is simply a matter of finding out the answer from the question. Usually if I have a good question, finding the answer is not too difficult. This means that 1OI is rather easy to deal with. Or to put it another way: we do not have to spend much time or energy finding out 1OI. Therefore, significantly improving process for 1OI does not make much sense, because we would be improving something that is already pretty good, and one of the golden rules of process improvement is always improve the area that is least effective first.

That leaves us with 2OI. Using a process to improve 2OI makes sense. The problem is we cannot really have a process for 2OI (see First Law of Software Process).

We can parse this argument further, but it still remains that the place where process is needed is the place where it is least effective.

We can define a *meta*-process for 2OI (see Exhibit 8). Many purported development processes are really meta-processes. A meta-process does not tell you what to do; it tells you what kind of thing to do (see Exhibit 9).

A few things can be noted here:

- The process is *much* bigger than the meta-process.
- The meta-process covers a much wider range of problems and solutions (for instance, we *always* gather requirements from the customer, no matter what system we build).
- The meta-process does not really tell us anything we did not know already (for the most part).
- The explicit process, while very useful and direct, only works for certain types of systems, and maybe only for one type of system (for instance, a system that contains a C24601 record and a user or other resource named Bob Smith who knows the exact format of this record).

The meta-process does not help us in a concrete fashion, but the definitive process only works in a very narrow field (in fact, we have probably already asked Bob for the record — that is probably how we know who to ask; so we might have to question why are we asking him again).

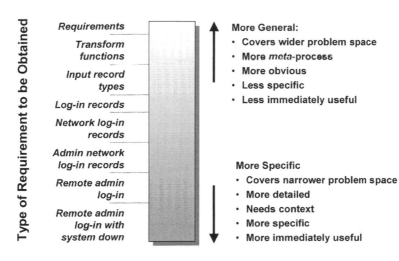

Exhibit 8. Process-meta-process hierarchy.

Exhibit 9. Examples of processes vs. meta process.

Activity to be done	Meta-process	Process
Find out what the customer needs	Gather requirements from the customer	Call Bob Smith at 555-1515 and ask him to tell you exactly what the format of the C24601 record is
Translate the design into code	Code the system	Using Microsoft C++ compiler V6.0 running under NT, for each unary function statement starting with <st…> code the state structure logic from the supplied state chart as shown in Std procedure 6.1.3.3, etc.

What we have here is a demonstration of the Second Law of Software Process:

We can only define software processes at two levels: too vague and too confining.

The meta-process is the *"too vague"* level and the detailed explicit process is the *"too confining"* level. In reality, of course, process definition is not discrete at two levels; it is defined in a continuum.

In Exhibit 8, the processes on the top are more "meta," while the processes further down are more "process." Telling someone to go define requirements does not help them much; even telling someone to identify the transform functions or to categorize the input record types, while more specific, is also not very helpful. Most systems contain transform functions;

systems that are dealing with transactions or packets will certainly process different types of input records. As we can see, there is a continuum of detail getting progressively more specific to the system being built as we move down the detail scale. At the bottom, explicitly telling someone to get the structure and content of a remote Administrator log-in signal while the system is down is much more useful, but the definition of the process presupposes quite a bit:

- That this system does accept input
- That at least one type of input can be referred to by the label *"log-in signals"*
- That an entity or user known by the label "Administrator" exists in the system or its environment
- That the transform process of "log-in" is authorized to the Administrator
- There is at least one mode of processing for the Administrator referred to by the label *"remote"*
- The system is saving some of this information in *"records"*
- The input does have a structure of some sort
- The system can be in the state of *"down"*

There is a lot of potential information that occurs "between the lines" that might lead directly to 1OI questions (such as *"What other modalities exist for Administrator log-in apart from 'remote'?"* or *"What other user types are there apart from Adminstrator?"*).

Obviously, the process at the bottom does not "work" for a system that does not conform to these criteria, while the meta-process at the top works for all systems. This results in a paradox of process:

The Process Value Paradox

> *Process Value Proposition 1: The value of the application of a process is in direct proportion to what we already know about the system.*

If we know a lot about a system, we can have a process that is rich, complete, detailed, and implementable. We can define a process in great detail that is very "valuable" in showing someone exactly how to create the system. The reason for the high value is quite simple: the *process contains knowledge*. Specifically, it contains (at least some of) the knowledge of what we are trying to do. It is reasonable to assert that the most valuable process is one that contained *all* the necessary knowledge — including the knowledge of how to apply the knowledge (which is exactly what an executable does) (see Exhibit 10).

By applying a process that contains a lot of knowledge, I can transfer this knowledge into my deliverable or into the activity of creating my deliverable. The alternative is that if I do not have a process that contains sufficient

Exhibit 10. A software wizard.

A typical software "wizard" is an executable process. It contains the knowledge and the context expanded to the level whereby anyone with a reasonable amount of knowledge of basic computers can execute it.

Consider how much knowledge would have been required 10 or 15 years ago to install a modem driver in an IBM PC. To make this system work, the user would need to know:

- The type of modem and its primary characteristics
- The appropriate modem initialization strings for the particular modem
- The interrupt line (IRQ) to be used on the PC
- Other IRQs being used on the PC
- The IO port address on the PC
- The send/receive characteristics of the system being accessed
- The terminal emulation to be used, the baud rate, number of data bits, whether it uses parity, number of stop bits, whether it employs hardware flow control, etc.

And there are a lot of other factors "between the lines" here, such as how to detect interrupt conflicts and reassign IRQs.

With modern setup wizards, the user often needs to know nothing more than:

- I have a modem I wish to install
- I know how to click a mouse button

The reason the user can now get away with knowing a lot less is that the software wizard contains the knowledge.

---

knowledge, I personally have to find the knowledge here and now. This invariably takes time and effort away from acquiring the *system* knowledge. Given the finite amount of time we have to find *all* the necessary knowledge, it almost certainly means that the knowledge content of my final system must be less. That is, the final system has less functionality, is less usable, is not documented as well, has more defects, or any other of the valuable knowledge attributes we expect in the system.

Meta-processes only contain knowledge about *types* and not about the specific system I am trying to build. The more meta, the less useful, because the process leaves me to find out the difference between the meta knowledge and the necessary final knowledge. So the more *meta* the process is, the less immediately valuable it tends to be.

How does the knowledge get into processes? It is usually by executing some version of that process and determining from the execution what works and what does not. It may be a close approximation (a "bootstrap") of the process, or it may be a "meta" level version that becomes progressively more explicit as I get closer to the right answer. It is possible I have acquired the process knowledge on a different system or an earlier system. Someone else may have acquired the knowledge on a very similar system and made it available to me, either by telling me about it (brain–brain transfer of knowledge), writing a book about it which I read (book–brain transfer) or created scripts which I can use (the executable software form). Obviously, both the "amount" and "quality" of knowledge in a process is proportional to the similarity of the systems being worked when the process was created and the system I am trying to build using the process.

Using Systems to Build Processes

We usually think of using a process to create a system, but it also goes the other way. In fact, the only legitimate way to create a process is to use a system to prove the process. We can create meta processes through analytical activity — we can just sit down and think up the process. But we will not know if the process truly works until we try to use it for the purpose it was intended, which is building a system. In a real sense, then, we create systems using processes, and define processes by building systems (see The Reflexive Creation of Systems and Processes in Chapter 1).

Because we create or at least validate our system building processes by building systems, the amount of knowledge contained in a process is proportional to what we know about the system. The amount and quality (applicability to the task) of knowledge in a process is the only genuine measure of value in a process.

If we do not know much about a system, we might have to make do with a higher-level (more meta) process. Such processes do not give us much. The job of the systems developer is to learn, and the meta process does not help with that, because it is unable to clearly state what knowledge I should acquire (because I do not know much about the system). A meta process still leaves me with 2OI. Therefore we have Process Value Proposition 2:

> *Process Value Proposition 2: The value of a process is in direct proportion to what we do not know about the system.*

Arguably, if I already have the knowledge, I do not have much need of a process. This is why experienced engineers tend not to use restrictive processes, and expert users do not usually use wizards. Helping me implement knowledge I already have is fine, but it is not really what I need — I need help finding and implementing knowledge I *do not* already have. So the best process is one that works when I do not know much about the system I am trying to build. Unfortunately, Process Value Proposition 1 is in direct contradiction to Process Value Proposition 2. We can resolve the apparent paradox by restating the propositions slightly:

> *Process Value Proposition 1 Restated: The value that can be provided through the application of a process is in direct proportion to what we already know about the system.*

Process Value Proposition 2 Restated: The value that is needed in the application of a process is in direct proportion to what we do not know about the system.

This restatement removes the self-referential paradox by separately addressing the two sides of the equation:

1. How much help can be provided?
2. How much help is needed?

It does not resolve the general dilemma of process which is that, in general, process provides the most assistance where it is least needed.

Other Problems with Process

There are other problems with process, apart from this dilemma. These are related to the activity of devising process, who devises it, and what they do with it when it has been devised.

How Do We Get Process? We can only devise processes for things that we know how to do and we can only know how to do something by having done it successfully. Like many of these observations, this is not a strictly rigorous truth. For instance, we can learn how to do something right by doing it wrong and being able to recognize the differences. We can also learn how to do something by successfully (or unsuccessfully) doing something similar and interpolating the differences. We can even sometimes learn how to do something correctly through sheer blind luck; although it is unlikely that we could successfully build a larger, more-complex system simply through this method. Even given these scenarios, however, we could argue that unless we do it right at least once, we have not proven that we can do it at all; therefore, we have not validated the process used or generated.

In the systems development field, it means we must have already built something very close to what we are building now. Again, one could argue, if we have already built it, why are we building it again?

The processes we use on our current project can only have been devised on earlier projects. Herein lays the Lemma of Eternal Lateness:

The only processes we can use on the current project were defined on previous projects, which were different.

And at least to some extent things are different between the project in which the process was proven and the current project. Therefore, to some extent, the processes will not work as well. Actually, this is the only useful extent, because the differences are what separate the current project from the earlier one — they are why we have a current project at all. The more different the projects are, the more the processes will tend not to work.

And it is only in the differences that we can actually acquire (new) knowledge.

This is simply a restatement of the Process Value Paradox.

Who Devises Processes? On several occasions in my career, I have been a software "process engineer." I do not wish to impugn process engineers, but I have seen problems with this setup. In many cases, processes are devised by process engineers (including myself), but often they are not the people who are creating the system. These engineers are sometimes even offlined strictly to define the process. The developers are too busy doing the work and sometimes avoiding the process. When process is developed by people who do not actually employ it, several things happen:

- The process engineers lose sight of the detailed application that makes process valuable.
- Not having access to the detail, they are forced to work more at the *meta* level, which is easier for them because they do not have to factor actual domain knowledge into the process.
- Because they are usually not employing the process they are devising,* they may lose the ability to validate that the process is actually helpful.
- Almost inevitably, a mindset creeps in that if process is good, then more process must be *better.*
- Process becomes important to these people, not for the value it brings, but because it is the reason they are employed.
- The definition of the process is left at the description level, in book form, not the executable level. There are several reasons for this:
  - It is easier to describe something than to make it actually execute.
  - There is a lot more knowledge we would need to get to be able to factor our process knowledge to the level where it will actually execute. This would greatly increase the effort and time to produce the process.
  - In attempting to actually get something to work, the process engineers must to a certain extent become development engineers. This is sometimes outside of their mandate as process engineers.
  - This leaves the actual job of making it work (i.e., finding and applying the additional knowledge) to the development engineers using the process. This is a very safe place to be — for the process engineers. If the process works, the process group can claim credit; if it does not work, the fault can be laid at the feet of the development engineers for not implementing it properly.

*This is actually quite common in my experience — software process engineers who do not use a process themselves.

– If the process is made highly specific, it often means the process cannot be easily used across wide swaths of the organization. In order to "maximize" their effect, most process groups look to assist larger rather than smaller constituencies.

I do not mean to be unfair to process engineers. It is a difficult job, and one that, in my experience, is rarely given the resources, authority, and support necessary to make it really successful. But as with many offlined "support" groups, there is a strong tendency for process groups to become marginalized within an organization. Part of the problem is the way we go about developing process; the other is our expectations — what we are asking process to do.

Given these issues, and the one that follows, there is a tendency in many process areas to devise more and more high-level, disconnected, vague, paper-intensive, descriptive, incomplete, and unproven processes whose value when applied is questionable and certainly not proven. On the occasions where detail is attempted, it is inevitably based on previous projects, not the current situation. Because process engineers are rarely required to prove the value of the processes they define, the process detail tends to become constraining rather than value adding. It is not surprising that developers often rebel against the processes that are defined this way.

Where Do We Put Process? The final issue is what do we do with the process once we have developed it? For this, I refer to the third and last of the Laws of Software Process:

> *The very last knowledge to be considered as a candidate for implementation into an executable software system will be the knowledge of how to implement knowledge into an executable software system.*

When one could reasonably assert that the job of the software developer is to extract knowledge from brains (talk to the customer) and books (read the specification), and transcribe it into an executable form, then the fact that much of our development process ends up on paper is ironic, to say the least.

Why is this? The question baffled me for a long time. One of the more commonly accepted organization process models prescribes that organizations should create "an approved documented process." For me, and I suspect most people, "documented" means "on paper." That is, there is some implication that the target of the process will be a descriptive document or process manual. A while ago, I discussed this with a quite well-known process guru, because it seemed to me just a license to kill trees. I thought it should read "...an approved automated process."* The guru's

---

*In defense of the SEI/CMM, from which this was taken, it does address tool and executable use, if obliquely, at the lower levels. There is an entire Key Process Area (Technology Change Management) devoted to exactly this.

Exhibit 11. Process and the Five Orders of Ignorance.

Order of ignorance	Effectiveness of predefined process	Source of process	Type of process	Process medium
0OI: Proven answers	Very high	Prior system development	Deterministic	Highly automated
1OI: Known variable questions	High	Prior system development + analysis of current system	Variable substitution	Automated with variable substitution
2OI: Unknown unknowns	Low	Discovery and process analysis	Strategy based	Human based
3OI: Unknown processes	Irrelevant	Similarity of process target	Meta process	Human based
4OI: Meta level	Irrelevant	Variable	High-level conceptual	Human based

rational defense of this was as follows: we have to understand something before we can automate it, and unless you can document it, you do not understand it. I can certainly appreciate the reasoning behind this thinking, but I also think it is quite wrong. We routinely build systems before we fully understand them. In fact it is only for 0OI and 1OI systems that we could ever understand them entirely in advance. Building systems without having complete information up front is the norm, not the exception. As I will cover in a later chapter, it may be the only way we can build certain kinds of systems, and the way in which the systems of the future must be built.

The Purpose of Process

It is evident from the foregoing that the purpose of process is limited in many ways. Because the effectiveness of process is determined by the degree of unknowns we can map process onto the Five Orders of Ignorance (see Exhibit 11).

Summary

It might appear that the outlook for process is bleak, given its apparent limitations. But that may not be so. Process has, I think, a very strong role to play in the future, but it will probably work in a different way for a very simple reason: it does not work very well today. But the fact that process does not currently work too well is not so much the fault of process, but what we are asking process to do. The future of process will reflect vastly increased executability, domain specialization, executable meta-process elements, and careful consideration of the value proposition. Indeed, I think this is happening today, except it goes under the guise of commercial off-the-shelf (COTS) package implementation, specialized language creation and use, tool building, along with a liberal dose of glue code written to bridge the meta-to-specific gap or the domain-domain translation. Driven by directives such as SEI's Technology Change Management Key Process Area, perhaps software process engineers will eventually revert to being software engineers.

Chapter 3
The Meaning
of Methodology

meth·od·ol·o·gy *n* **1:** *a body of methods, rules, and postulates employed by a discipline: a particular procedure or set of procedures* **2:** *the analysis of the principles or procedures of inquiry in a particular field*

— *Webster's New Collegiate Dictionary*

The IEEE Glossary of Software Engineering Terminology (IEEE-STD 610.12) does not actually have a definition of *methodology,* which is quite surprising given the importance of the subject and the amount of copy it generates. The closest IEEE's Glossary comes is *method standard,* which really is not the same thing.

Methodology is a word that is used quite extensively in software circles. Not only are there differences of opinion on methodologies, there are differences of opinion on the meaning and scope of the word itself. Methodologies range from loose sets of guidelines to multi-volume treatises that purport to define and control all aspects of creating systems. The definition I will use is that a methodology is the framework in which thinking (about the problem, context, solution or anything else that is relevant) is done. There is an abundance of methodologies out there: old ones, new ones, big and famous ones, tiny and obscure ones. Methodologies have been named for the person who created or popularized them (e.g., Yourdon) or named for some aspect of their reasoning (e.g., OO). There are graphical methods and text methods and table methods; empirical methods, heuristic methods, and scientific methods. There are methods that lots of people use and ones that no one uses.

Sometimes, although recently less than of old, methodology has been the field in which some of the conceptual and philosophical battles of software engineering were fought. Methodologies have often been the arena in which the gurus and thought leaders of software dueled. Their weapons were plastic diagramming templates, CASE tools, overhead transparencies, and articles in ACM's *Communications* or IEEE's *Software.* At times in the evolution of the software business, methodologies replaced each other at the rate of a banana republic changing dictators. A friend once commented that methodologies are like queen bees; it seems that each must sting all the other methodologies to death in order to survive. Few subjects, except perhaps programming languages, generate so much patriotic fervor on the part of their adherents and emotion in their defense. Yet many of the methodology differences were slight, even cosmetic. Early CASE tools such as Excelerator boasted that they supported both the Yourdon and the Gane-Sarson conventions of "Structured Analysis." In reality, what these tools did was convert all circular "process" icons (Yourdon convention) in the "Data Flow Diagram" graphical models into rounded-corner squares (Gane-Sarson convention). The real difference between the two methodologies was actually related to the rate of functional decomposition, which is a thought process, not a notational convention. Nevertheless, each camp had its quota of adherents and detractors.

I would like to present a slightly different view of methods here, and maybe shine a little light on this sometimes foggy scene.

Third Order of Ignorance Processes

To cut to the chase, I contend that all methods are Third Order Ignorance processes. The Third Order of Ignorance is defined (in the first person) as:

> *I have Third Order Ignorance (3OI) when I do not know of a suitably efficient way to find out that I do not know that I do not know something.*

Basically, the job of processes at the 3OI level is to convert Second Order Ignorance (2OI) into either First Order Ignorance (1OI) or Zeroth Order Ignorance (0OI). That is, a 3OI process operating on a problem domain translates what we do not know we do not know into either questions (1OI) or answers (0OI).

We see two cycles here: (1) to find out that we do not know something (to find the question), and (2) to find out the answer (see Exhibit 1). These correspond to reducing 2OI into 1OI and then into 0OI. This occurs as follows:

- *Get Context (Questions).* Exploring in the 2OI domain, using type-questions, tests, observation, interaction, analytical techniques, and even blind luck, we somehow learn that there are things we do not know. The act of discovering this is the first part of the 3OI process. It is usually a bootstrap activity. Generally we do know *something* about the system — a lot if it is a 1OI system, much less if it is a 2OI system. By attempting to classify our meager knowledge against reality (whatever and wherever that may be) we start to find out more about what it is we do not know. Specifically, we find out the context or framework of our lack of knowledge. It is at this point that we often start to realize that perhaps we do not know as much as we thought, or the problem is bigger and more complex than it looked like to begin with.
- *Get (Specific) Questions.* The next cycle uses the contextual questions (against the environment, not the methodology!) to drive out

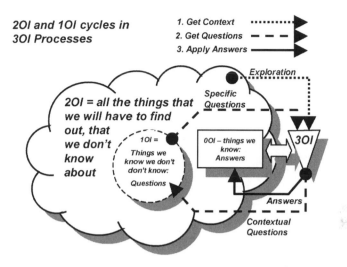

2OI and 1OI cycles in 3OI Processes

1. Get Context ⋯⋯▶
2. Get Questions ─ ─ ─▶
3. Apply Answers ──▶

Exploration

Specific Questions

2OI = all the things that we will have to find out, that we don't know about

1OI = Things we know we don't don't know: Questions

0OI – things we know: Answers

3OI

Answers

Contextual Questions

Exhibit 1. 0OI cycles.

---

the specifics of what we do not know. In particular — the detailed questions that will allow us to obtain an answer from the environment.

- *Get (and Apply) Answers.* The final and perhaps even trivial step is to obtain the answers to the questions and then appropriately apply them to the system (i.e., complete the design and code).

These activities are in approximate descending order of difficulty — specifically identifying one's area of ignorance is in many ways the hardest task, getting the answers the easiest. The purpose of a methodology is to provide a framework in which to construct or populate our knowledge as we get it. Most methodologies allow for certain kinds of verification (although rarely validation) of the knowledge structure and even a small amount of the knowledge content. Specifically, by examining the parts of the methodology structured knowledge store that are populated (with knowledge learned) and unpopulated (with knowledge yet to be learned), we can usually recognize where our knowledge is deficient and generate some level of question.

Methodologies can provide us with useful type-questions. A method that requires us to build, for example, a system state behavior model will require us to ask questions related to the operational states of the system and the transitions between those states. The questions prompted by the unpopulated methodology must naturally be high-level type-questions such as *"what operational states can the system have?"* and *"what different ways do you want to transition from this screen to that screen?"*

The Job of Methodology

The act of getting a question answered is usually much easier than recognizing the conditions under which we have to ask a question — that is, getting the question is harder than getting the answer. Because the main work is in defining the question in sufficient detail to elicit an answer, we can infer the *real* job of a methodology:

> *The real job of a methodology is to tell us what we do not know.*

The finding and fixing of bugs in programs while testing is a good example of this 3OI (2OI) → 1OI, 0OI cycle. There are two discrete stages to testing:

1. *Find a bug.* The bug manifests itself through some externally identifiable event such as a system crash. I call this moment *an epiphany of knowledge*. Basically, the system is telling the tester that there is something he or she does not know. (*Omigosh, the system crashed! What went wrong?*) Well, we do not know what is wrong. Yet. But we *do* know something is wrong. Until this event occurred, we did not know something was wrong, even though it was. Simply stated, we had 2OI. This event, or more correctly the activity we were conducting to cause the event, is the 3OI process. What it has done is illuminate our ignorance. It has converted 2OI into 1OI.

2. *Fix a bug.* Now the work begins to find out why the bug occurred. Note that we do not have this information. Yet. But we do have some information about the crash, and we do have a series of increasingly relevant and pertinent questions: *What was the system doing when it crashed? What inputs were being processed? Who was running it? What else was running?* These questions are backed with explicit data relating to the event at hand: the time, memory dumps, input transactions, traces, etc. These specific questions indicate we are now in the state of 1OI. Getting the answers to these questions is another part of the process. Tracking down the bug and answering the question "*what would it take to fix it?*" converts our 1OI into 0OI.

So the primary purpose of this 3OI process (in this case the activity of testing) is to tell us that we *do not* know something, not that we *do* know something. The same is true of other methods, including the well-accepted graphical analysis and design approaches. That the application of methodologies derives questions rather than answers is a fact that is not often acknowledged by methodologists or perhaps even understood by practitioners using a methodology. It is common to see methodologies and their associated tool sets advertised like this: "*Use my Aspect Oriented Widgets Framework Pattern and you'll get the right answer!*" However, it is not possible for methodologies to provide the answer — they simply do not contain the answer (see the "Dual Hypotheses of Knowledge Discovery," Chapter 1). In fact, with luck and discipline, use most methods correctly and you will get the right *question*. As simple as it is, this can be a difficult concept for many adults to accept in practice because:

- All software is simply a representation of knowledge and it is the acquisition of this knowledge that is the real activity of software development.
- All software artifacts (requirements documents, design documents, code, test plans, management plans, execution scripts, compiler parameters, etc.) are knowledge repositories of various types.
- Using a methodology is applying a specific process and mindset to populate these repositories with knowledge through a combination of analytical activity and interaction with the target knowledge domain.
- The methodology does not and cannot contain the answer; all it can do is to help us to determine if we have the answer. It usually does this in several ways. Basically, the methodology does not provide the answer. *It tells us whether we have the answer.* This is a very important distinction and one that is often missed.

So the key output of using a method is to find out, at the end of the day, what our level of ignorance is. This is not an easy thing for adults to hear. Most of us, myself included, like to use processes that tell us how smart we are. We like to work in areas that allow us to demonstrate competence, and to show off our skills, knowledge, and expertise. We simply do not like to use processes that shine a light on what we do not know and thereby expose our ignorance. That, however, is the job of a methodology.

A Test System

Let me illustrate this ignorance illumination with a couple of examples. First a specific experience:

> *"Here's our high-level process flow for this system,"* the team leader said as he put up the next transparency. *"As you can see, at the very highest level, there are three essential processes."* He pointed to the overhead.

The scene was a high-level review for a testing system for a cellular telephone switch. Assembled in the room were a number of developers and others. The requirements and high-level architecture were developed using a fairly well-accepted methodology for this kind of system (the Hatley-Pirbhai method, in fact). The high-level process flow (a data flow diagram) looked like the diagram in Exhibit 2. This is a great over-simplification, but it shows the essential transforms of setting up the system, testing it, and then tearing it down.*

---

*This is very simplified. For those methodology eagles, I have not included the flow names (which is a no-no) because I am not trying to be rigorous. Readers familiar with the H-P method will recognize that the team is "enhancing the essential transform model" by adding IO transforms front and back.

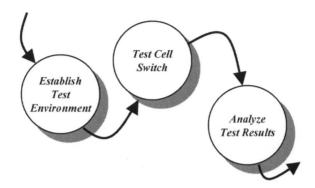

Exhibit 2. Test cell switch DFD 0.

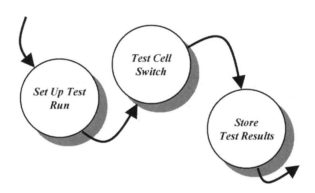

Exhibit 3. Test cell switch DFD 1.

So far so good. The next level, a decomposition of the central transform Test Cell Switch again simplified a lot, looked rather similar (see Exhibit 3). Here, at the decomposition of the central transform, we see the activities necessary to support the testing activity: each test has to be retrieved from the test environment and then, after testing, the results of the tests are stored back in the environment for analysis (see Exhibit 4). Taking the decomposition of the central transform again we see something looking suspiciously like the higher level. Again, the actual picture had a lot more than three "processes" (transforms) on it. Here they are extracting a test command from the test run, running it, and posting results.

The fourth and final level looked like the diagram in Exhibit 5. At this level, the system is parsing a test command from the test command string, running a test, and then obtaining the results from the stack.

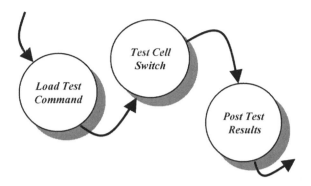

Exhibit 4. Test cell switch DFD 1.1.

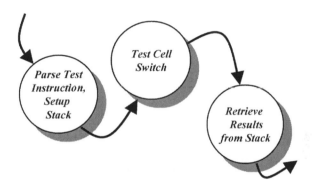

Exhibit 5. Test cell switch DFD 1.1.1.

What is going on here? This team had defined a large quantity of transform behavior, almost all of which was related to *setting up a test, not to running a test!* In fact, they had done a lot of work and gone down many levels of analysis without answering the question "*what does it mean to test a cellular telephone switch?*"

Because testing the switch was the actual purpose of the system, clearly something was not being done. But why? The answer lies in our desire to be right. Basically the team was responsible for developing the setup and teardown, so they could themselves answer the questions posed by the model they were trying to build. The central transform, which is the reason the system exists, they did not have answers for. They were not in control of this aspect of the system. To get the answers, they would have to look at the "outside world," which in this case was a whole organization of hundreds of engineers who were at that moment designing and building the switch. So the system to be tested and the test system were being built concurrently. Test system requirements were changing hourly. Clearly, for the

45

engineers designing the test system, this was not a high-quality source of information. In order to feel competent and to feel like they were getting something accomplished, they concentrated on deciding what they could decide and building what they could build. Unfortunately, this was not what was required.

The process and methodology they were using was highlighting what they did not know. This was quite uncomfortable for them and they responded as many of us would do, by avoiding it altogether and working on something on which they could "make progress," on something they knew.

For most of us, given a straight choice of working on something that is easy, something that plays to our strengths and demonstrates how competent we are, and working on something that is hard, something we have no clue about, and ultimately shows us and everyone else just how little we understand about the system, we are probably going to choose the former.

This team had spent all its time working on its area of expertise (where it was likely to learn nothing new) rather than its area of nonexpertise (where it would certainly learn a lot). This is not only a natural, human tendency; it is also exacerbated by some of the pressures we experience in development, the desire to demonstrate "progress" and most of all by the organization's and management's expectation of producing a product.

The second example is more generic, but I will continue using data flow diagrams (DFDs; leveled transform models) as my method. This is not because I like DFDs as a model or think they are a good method, but because they are one of the simplest and best-known graphical modeling conventions.

Exhibit 6 shows a "bad" (although "correct") DFD. It is highly unlikely that anyone would present such an egregious model for inspection. While it has labels, assuming they are uniquely named and the model fragment might be "correct" in terms of the syntactic rules of this modeling approach, it is obviously not a "good" DFD.

As unlikely as it is to see the DFD in Exhibit 6, I cannot count the number of times I have seen offerings such as Exhibit 7 or variations on it. The two DFDs are almost equivalent. In fact, we could argue that the first might be better because it is actually more honest about the (lack of) quality of the information it contains. While the second might be a "correct" DFD, it is an almost useless DFD. There is a simple reason for this: it contains no knowledge.

A developer would not know any more after looking at the model than he knew before looking at it. The model shows that there are inputs and outputs and the system "processes transactions." Well, every system ever built accepts inputs, produces outputs, and "processes transactions" in some way. The key issue is not that it has inputs and outputs but what

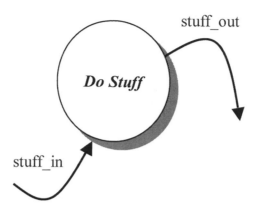

Exhibit 6. Almost useless DFD.

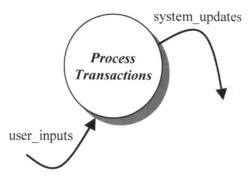

Exhibit 7. A "correct" DFD.

exactly *are* the inputs and outputs? The specification is not that the system "processes transactions," but exactly what the transactions are and how they are processed in *this* system.

Given that software development is a knowledge-acquisition activity, the author of this model obviously has not acquired the particular knowledge of this particular system. Because acquiring this knowledge is the goal of the analytical and requirements-gathering process, clearly something is missing. Such knowledge-deficient models sometimes occur because a software process dictates that the developers produce a model at a given stage of the project. So they produce a model; not a useful model, not the correct model — simply *a* model.

This leads to perhaps the most-important observation about methodologies. This DFD, while knowledge-light, does in fact contain one very useful piece of information — assuming that the model is the best job we can do of describing the system at the time we drew the model: it tells us that we do not have the answer. That is, attempting to produce the output required by the methodology does not necessarily give us the knowledge, it *tells us whether or not we have the knowledge.*

In this case we do not. We can tell this by the nonspecific nature of the model components. What we now do know is that we do not know enough. By carefully and honestly using the methodology, we have transformed 2OI into 1OI. I do not have the answer, but now I know that I do not have the answer. And I may know some of the questions: *Who is the user? What inputs come in?* I have somewhat localized my ignorance — I know a little better where to look. If I have a part of the model that contains detailed and relevant knowledge and another that does not, I should concentrate on the areas I know least, on the parts of the model that contain least knowledge, that are most vague.

The Maturity of Testing

Paradoxically, it seems we could measure the effectiveness of a method, not by how much it demonstrates what we know, but by how much it demonstrates what we do not know. Of all methods in common use in software development, only the act of testing seems to have made this philosophical leap. It is now pretty well accepted that the job of testing is to find bugs (show what we do not know), rather than prove the system works (show what we do know). The insistence of the newer "agile" methodologies on the early development, testing, and even delivery of real executables is supporting the same contention.

To apply this concept globally in an organization might look rather weird. In the development of graphical requirements and design models, would we end up rewarding people for doing "bad" models rather than good ones? *"Excellent job in constructing this model, Jim. Obviously, you don't have a clue about what you're doing!"*

As ironic as this sounds, if we apply this logic to that part of systems development that is currently populated with graphical modeling activities, it is increasingly the reality in testing. In testing we have learned to recognize and reward the identification of defects. It would be a poor testing organization that punished the uncovering of problems. The other software development methods of requirements definition, design, and coding have not reached this point. Yet.

Summary

This is the meaning of methodology. Methodologies exist primarily to show us our ignorance and to identify what we do not know. Certainly, there are other advantages to methodologies — the discipline they impose and the framework they provide for structuring our thinking are very valuable. Close inspection of the results we obtain from this discipline often shows that there are some costs associated with applying the methods. Some of this is the cost of learning the methodology and syntax. Some of it is in the constraints the methods apply to our thinking — while the discipline helps us categorize the information we need, as in any other process, it may inhibit our understanding of aspects of the system not fully covered by the methodology. But the bottom line is always that methods do not do the work, people do; and methods do not highlight our knowledge but shine a bright, glaringly uncomfortable light on our ignorance. And we do not like that.

Chapter 4
The Logic of Life Cycles

All the business of war, and indeed all the business of life, is to endeavor to find out what you don't know by what you do.

— Arthur Wellesley, Duke of Wellington
Croker Papers (1885), vol. iii, p. 276

The software profession's first attempts at defining a life cycle for the development of software were unashamedly based on the assembly line concept that dominates manufacturing (see Exhibit 1). The fact that many of the businesses that moved into the area of software in the 1960s and 1970s were manufacturing industries reinforced this philosophy. People built the new product like they built the old product; they managed the way they were used to managing. Also, the nature of the systems being built at the time tended to reinforce the idea the software was a product to be produced, and that the production of this "product" had discrete phases through which it would pass before being shipped to the customer. One of the common characteristics of these systems was that the user's requirements were often well defined and quite static. The computerized systems of the time often replaced existing systems, some of which were fully operational, albeit on paper. Even many of the engineering systems of the early computer decades of the 1950s through the early 1980s were deterministic endeavors in that the target functions of the systems were well understood, well defined, largely identifiable, and quite predictable. This was the era of the large COBOL systems, of the perennial designs and redesigns of payroll and accounting systems.

The Assembly Line

Winston Royce* was one of the first to identify "standard" sequences of activities in the creation of software. His documentation of the basic value-adding and feedback steps known as the "Waterfall Model" (see Exhibit 2) remains, to this day, arguably the most commonly used model for the planning and management of software development.

*Royce, W., Managing the development of large systems, IEEE WESCON 1-9, 1970.

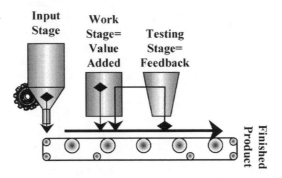

Exhibit 1. Assembly line process.

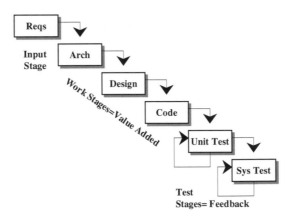

Exhibit 2. Waterfall Model.

The premise of the Waterfall Model is simple:

- *Discrete stages.* The model has well defined and separated stages that are usually managed differently, and may employ different team members or even organizations.
- *Requirements stage.* The *what* of the system is defined through some research, questioning, and analytical activity. The research usually operates on the user's environment, the questioning of the user or specifier of the system, and the analysis is done on the answers obtained from the environment and user. The implication of this life cycle model is that the combination of these activities renders the requirements "complete" and "usable." "Complete" means that the collected requirements fully describe the needed capabilities of the system, and "usable" means that the context and format of the requirements are sufficiently consistent to allow the later activities of architecture and design.

- *Architecture stage.* The first part of the *how* of the system. The requirements are somehow factored into a high-level "executable" description and folded into knowledge of general systems design to produce a high-level systems design that will fulfill the requirements while operating within the target production environment constraints.
- *Detailed design stage.* The second part of the *how* of the system. Generally, the high-level design is decomposed into smaller subsystems and modules, whose internal design is decided. At this point internal systems ("design") knowledge tends to predominate over the user and operational environment knowledge, although the design must (should) support the requirements at all times.
- *Code.* The last part of the *how* of the system. In this stage, all the knowledge from the previous stages is translated into some executable form. Generally, a certain amount of additional knowledge such as language capabilities and limitations or target processor operation is added at this point.
- *Unit test.* The first of the "feedback" stages. Here the operation of the coded module is compared against some set of expected functions and outputs. Any differences are presumed resolved through a "recoding" activity. This is repeated until the operation of the product is considered close enough to specification to proceed to the later feedback stages.
- *System test.* There are usually several stages of this type of "feedback." The modules are aggregated in increasing size, quantity, and complexity, and a variety of testing functions are performed against the combinations. These typically include integration test of combinations of modules up to the subsystem level; functional system test of the full system; user-oriented system test, often run against user-supplied data; and alpha and beta tests run in the users' environment. There may also be load tests to ensure the system loads in the varieties of user target environments; acceptance tests run to certify the system; performance tests to prove performance and capacity levels; and many other flavors of feedback.

Finally the system is certified and is released to the user.

This model is quite logical and, depending on the level of abstraction, may be quite useful, even if not very "accurate" in the sense that it reasonably explains, predicts, and explicitly helps control the actual tasks being worked. Certainly it makes sense for us to understand *what* we are building before we try to build it. It is equally hard to see at first glance how we can test a system to prove it works before we have built the system. Variations and modifications of this model abound. Most Waterfall-based process models in actual operation include a number of mechanisms for tighter control of feedback, avoiding having to wait until close to the very end of

THE LAWS OF SOFTWARE PROCESS

the development activity before the knowledge (requirements, design, etc.) is verified. These mechanisms include close cooperation between developers and users in, for instance, joint application development (JAD) sessions or through requirements, design, and code inspections. These are all fine methods and very useful. Their application has allowed the Waterfall Model to be used quite effectively for decades, with some qualification.

But no matter what adjustments are made to this life cycle model to make it more useful and applicable, it will not be "correct" or even "accurate." There is one simple reason it can never be "correct" — it is a model (see Exhibit 3).

Models are *always* simplifications of the things they are modeling. The only way a model could be as complex as the real thing is if it actually were the real thing, in which case it would no longer be a model.

The very act of factoring knowledge into any model tends to change the knowledge. For instance, one of the limitations of any textual form of knowledge is that it is always *de facto* in sequence. A word follows a word, a sentence follows another sentence. Even if we rearrange the words and sentences, words still follow or precede other words. Sequence is inseparable from text. Given that unavoidable characteristic, *any* list of tasks or functions written down in words must follow some sequence. Consider the following list: Define Requirements, Develop Architecture, Design Modules, Code Modules, Test Modules, Test Module Interfaces, Test Subsystems, and Test System; simply writing them down forces a sequence. The fact that the tasks or phases are written in a sequence strongly implies that they should be executed in that sequence. Given this particular list, the order in which the Waterfall phases are placed is easily the "most logical." That is, one could more easily make a case for the phases to be in this sequence than in any other, although for any given instance of systems development, it might be entirely possible that we would execute the phases in a different order.

Therefore, text documents using words are good for describing sequences; but they are not as good for describing activities that might not fall in a sequence that can be executed at any time, that can be executed concurrently, that are event-determined in real time, or that are predicate-based.

Exhibit 4. Baking Cookies

Chocolate Chip Cookie Recipe

Ingredients: 1/2 cup butter; 1/2 cup brown sugar; 1/2 cup white sugar; 1 egg; 1/2 teaspoon vanilla; 1 cup flour; 1/2 teaspoon salt; 1/2 teaspoon baking soda; 1/2 cup chopped nuts; 1/2 cup semisweet chocolate chips.

Gradually add sugar to butter and beat until creamy. Beat in egg and vanilla. Sift and stir in flour, salt, and baking soda. Stir in nuts and chocolate chips. Drop 2″ round batter onto a greased cookie sheet. Place in preheated oven at 375º for 10 minutes.

A simple example of this is the activity of following a recipe for baking cookies, shown in Exhibit 4. Everything goes well until the "Place in *preheated* oven" step. In an ideal implementation of this system, the activities of mixing the cookie ingredients and heating the oven are concurrent. In this particular recipe, the "preheat" step is out of order and appears dependent on the mixing steps. Slavishly following the recipe format will lead to the prepared batter sitting and waiting for the oven to heat. Good cooks know this and they will carefully read the instructions first, mentally converting them from their linear form in the recipe to a combination linear-dependent and concurrent-independent form in their heads before they start cooking. Sometimes sequence is irrelevant, and preparation can be batched — with all the mixing done up front. But in many recipes the mixing must be done immediately prior to use.

Given this, one of the advertised limitations of the Waterfall Model is its "enforced" sequence of phases, which may only be a convention of the form in which we present it.

This is, in fact, the case with the IEEE Standard 1074 (Standard for Developing Software Life Cycle Processes),* which appears to recommend a Waterfall Model but phases may be ordered as needed. This linear phase limitation of the Waterfall Model is commonly overcome by "overlapping" the phases in some diagrammatic form (it is not possible to do this easily in text).

This overlapping signifies a certain amount of concurrency in the tasks in each phase. There are several things implied in this use of the model:

- There exists a level of detailed tasks below the phase level that is not being shown.
- There is dependent behavior between some elements of phases that cause sequence (the nonoverlapped sections).
- There is some independent behavior between tasks and products that allows concurrency (the overlapped sections).

*IEEE Std 1074-1997, IEEE Standard for Developing Software Life Cycle Processes, IEEE, Piscataway, New Jersey, 1997.

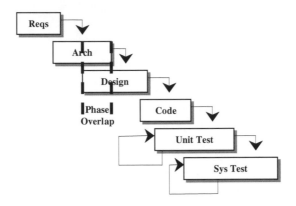

Exhibit 5. Overlapped Waterfall Model.

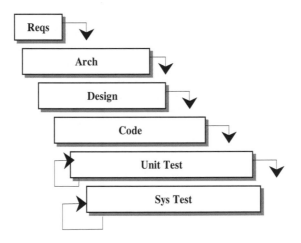

Exhibit 6. Massively overlapped Waterfall Model.

- The general trend of activity follows the Waterfall approach (i.e., "what" is determined before "how").

- There remains an implication that once a phase is "completed," it is not reentered (i.e., the work inherent in that phase does not need to be repeated).

In Exhibit 6, the phases are so overlapped that the concept of "phase" starts to disappear. Modern software development, consisting of rapid-cycle development and test, sometimes resembles this at the highest level — the development is actually in "all" phases at the same time. Nevertheless, adjustments of this kind are routinely made to try to make the aging Waterfall Model fit modern development paradigms and modern software realities.

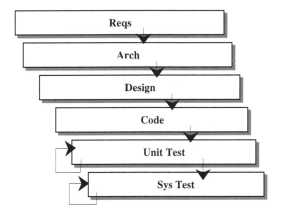

Exhibit 7. Fully overlapped model.

Nevertheless, the fact that both the Waterfall Model and the adjustments to it are both pragmatic and useful does not mean that the model is "correct."

In fact, Exhibit 7 might be the most "correct" model for many modern development environments. At any given time *all* activities (requirements definition, design, coding, and testing) may be occurring all throughout the project. This "phaseless" model is never used in practice. Why? Because it has no phases; therefore, while it might be "accurate," it is not *useful* as a management tool.

Accuracy in respect to direct one-to-one correspondence between the "real world" and the management model may be less necessary than we think and also less achievable for some very simple reasons.

Shooting Down Zeppelins

A simple metaphor may explain this. In the early years of World War I, German airships known as "Zeppelins" were used to bomb Paris and London. While they were the only long-distance bombers available at the time, and caused quite a bit of panic, they were not very useful as a military device. Essentially, they were large, slow moving (85 mph), and very fragile bags of highly explosive gas with a maximum operational altitude of around 14,000 feet and a very small payload (about 4000 lbs. of bombs). Needless to say, they were rather susceptible to ground or aerial fire. In fact, the first Zeppelin involved in a bombing raid over Liege, France, in 1914 was brought down by ground-based artillery fire.

If we look at what is required to bag a Zeppelin, we see that it is a quite deterministic problem and that success is mostly a matter of the prior measurement and processing of known information.

57

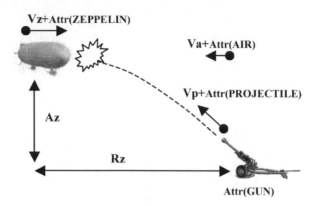

Exhibit 8. Shooting down zeppelins.

Exhibit 8 illustrates this system in operation. To hit a Zeppelin (assuming that you have a cannon of suitable capability) requires the following information:

- *Attributes of the target.* These include the velocity (speed and direction) of the Zeppelin, its altitude, distance, and angle downrange; to a certain extent, we might need to know the size of the target, and to a lesser extent its construction (this was not very important because the skin of a Zeppelin could be pierced by a dart, which were, in fact, actually thrown at the airships by attacking fighters). Also to a lesser extent, knowledge of the maneuverability of the airship might also be useful.

- *Attributes of the cannon.* These include muzzle velocity, and perhaps such things as rate of traverse and elevation.

- *Attributes of the projectile.* These include its shape and how that shape affects its air resistance and trajectory. If it is an explosive shot, then the effective range of the explosion would be useful. Also critical, although very difficult to calculate, is the performance of the projectile through the air.

- *Attributes of the air.* These include obvious data such as wind velocity, its density, its temperature and humidity (which effects density and viscosity), and complex information such as thermal and density variations related to altitude.

Assuming that the anti-aircraft artillery (AAA) is sufficiently powerful, success in shooting down a Zeppelin is largely a function of the accuracy of measuring these variables, calculating their relationships, and usefully relaying this information to the gunner at the point of firing. The resulting behavior in some ways resembles the Waterfall Model (Exhibit 9).

Exhibit 9. Comparison of zeppelin and jet plane.

Attribute	Zeppelin/cannon	Jet plane/missile
Speed	Slow with respect to projectile	Similar order of magnitude
Identifiability/acquisition of target	Easy, certain	Difficult, uncertain
Maneuverability of target	Very little	Very great
Countermeasures	Very few, ineffective	Many, quite effective
Target payload	Small	Large
Maneuverability of projectile	None	Significant
Total projectile payload	Large	Small
Location of control	100 percent with gunner	Divided between gunner and projectile
In-process data collection and feedback	None	Continuous

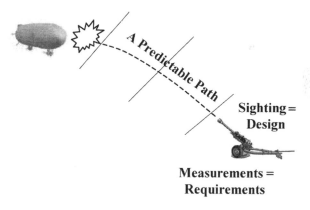

Exhibit 10. A deterministic path.

Shooting down the Zeppelin is an example of a *deterministic* system (Exhibit 10). That is, knowing the precursors (variables) in advance and in sufficient detail ensures that we can accurately predict the behavior of the system from that point onward, at least within the typical operational limits of control. However, many systems are not so deterministic.

We no longer attempt to shoot down Zeppelins, and Zeppelins are no longer used in warfare for very obvious reasons. We now attempt to shoot down very fast, often low-flying and highly maneuverable jet fighters and bombers that may have the capacity to employ countermeasures to any attempt to hit them. This makes for a somewhat more-complex situation.

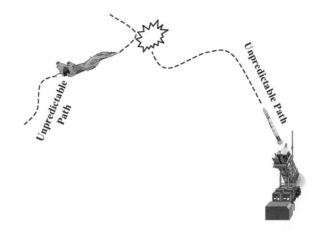

Exhibit 11. Shooting down jet planes.

Shooting Down Jet Planes

Exhibit 11 illustrates the modern situation — attempting to shoot down a supersonic jet fighter-bomber. First, it is unlikely that we would attempt to shoot down such a fast-moving jet plane using ballistic ordnance. If we did use AAA, we would certainly not shoot just one projectile, see where it goes and then shoot another (which would be the equivalent of completely building a system and then testing it to see if it works). If we used AAA at all, we would fill the air with projectiles hoping to get a lucky hit. More likely, we would use some kind of missile, either ground- or air-launched, that we would be able to track, acquire or "lock-on" to the target, and maneuver postlaunch to hit it.

Here we see the fundamental difference with the Zeppelin scenario. First, the missile *will* change direction after launch. Second and critically, the airplane will almost certainly respond to the missile launch and tracking by changing direction, by taking evasive action. The missile will respond to this change of direction by itself changing direction. Here is the critical difference: the missile causes the plane to change direction and the plane causes the missile to change direction. In the case of the Zeppelin, the airship's speed with respect to the ground shot was very slow. In the case of the jet plane, the speeds of the plane and missile are much closer. Because each variable causes changes in the other variables, it is intrinsically a nondeterministic system. This means that we *cannot* know in advance exactly how the system will function.

Other interesting points are that, at the point of launch, we cannot know where in space the missile will intercept the plane. However, to be successful we do not *need* to know where in space the missile and the plane will come together, as long as we have a reasonable certainty that they will.

Exhibit 12. Zeppelin projects.

Attribute	Project version
Speed	Typically long-cycle, low rate of change
(Target) Requirements	Well defined, defined in terms of system function, extant source of detailed requirements, well defined analysis methods
Requirements changes	Low rate, static
Change response to system construction (countermeasures: reaction of target to system)	Low or irrelevant
Target payload (delivered functionality)	Typically low business value
Maneuverability of project (flexibility of process)	Typically well defined and rigid
System size (payload)	Typically large number of lines of code
Location of control on project	Usually single hierarchical and controlling resource management
In process data collection and feedback (process correction)	Typically low, often long term, even after project finishes

There is also an increased probability that the missile will not hit the plane at all, which is why air forces employ jet fighters and not Zeppelins.

Here is the metaphor: the Zeppelin represents the "old" software projects of perhaps 25 years ago (see Exhibit 12). Many of them were "slow moving" and deterministic. The target was obvious. Key variables were easily identifiable, their values were readily collectible, and much of the knowledge was available in advance. Given the nature of what we were trying to do back then, the straight Waterfall Model worked quite well. Certainly, the average rate of change on projects was usually well within the limits of our ability to respond to those changes. This period in software process evolution between 1975 and 1990 was also the "Renaissance Period" of software process and methodology.

While there have been great advances since then, it was during this time-frame that the foundations of software engineering were laid: the first attention to process and methods, an explosion in the number and concept of programming languages, the first software development tools above the level of text editor and compilers appeared. Even such "modern" developments as Object Oriented languages and development, the mouse, GUIs, the Internet, inspections, testing methods, etc. were first defined and made useful.

We can make a good argument that the predominant type of project at that time was of the Zeppelin type. Being Zeppelin projects, they gave rise to anti-Zeppelin processes. Even more damning, the apparent success of

Exhibit 13. Jet plane projects.

Attribute	Project version
Speed	Typically short-cycle, high rate of change
(Target) Requirements	Poorly or loosely defined; defined in terms of business need; no single source of detailed requirements; loosely defined analysis methods
Requirements changes	High rate, volatile
Change response to system construction (countermeasures: reaction of target to system)	High change rate, continuous, even higher rate close to completion
Target payload (delivered functionality)	Typically high business value
Maneuverability of project (flexibility of process)	Requires highly flexible process
System size (payload)	Variable, often small number of lines of code written
Location of control on project	Distributed between users, resource management, technical architects, and development team
In-process data collection and feedback (process correction)	Variable; if low in capability, will hamper development and result in defects and customer dissatisfaction

the Zeppelin processes reinforced the already prevalent idea that software was really a product to be produced. Many of today's leaders and executives grew up in this era, and absorbed this mindset. Many of the underpinnings of current software engineering are built on the foundation of predictability, as the foundation of early twentieth century physics was built on the predictable, mechanistic and deterministic models of physicist Isaac Newton. The trouble is that these processes simply don't work well for shooting down jet planes (see Exhibit 13).

The True Life Cycle

We have seen that software development is really a knowledge-acquisition activity. Therefore, the life cycle is most correctly defined by the following:

- *Tasks:* A sequence of learning activities, the results of which are captured (stored) in "work products."
- *Work products:* A set of knowledge repositories of various kinds containing knowledge of various kinds.
- *Testing* (or other feedback cycles) has two parts:
    - The *verification* of the format of the knowledge repositories against a set of syntactic conventions that are largely defined by the constraints and structure of the repositories.

- *Validation* of the content of the knowledge repositories against some other equivalent source of knowledge, based on the knowledge present in the target domain.
- *Phases:* Groups of logically related activities with (relatively) clearly defined start and end points. Related elements constituting phases may include:
  - Similar tasks or activities.
  - Similar or related knowledge sources.
  - Similar or related knowledge types.
  - Similar or related knowledge components or content.
  - Related knowledge repository elements. These elements may be related by convention (as is the case in many methodologies), but usually have some knowledge components that are interdependent. Often, the collection of these knowledge elements constitutes one of the phase "deliverables," such as a system test plan.
  - Similar or related knowledge-gathering responsibilities. These may also be by convention. Commonly they may be a result of the division of work within an organization, based on some logical separation of domain function or product architecture, or they may arise from the skills and experience of the people assigned to the job.

    The "termination" activity of a phase is often the validation and publication of the repository of the knowledge obtained during that phase. These publications include such repositories as the contract or statement of work, the functional requirements, the architecture model, detailed designs, program specifications, executable source code, test plans, and many others.
- *Task and work product dependencies:* A natural occurrence of the learning activity that usually happens when a higher-order abstraction or context of knowledge must be obtained before the detailed knowledge can be found. This often happens when there is dependency in the knowledge content of parts of the system. It is often related to the need to discover the question (resolving 2OI) before discovering the answer (resolving 1OI).

Exhibit 14 displays the most-simplified and generalized knowledge-acquisition model. In its simplest form, the job of software development is to reduce the number of unknowns to zero by the time the system is delivered. It is a process of knowledge acquisition and ignorance reduction. It is also a *continuous* process rather than a punctuated or continual process. This means that moment-by-moment on the project, ignorance is identified, questions are asked, answers are obtained and validated, and knowledge is acquired. Different knowledge may be most effectively acquired at different times using different techniques, and certainly there are periods

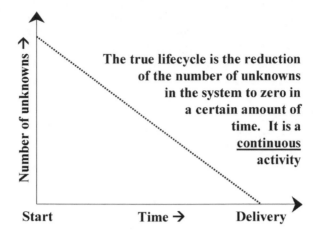

The true lifecycle is the reduction of the number of unknowns in the system to zero in a certain amount of time. It is a <u>continuous</u> activity

Exhibit 14. Generalized life cycle model.

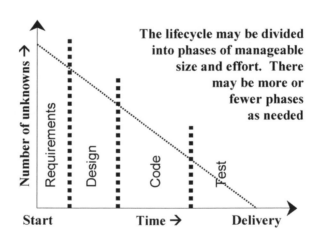

The lifecycle may be divided into phases of manageable size and effort. There may be more or fewer phases as needed

Exhibit 15. Phase: Waterfall.

during the development cycle when knowledge is acquired more rapidly or more slowly than at other times.

But anyone who has ever participated in a software project knows that the moment a requirements specification is published, it is out of date. Sometimes before the ink is dry, new knowledge is obtained or the old knowledge in the document is refuted in ways that render the specification incomplete and to some extent "wrong." The attempt of life cycle models (Exhibit 15) to punctuate this continuous process, to make a batch system out of a real-time system, is one of the greatest difficulties that any life cycle model presents to us. The model shows phases, beginnings and ends,

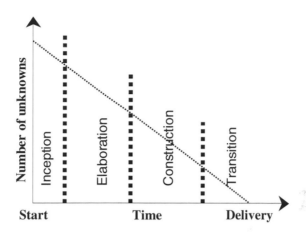

Exhibit 16. Phase: Rational Unified Process (RUP).

starts and stops, documents being "completed" and signed off. The real world has knowledge being constantly identified, refined, tested, added to, corrected, and refuted. The "disconnect" between the model and the real world that the model is attempting to portray is the source of many of our management woes.

We can have more or fewer phases. They may, almost arbitrarily, have different names. While different life cycle models attempt to group similar tasks and work products as described previously, the phases are simply conventional discrete overlays on the continuous process of acquiring knowledge. We can substitute the Rational Unified Process (RUP) phase names for the Waterfall phase names (see Exhibit 15 and Exhibit 16) and, while we may look for subtly different kinds of knowledge in different ways with different life cycles, the underlying reality of continuous knowledge acquisition still pertains.

We can have more or fewer phases, we can reorder them, we can define the knowledge-to-be-gained differently, and store the knowledge obtained in different modalities. We can retain the information we have learned and collected in documents, in project plans, in peoples' heads, in CASE tools, in test plans, or in executables. But we are still continuously acquiring and refining the knowledge.

We can also see clearly what happens when we deliver a product too early. Simply by moving the delivery date to the left (shortening the development cycle), we are just moving the discovery of unknowns into the user's environment. The number and type of unknowns we have effectively acquired is the measure of the functionality the system provides. The number and type of unknowns that remain undiscovered (2OI) or unresolved

65

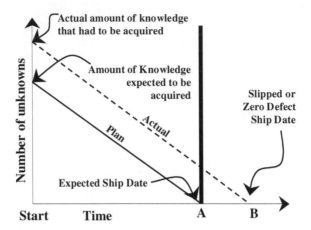

Exhibit 16a. More knowledge required.

(1OI) is a direct measure of the defects delivered to the customer. That is, quite simply, what a defect is — it is an unknown.

Quite commonly, we underestimate how much knowledge we have to obtain to deliver the functionality to the customer (or overestimate our current knowledge, which is the same thing). In this case, we have the situation shown in Exhibit 16a. The amount of knowledge (the Y-axis) turns out to be higher than we thought at the time of project planning. Assuming that our rate of knowledge acquisition is the same as planned (often an unwise assumption) means that at some point in the project we are faced with some choices:

- Ship the product at the original delivery date (point A) and also ship a bunch of defects.

- Resolve the defects in the development environment and ship later (at point B).

- Arrive at some compromise date between A and B that eliminates the worst of the defects while not shipping too late.

Another common project ailment is that the knowledge may turn out to be harder to get than we thought it would be. This negatively affects our "knowledge discovery rate" (see Exhibit 17). In this simple model, the result is the same as in Exhibit 16; we are faced with shipping defects or slipping the delivery date.

Usually, a combination of these occurs at the same time: it turns out that there is both more knowledge for us to get *and* it is harder than we thought to get it.

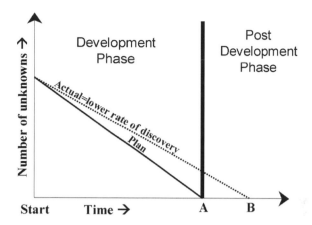

Exhibit 17. Knowledge is harder to get.

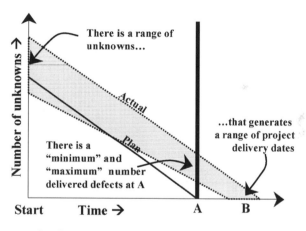

Exhibit 18. Range of unknown unknowns.

A More-Complex, Generalized Model

Unfortunately, our woes do not stop there. There are a number of other factors that affect how our project may run, including:

- Unknown unknowns (Second Order Ignorance)
- Knowledge variability with time
- Design dependence of knowledge
- Variability in the rate of learning with time

The effects of these are shown in Exhibit 18 through Exhibit 22.

Range of Unknown Unknowns

This is simply the result of Second Order Ignorance (see Exhibit 18). For projects with many "new" variables, we can expect this to be high. For

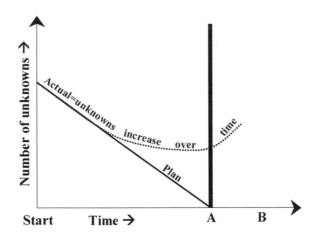

Exhibit 19. Knowledge variability with time.

projects with few "new" variables (Zeppelin projects), it is low. This generates a range of unknowns that cannot, by definition, be explicitly measured at the beginning of the project. Typically, both the number of unknowns and the likely range of unknowns will diminish as time goes by and the project acquires the necessary system knowledge (this assumes that the other factors do not come into play, of course). The result of this is a range of delivery dates, each with an associated likely range of delivered defects (unknowns still to be resolved).

Knowledge Variability with Time

This is becoming more and more common in modern development (see Exhibit 19). Simply due to the fact that time is going by, certain key knowledge components change. Different business realities change the customer's requirements, new technologies invalidate the old architecture, new processors or language allow new capabilities and change expectations. This rate can get so fast that it is functionally impossible to deliver "zero defect" systems because the target (and therefore the definition of what a defect is) is changing faster than our ability to deliver to that target. Too rapid a rate of change may simply invalidate the feasibility of even attempting the development of a system, unless extremely rapid development techniques are available. This rate of change of external knowledge is the primary driver of "Jet Plane" projects.

Design Dependence of Knowledge

This is often related to the knowledge variability with time, but is more often caused by design decisions that *we* make (see Exhibit 20). For example, as a result of deciding to implement a homegrown security package rather

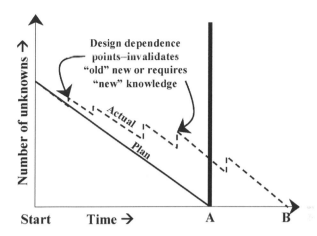

Exhibit 20. Design dependence of knowledge.

than attempting to modify an available one, we may find there is much more that we have to learn. The design decision predicates additional work necessary to support it.

Indeed, this sometimes happens when using system components that are already available. We think we will save a great deal of time (read "have to learn less") by purchasing and modifying an existing package, only to find later that the package does not do what we need, and we are forced to spend considerable time in research or experimentation (read "acquiring the knowledge") to find out how to make it work. This causes "hiccups" in the actual project progress, where the amount of work remaining suddenly jumps up.

Variable Rate of Learning

This is similar to the "knowledge is harder to get" scenario in Exhibit 17 (see Exhibit 21). However, rather than the whole project being harder than we thought, our ability to extract and process knowledge from the environment fluctuates over time. There are many reasons this can occur. Probably the most common is the addition and subtraction of people from the project. The new people have to be trained in the project's processes or existing knowledge, so knowledge acquisition is done in that arena rather than on the discovery of new knowledge pertaining to customer's system. The development engineers take time off from discovering their own knowledge to train the newcomers. Experienced, high-capability engineers (who can learn fast) are replaced with less-experienced engineers who take longer to acquire the necessary knowledge. There are two sides to this: it is possible to speed up knowledge acquisition as well as slow it down, and

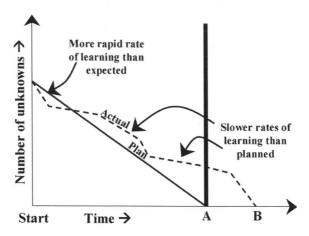

Exhibit 21. Variable rate of learning with time.

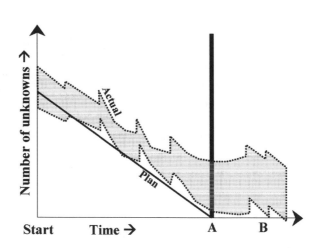

Exhibit 22. All life cycle variables combined.

it is not uncommon for projects in trouble to be staffed with "SWAT teams" of highly skilled developers who can accelerate the final stages of a project.

All Variables

Exhibit 22 shows what happens when all of these factors come into play at the same time on the same project. What we see is a very complex, discontinuous function that may be highly unpredictable. This is, in fact, what happens on many projects, and why managing such projects is so hard. It also explains why projects run so late so often.

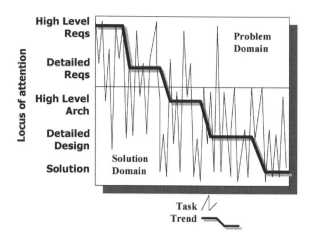

Exhibit 23. Task level variation and project trends. (Adapted from Curtis, B., Iscoe, N., and Krasner, H., A field study of the software design process for large systems, *Communications of the ACM,* 31, 11, 1988.)

The analogies of the development life cycle with a walk in the woods or the shooting down of a jet fighter are appropriate. All activities have some measure of predictability and some measure of unpredictability. There are factors that are known and factors that are not known. The relative quantities of known and unknown factors determine how predictable the system can be. In any discovery activity, there must be significant uncertainty at the beginning, and considerable variation in the unfolding of the discovery. It is this that makes software development a discovery activity. There must also be "wrong turns" and backtracking. In the event that the unknowns are unknowns of type, there may be substantial investment in process development, as the team searches for the optimum process to uncover what is not known.

In Exhibit 23, we see the relationship between the project level activities and the tasks. Through time (the x-axis) on a project, the "locus of attention" — the actual task being worked at a given point in time — may vary across the problem-solution domain spectrum. One moment the project may be working on high-level requirements, the next moment it might be working on a specific design or implementation of a particular function. A moment later, the team could be discussing how to test, followed by how the user will respond, followed by what additional business functions are required by the customer to support this implementation, followed by how the team will support a postimplementation customer training activity. What the project is doing is pursuing a line of logical reasoning and discovery related to a specific requirement or type of requirement. More often than not, the reasoning and the tasks associated with it are clumped together by the function rather than whether the thought process addresses the problem (requirements) or solution (design, code) or proof (test) domains. Therefore the *actual work being done* does not follow a convention of abstraction from the problem through the solution domain as expected by the Waterfall (and most other) life cycle models.

However, if we take a "moving average" of the locus of attention particularly over a larger period of time, e.g., several months, we will usually see that the projects on average and as a whole do tend to follow a general-to-detail and problem-to-solution trend. The implications of this are quite simple: generalized life cycle models are suitable for general trends in projects, much less suitable for detailed task assignment, and may not be useful at all for detailed task tracking.

Summary

The bottom line for system life cycles is that, while they are useful as general guides for large scale work and for averaging activities, they are primarily *management models* rather than development models. Indeed, their primary purpose has always been the assignment and control of resources and the reporting of status rather than to model a close relationship to the nature of the work being done on projects.

The fundamental challenge for all management models is that they are models and therefore only subsets of reality. There is an error which scientists are prone to make called *"the fallacy of identification."* This occurs when there is a failure to differentiate between a model of something and the thing itself. The primary job of scientists is to create models that reflect certain characteristics of reality. The model is the *result* of the scientists' efforts. It is common for them to then mistake the model for the thing that is being modeled. This is natural, because the model represents the sum of the scientists' thinking on the thing. The model, though, remains a model and is not reality. There are always severe limitations inherent in being a model. In software development, the fallacy of identification occurs when management believes the life cycle model and the project plan are the project. Developers can also be guilty of the fallacy of identification when they view their development models as being the system itself rather than a representation of the system. Both contain knowledge, both may be useful, but both are also "wrong" and their limitations must be recognized.

Chapter 5
Of Methods and Models and Minds

By different methods different men excel
but where is he who can do all things well?

— **Charles Churchill 1731–1764**
Epistle to William Hogarth

I should have no objection to this method.

— **Laurence Sterne**
Tristram Shandy

In the olden days, the method and the model were the same thing and the mind was hardly considered at all. The classical texts of software development methods mostly concerned themselves with modeling conventions: what icons should be used to represent what? What connections can link these icons? What do the connections represent in the "real world?" If we want to apply syntactic rules to the creation of these models, what rules would be most useful and most pertinent to the job at hand?

The "methodology" books tended not to talk too much about the methods of using the models, as if by simply defining the model conventions people would be able to use them. They did not much discuss the mental disciplines and even the intellectual constructions required to actually use the models. They even more rarely talked about the people who would employ those methods.

Models of Convention

Humans always use models. We are physiologically incapable of dealing with "the real world," whatever that might be. Instead, what we do is build intellectual models of the real world, which we then manipulate. Executable software systems are themselves intellectual models. The precursor work products that we build (or more correctly, populate with knowledge) prior to developing the executable version of the knowledge are also models, although with different rules and syntax. All types of models by their very nature are *conventional*. That is to say, the models operate under a set of model conventions that we choose. We are in charge of defining what the models are, what they will look like, what rules they will use, how they will operate, and what they will represent. Traditional software methodologies, especially in the IT field, focused mostly on the structure of, and operation against, persistent data stores. The simple reason for this was that most IT systems were, and in large part still are, data analogues of real-world entities. The most important knowledge to obtain in such systems is the nature of these entities, what functions can be performed against them and what relationships they have with one another. Classical models arising from this focus were the Entity-Relationship models and the transform models known as "data flow diagrams." There were, and remain, some issues with the usability of these models; for instance, the connotation of movement given by the word "flow" is not a particularly apt metaphor for data, because in the real world data does not, in fact, flow. Nevertheless, these models became very popular, at least in the sense that they were used extensively. Some legacy of their usage remains in modern methods.

In the years since, a greater variety of modeling conventions has arisen. Dissention regarding the format of models seems to have lessened and something of a consensus modeling approach appears to be precipitating out of the cloud. The most popular at present is the convention set known under the rubric of Universal Modeling Language or UML.

The choices we make of what models and what modeling conventions to use to understand a particular problem are very important. This is because, as we endeavor to populate our model repository the model formats, content, and syntax we choose largely defines what information we expect to retrieve or discover. It also greatly colors our thinking about what knowledge we are retrieving. If the model stresses one aspect of the system and ignores another, we are likely to stress and ignore the same attributes. If the model has certain physical or logical characteristics, they will certainly affect our final model representation and will probably affect how we collect the data and populate the model. Practitioners of model syntax and developers and users of models tend to equate the model with what they are modeling — a syndrome known as *"the fallacy of identification."* There is a simple reason for this: after investing significant effort in learning the model's precepts, the model becomes the practitioner's way of thinking about the problem. Whenever we invest energy in learning a new language, that language becomes embedded in our reasoning process and can actually become the way we think about things. This partly explains the "methodology wars" that have occasionally broken out. When you say to someone, "your model is not as good as my model," you are *de facto* saying "your way of thinking is not as good as my way of thinking." Not only is this a somewhat contentious statement that will generate significant resistance on the part of most people, from the perspective of *our* model, it is quite correct.

Of course, if we use our model as a modality of thinking, our model will always be "better" than another, simply because it maps onto our model evaluation criteria better. For each of us, our own modality of thinking will always be easier, more rational, and more *internally* consistent. Other people, using their models for understanding or evaluation, will not comprehend how our model is better any more than we appreciate that their approach is better. Because the model and the thinking modality go hand-in-hand, to other people using different models, it will seem to them that their way of thinking is better. Hence the methodology (and language) wars — they were not so much about models and syntactic conventions as about thinking.

It is a fact of human existence that we tend to hold on to our way of thinking sometimes in spite of glaring evidence that it is inadequate, and we will sometimes vigorously defend the thinking status quo. This type of thinking explains the chauvinism that afflicts models and languages. Ask a UNIX aficionado which operating system is "best," or get an ADA programmer to describe what a "good" language should look like. The answers will not astound you.

Models of Numbers

To understand the role of models in our lives and our understanding, it might be useful to look at one of the very first and most basic models that the human race uses: integer numbers. Our use of numbers and the associated activity of counting are so ingrained that it appears to us to be something of a fundamental law of the universe. We become so practiced at applying this simple model to simple situations that, most times, we do not even realize we are using a model that is entirely conventional (although founded in some very logical observations and deductions). Numbers are also a good example of the limitation of models. If I count the number of people in the room, I understand and accept that I am merely operating on the cardinality of the people. Counting the number of people does not measure their combined weight, although I might be able to calculate an average or likely range. It certainly does not determine their moral basis, religious convictions, ethnicity, or eye color. We do not expect counting to do these things for us and we accept that if we wanted to count such attributes we would use different measures and counting methods. We never view the fact that numbers do not measure eye color as a limitation of the number model, because we would never try to use it for that purpose.

This is an example of the sometimes-different standards that software and systems models seem to be held to, compared with other models that operate in other domains. We do not expect Kirchoff's Laws to explain fluid dynamics; we do not try to apply the units of measurement of mass to estimate distance. But for a variety of reasons, systems modeling approaches have had some implicit expectation that they should map onto all aspects of the system's behavior.

THE LAWS OF SOFTWARE PROCESS

Numbers only operate on a rather narrow range of observable phenomena, and our ability to use even this simple model system is severely limited by our physiology. Dr. George A. Miller published in 1956 an interesting paper that strongly inferred that humans possess a "number bandwidth" of around seven inputs.* The range of this bandwidth Dr. Miller measured as seven plus or minus two. This means that humans can reasonably accurately determine and differentiate (and presumably process) between around seven things: seven tones, seven tastes, seven objects, etc. Because we have been able to create devices and systems with significantly more than seven elements, obviously this is either not an intrinsic property of all humans or we have found ways to compensate for our limitations. When we look closely at our numbers model, we can see that it is an example of how we modify models and migrate between them quite effortlessly, once we have defined the model and learned how to use it.

Consider the number 1024. It is a lot bigger than the number seven — about 147 times bigger in fact. Personally, I understand this number quite well, which would imply that Dr. Miller's assertion is incorrect. But 1024 is not one thousand and twenty-four things. Exhibit 1 shows one thousand and twenty-four things. The number 1024 as depicted is either one thing or four things that *represent* one thousand and twenty-four things.

For most of the human race, 1024 is four things. Many people in the software business would recognize it and deal with it as one thing. The difference is the *meaning* and use applied to the number. For people who do not deal with binary systems, 1024 is not a special number; 1000 is significant but 1024 is not: 1000 is "important" because to people it is a number of the form $number\_base^n$. 1024 is also of this form but of a base that most people do not use. Neither, of course, is the number 823543, which is not an "important" number unless we happen to operate in number base 7 (823,543 is 7^7, described in decimal base; in base 7, of course, it is 10,000,000).

The human brain cannot deal with large counts. We cannot deal with numbers as portrayed in Exhibit 1, especially if those numbers are randomly distributed, as they are in Exhibit 2. The careful ordering shown in Exhibit 1 does allow us to use some of our brain's processing modalities to estimate the number of lines. Disordering them as in Exhibit 2 prevents that brain function from working.

Dr Miller's seven plus or minus two applies to numbers as much as to anything else. We cannot reasonable process the number:

$$102479634087802019738498$$

as it stands because it seems to be "too big" to fit in our input processing buffer. Therefore, to deal with it, we must process the input somehow.

*The Psychological Review, 1956, vol. 63, pp. 81–97.

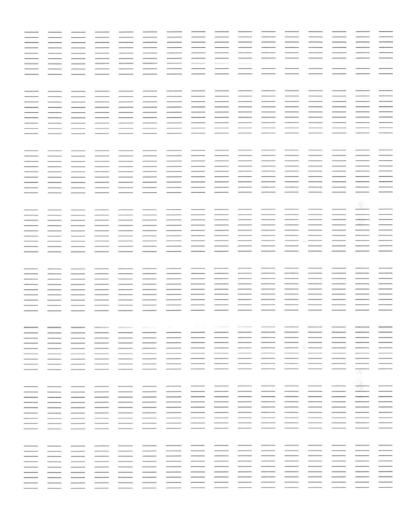

Exhibit 1. One thousand and twenty-four things.

Counting

There is evidence that we cannot "recognize" much above the number 4 in terms of simply processing visual input. We deal with larger counts by, well, counting. We use counting so often (along with our base 10 counting model) that it is largely effortless and seems to be something akin to a characteristic of the universe. It is not. Counting is entirely a human invention, just one that we have practiced so often it seems "natural." The "natural numbers" are more natural to people than they are to nature. Counting is a place-holding activity. We usually process ordered strings and define our place on that string (the count) by assigning it a number from our "sequential" number model. Counting is less effective when we are assessing characteristics of dissimilar items, there is no obvious sequence, there are part-counts, etc. There

Exhibit 2. A large number of random things.

are populations in the world, even in modern times, whose native languages contain only words for one, two, and many.* While it appears that people in these societies understand parity in number counts quite well, their ability to actually count and perform the associated arithmetical calculations is severely limited because they do not possess a mental model that accommodates such reasoning.

*Ifah, G., *The Universal History of Numbers,* John Wiley, New York, 1999, p. xix.

Chunking

One of the primary mechanisms the brain uses to generate limited order out of large-scale chaos is to "chunk" information by aggregating it in some way. This aggregation reduces the sheer number of units being dealt with by dealing with some collections of units as units themselves. Sufficient chunking allows the number of objects to fall within our bandwidth. We can see the effectiveness of chunking by comparing Exhibit 1 and Exhibit 2. We can "understand" Exhibit 1 much better than Exhibit 2 because the careful ordering of the rows and columns chunks the data for us into smaller numbers of aggregates.

We very obviously see chunking in our numbering conventions. The very big number discussed previously becomes:

$$102,479,634,087,802,019,738,498$$

One of the prices we pay for this simplification is that we must learn both the "counting" and the "chunking" methods in order to be able to employ them. People who have not acquired these skills cannot employ these models and methods and are generally less able to make use of the numbers. The number base is quite arbitrary (although base 10 has a lot to commend it, not least being the normal number of fingers on a person's hands), and the chunking method is also conventional. Mainland Europeans, for instance, will chunk differently:

$$102.479.634.085.802.019.738.498$$

Neither the use of commas or periods as thousand-chunk delimiters is "better" than the other, although proponents of both can (and do) devise logical arguments as to which is most natural. Of course, whichever you have learned will be most natural to you.

This number, even with the addition of the delimited chunking, is probably on the far side of comprehensibility. To fit this number within our "span of absolute judgment," as George Miller described it, we have to switch models:

$$1.025 \times 1023$$

This switch to a scientific notational model moves the number into our band of understandability. There are several things we must note about this model:

- It is a *different* model than the integer "natural number" model being used earlier.
- The different model has different (although related) rules for performing operations such as multiplication and addition.
- The models obviously have different characteristics and strengths.
- Both models are "correct" and map perfectly (in the context of each model's rules) onto the target domain.

The integer model is not "better" than the floating-point model, nor is base-10 arithmetic "better" than base 2, base 7, or base 60. The practical value of any model is not its "correctness," but its usability. As George Box observed: "All models are wrong."

Some models may be more "wrong" (read: harder to use) for certain purposes than others. Consider using the Roman numeral system when performing a multiplication or division calculation. The calculation:

$$\frac{LXXII}{XII}$$

is functionally equivalent to the same in decimal notation:

$$\frac{72}{12}$$

It would be possible to perform the calculation in Roman numerals, while staying within the constraints of the Roman numeral system. We could write a computer program that would parse any Roman numeral string and divide it by another Roman numeral string. While it would be difficult to do this while internally (to the program) retaining the Roman numeral format rather than slipping into decimal or binary, it is possible. We would not do it, however, and if we did, the program would be unnecessarily complex and prone to error. The translation: Roman → Decimal is quite straightforward. Once done, the calculation 72 ÷ 12 is quite straightforward. If the calculation is attempted before the translation, however, the task is rather difficult.

This is the role of modeling in systems: to translate the knowledge format from (usually) a narrative text model into a more–structured, graphical representational model. This translation, while not easy in itself, makes later translations, calculations, and factoring (into an executable system) much simpler.

It is obvious that all activities we engage in when we develop systems are *modeling* activities:

- *Create the model.* We decide on or create the model syntax and components.
- *Populate the model.* We map our observations of the problem or solution onto the model conventions.
- *Verify the model.* We populate and verify the model contents by parsing the populated model against the models "rules."
- *Validate the model.* We somehow validate the model contents against the thing being modeled and make appropriate corrections. This is invariably an *external* referencing activity.

- *Translate between models.* We may also translate from model type to model type, or link different models together to provide the necessary views of different parts of the system.

Here we come up against a fundamental characteristic not of models, but of people. The real world is generally very complicated. Real systems have many different attributes that we need to understand if we wish to make them work properly: we must understand the classical system attributes of data structure, function, state, and event. We need to know the interaction between the system and its environment and its users. We need to understand the interaction between the system and its executable platform. We may even need to understand the operation of the system in the systems environment in which it operates and a number of levels: the transactional level, resource usage, even business activity. In some kinds of systems, we have to know how the processor works. We may have to create data transport mechanisms or learn how to use existing ones. We may use "standard" machine interfaces or design our own. This is a lot of information.

We might be able to define a single model that attempts to describe all of the above, but it would be very complicated.

What is required, of course, is a (somewhat) interactive *set* of systems models, the combination of which usefully describes as much of the systems behavior as necessary to allow us to:

- Learn what it should be.
- Learn what it could be.
- Interrelate elements of the models to determine if their different views highlight any systemic or logical inconsistencies.
- Translate from the model form into other ultimately and preferably executable forms. This includes, of course, the code form, but it may also include testing forms for both verification (internal consistency) and validation (external consistency) forms.

So much for the system; but viewing systems development as a knowledge-acquisition activity leads us to realize that we need to learn a lot more than just the knowledge of the system to make the system work properly.

Exhibit 3 shows an overall meta-model of domains within software organizations. There are some quite distinct "areas" where the type, quality, content, and location of the operational models are quite different from each other. Exhibit 4 shows some of the content of each of these levels.

The "General" models in the top domain of *Standards and Process Models* are usually meta-models. A good example of this might be the SEI CMM^SM. This model is, intentionally, a generalized model that maps onto elements in the *Standards and Process Models* area and some of both the *Resource and Environment Models* and the *Project Models*. Most classical systems

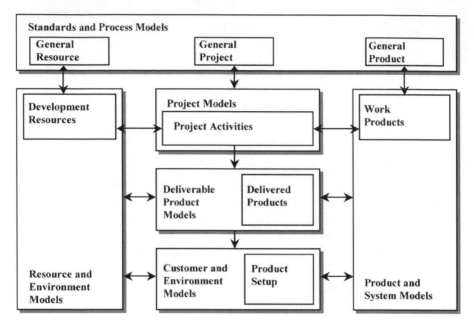

Exhibit 3. Generalized software process domains.

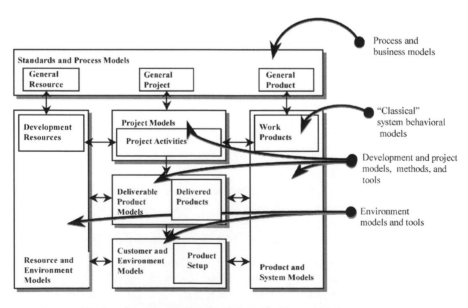

Exhibit 4. Software process domains and embedded models.

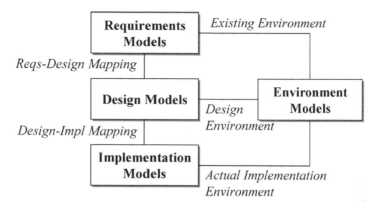

Exhibit 5. Typical system's model interactions.

engineering models are placed firmly in the *Product and System Models* domain, because they describe the expected behavior of the target system. The same models may be used in the *Deliverable Product Models* and even to some extent in the *Customer and Environment Models* area.

Of most interest to software developers has historically been the *Systems Models* in the *Product and Systems Models* area. These are the models that describe the required functioning and design attributes of the system to be built. Exhibit 5 shows some of the model types that generally occur in this domain and their interactions.

These models do not stand alone. We have models of the requirements of the system that interact with and influence the models of the design of the system. Requirements models are usually (depending on the system) populated models of the systems functions (transforms), what those functions operate on (data), and the circumstances under which they will be operated on (states). Some of these models are identified in Exhibit 5. The sources of information we access to populate these models also vary, sometimes considerably. The primary sources for the systems' functional requirements (see Exhibit 6) are usually some combination of the customer(s) and the business environment(s).

The primary source for *design* knowledge is quite different. As well as the source knowledge from the requirements (what the system must do), design knowledge often comes from engineering experience, heuristics, and the proven design constructs known as patterns. For the *implementation* models, which are usually transcribed in some sort of code form, the knowledge comes from knowledge of programming (how to use the language), from knowledge of program libraries (what additional language constructs are available that can operate in this domain) and from programming environments (how do we create executables in both the development and

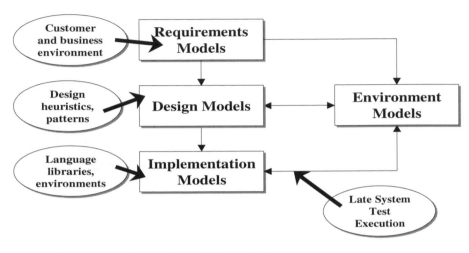

Exhibit 6. Sources of system's model population.

target domains?). We should also probably make a fine but important distinction between the knowledge necessary to transform the knowledge, and the knowledge being transformed. The knowledge represented in a fully factored set of requirements is *not* the same as knowledge of how to design a system that will fulfill those requirements. The design accounts for and supports the requirements, but it is not the same; ditto the implementation phase. The coding activity must support the design (which supports the requirements), but knowledge of coding is not knowledge of the specific system.

Some of these models must be bootstrapped. Fully understanding the target system execution environment usually requires a cyclic interaction between programming and detailed design and the environment itself. This in fact is why we do system and beta testing — to extract the knowledge to make the system actually work in the target environment. This is a reiteration of the Dual Hypotheses of Knowledge Discovery (see Chapter 1). In some cases, experienced developers will know (have the knowledge in their brain media) that certain environment configurations will or will not work. In many cases the developers will not already have this knowledge. They may be able to postulate an environment that is likely to work, but they cannot *prove* it unless they attempt to run the system in that environment, because the Dual Hypotheses state that you can only discover knowledge in an environment that contains it. The rapid develop–test cycle of modern "Agile" methods acknowledges this truth.

Within each model set, there are models that we adopt as conventions that hopefully will help us understand what the system has to do. The nature of these models is also conventional, although these conventions are starting to solidify within the profession of software development. This convergence of ideas is largely due to the following:

- People are realizing that there is more to be gained through the acceptance of a "standard" modeling notation than there is to be gained through continually "re-devising" one. However, this realization may not be quite as true as we think.
- There are certain systems behaviors that are universal and can be adequately defined using a consistent notation. For instance, all dynamic systems have "states" in which certain operations are active and others are inactive. These operations work to transform data, material, or energy in some way. If the object being operated on is data (and sometimes material), it often has a definable structure. Therefore, a notational set that includes provision for states, transforms, transitions between states, events causing transitions between states, data, and a variety of data structuring modalities can work for many systems. The understanding that all systems have these characteristics or, more correctly, can be usefully described using a fairly small set of notation primitives has resulted in a welcome convergence of peoples' ideas and practices in this area.
- Use begets use. As more and more practitioners learn common techniques, as more and more books are written on the subject, and as schools and colleges employ them as the basic building blocks for understanding systems behavior, they *become* the basic building blocks for understanding systems behavior.

It is becoming increasingly accepted that we need a *set* of models that work together to describe the system being built. But that is not all that is needed.

The Physical Nature of Models

Models are not only subject to the conventions adopted for their use; their usability is a function of their physical nature. Again, as with numbers, some of our models are in such common use that it is hard for us to see just where their limitations are, mostly because we *use* the self-same models for understanding. For a good example of the limitations imposed by the physical attributes of modeling media, we can look at one of our primary knowledge media, the book (see Exhibit 7). Simply putting knowledge down in written words *forces* a sequence on the knowledge. The only intrinsic physical relationship that text has with itself is *next-prior*. A word is after a word and before another word. A page is in front of another page or behind it. No matter how we move the words around, one is still in front

Veneris que secundus; haec generis princeps,

Caesar, quae moverit illum, erroremque suum

Tempora cum causis Latium digesta per annum
lapsaque sub terras ortaque signa canam. excipe
pacato, Caesar Germanice, voltu hoc opus et
timidae derige navis iter, officioque, levem non
aversatus honorem, en tibi devoto numine
dexter ades. sacra recognosces annalibus eruta
priscis et quo sit merito quaeque notata dies.
invenies illic et festa domestica vobis; saepe tibi
pater est, saepe legendus avus, quaeque ferunt
illi, pictos signantia fastos, tu quoque cum Druso
praemia fratre feres. Caesaris arma canant alii:
nos Caesaris aras et quoscumque sacris addidit
ille dies. adnue conanti per laudes ire
tuorum deque meo pavidos excute corde metus.
da mihi te placidum, dederis in carmina vires:
ingenium voltu statque caditque tuo. pagina
iudicium docti subitura movetur principis, ut
Clario missa legenda deo. quae sit enim culti
facundia sensimus oris, civica pro trepidis cum
tulit arma reis. scimus et, ad nostras cum se tulit
impetus artes, ingenii currant flumina quanta tui.
si licet et fas est, vates rege vatis h abenas, auspice
te felix totus ut annus eat. Tempora digereret
cum conditor Urbis, in anno constituit menses
quinque bis esse suo.

- **Only two physical relationships implemented:**
  - **Next**
  - **Prior**
- **Sequential**
- **No connection between physically separated concepts**
- **Single tasking, single threaded**
- **Poor chunkingól ow large-volume comprehension**

Exhibit 7. Physical characteristics of text models.

of another. This imposes on the knowledge a form of sequence *whether or not the knowledge contains that sequence*. The example of a cookie recipe in Chapter 4 shows some of the perils of this sequence. These perils are somewhat more pronounced when incompatible sequence is forced into engineering specifications. Other limitations of text documents are:

- *No connection between physically separated ideas.* There tends to be no connection between ideas that are physically separated in the document. If an idea is referenced on page 1, page 12, and page 243, that relationship is not easily evident while looking at page 1.
- *Single threaded, single tasking.* Because we are generally capable of reading only one word, paragraph, or page at a time, the text representation of the knowledge tends to describe it as if it were single tasking. While this is also inferred by *sequential*, they are not the same. It is very difficult to reasonably show both concurrence and pipelining (overlapped sequential tasks) in a text document.
- *Poor chunking.* In the absence of good editorial layout, many text documents do not chunk the material well. This requires our brains to absorb a lot of information and perform an internal chunking and cross-referencing activity before we can properly understand the document.

Many techniques have arisen to standardize text documents so that they stand some chance of overcoming these limitations. Some of these are shown in Exhibit 8. Some of the more obvious of the document conventions we routinely apply are directed at these limitations:

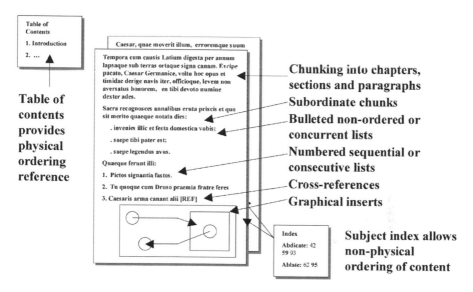

Exhibit 8. Modified text documents to overcome physical limitations.

- *Table of contents.* To provide a high-level overview of the physical ordering of the document
- *Chunking.* Into chapters, sections, etc.
- *Subordinate chunks.* To show levels of chunking
- *Bulleted lists.* To connote concurrence or equivalence
- *Numbered lists.* To show explicit sequence or ordering
- *Cross-references.* To provide in-text links between subjects
- *Graphic inserts.* To show the information in alternative ways that compensate for the limitations of the written word
- *Index.* At the end of the book to provide an alternative order of processing other than the physical order

Also, good authorship implies that the physical structuring of the document is relevant to the content: there is a logical order of the chapters, good annotation, etc. The use of graphics is an interesting one, because the combination of the graphics and the text allows a switching of modalities. Text tends to be good at detailed sequential descriptions but bad at concepts and nonsequential relationships. Graphics are good at showing concepts, but poor at detail. The combination of the two has long been recognized as delivering the most accurate depiction of the knowledge.

It is important to note, although we do not often recognize it, that within the document itself we are switching model conventions.

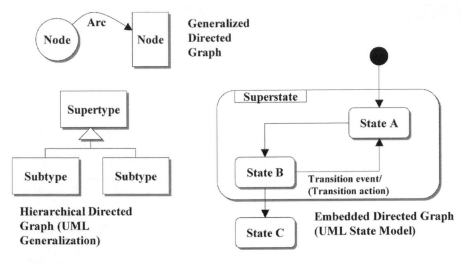

Exhibit 9. Directed graphs.

Most systems modeling approaches use a combination of graphics and text to describe the system in question. Exactly how that happens, and what each part means is where the model's conventions apply. It is also interesting to note that almost all models contain some form of directed graph. Exhibit 9 shows some types of directed graphs.

The notational system: the shape, size, and color of the nodes and arcs; the positioning and connection of the model elements; the syntactic rules for the elements; and, most importantly, what the model elements represent are the modeling conventions. But there are a lot more considerations to the use of models than simply what they look like and what they represent.

The Logical Nature of Models

A model is a representational system for describing the content, behavior, structure, function, or other collection of attributes of some requirements, some software, a project, an organization, a machine, or any other system. The word "model" can also mean a populated version of the same when the knowledge of a specific system has been transcribed into the model syntax. I will generally mean the generalized model language and syntax, except where specified otherwise. In the case of systems development, models are usually defined by methodologists or practitioners to allow them to more precisely or more easily describe the behavior of a system or set of systems they are investigating. As mentioned previously, almost all of our model types fall into one of two categories:

1. Textual lists with enforced or implied sequence. Models of this type include most forms of paper-type documents, most forms of code, lists of test cases, project task lists, etc.
2. Directed graphs, which are drawings that consist of icons or symbols that act as nodes, and some form of connector that attaches or links nodes together.

The meaning and purpose of the elements of the models is entirely conventional; we can choose what the primitives look like, how they "act," how they operate together to describe larger constructs, and what they mean in relationship to themselves and the outside world the models are supposed to represent. It is in this area that methodologists have traditionally dueled, with one model and its adherents claiming greater accuracy or coverage or applicability than another.

The "method" is the set of activities that *people* perform to use and populate the models. Obviously, the method is very closely aligned with the model, in that the requirements of populating the model rather define the activities necessary to populate it. For instance, if a particular modeling approach requires that an operational state model is constructed (for example, with stable functional states, transitions between states, and the events necessary to trigger those transitions), then the method will require that the practitioners investigate this kind of system behavior. If the approach dictates rapid and cooperative construction of operational code, then the method to be applied and the skills that are needed will be different.

One of the issues that has been rather ignored in the development and application of traditional methodologies is the role of the people in the process. Often, methods have been devised as if they are simply mechanical constructs or a theoretical mapping between two domains (the real world and the model conventions). More recently, and of critical importance to the Agile movement, the trend is to recognize that this activity is done by people, and that the model conventions are only a part of the puzzle. For instance, if a project requires the cooperation of a number of people, there is substantial work that must occur for people to integrate what they do. Obviously, this means that the modeled components must be *integratable*, which is often a function of the design of the model conventions, but it also means that people must communicate and make decisions about how the components go together. This is a human activity that is not specifically a part of the modeling conventions. Although most methodology proponents will rightly maintain that using the model helps with this, it does not actually do it; only people actually do it.

Therefore, the method includes all of the work necessary to use the model, but it contains a lot more. As well as the inter-person communication mentioned previously, it includes each person's cognitive understanding of the model syntax and use. It also includes their understanding of the domain to be modeled, the application of that understanding to the model syntax, their understanding of organizational and business constraints, their ability to process *other peoples'* understanding of the domain, model, etc. In fact, the method includes all of the work necessary for the whole project team to learn what has to be done cooperatively to build the system.

Because model conventions are, well, conventions, we can adopt whichever we choose. Our methods are adapted primarily to allow us to build our models in a presumably efficient way. Therefore our methods are also conventional.

Typically, of course, we would attempt to choose conventions that:

- Map reasonably well onto the problem (and solution) space.
- Have internal syntactic consistency.
- Allow useful partitioning of the problem and solution.

Also, the value of both methods and models are enhanced if they:

- Are relatively "easy" to use; this means the investment in learning the syntax of the model and process of the method is relatively small, or at least provides a positive reduction in the overall amount of knowledge that needs to be gained.
- Allow elements of the project or product to be disassembled and reassembled to facilitate division of work.
- Allow for translation into other work products and storage across a range of knowledge media (i.e., from brain to brain and book to software, etc.)
- Facilitate the management of the work products and their creation and population.
- Fit with peoples' modalities of understanding, work styles, communication, and behavior.
- Allow efficient validation of the knowledge.

Map onto Problem and Solution Space

This is the *sine qua non* of methods and models. The purpose of a model or a method of any sort (I will tend to use the two synonymously, because I believe they are so closely related that they cannot be usefully separated) is to establish an analogue of the work to be done. This means that both the logical and physical characteristics of the model and method align closely with the attributes of:

- The domain being investigated
- The system being built
- The environment in which the project team is working
- The project team using the models and methods

It is lack of attention to the last two points that has doomed more methods than anything else. The development and attempted implementation of highly complex methods and models can result in the project team having to learn more than if they did not use the methods. This is a net reduction in productivity, and unless the methods provide real value elsewhere, people will just stop using them. The lack of attention to the environment is the major objection that the Agile movement has been trying to address. A key element of the environment is the need for flexibility and for the method application to be done in some reasonable time, usually defined by a business constraint such as a committed delivery date or market window. Classical "heavyweight" methods did not do this. They often required enormous efforts that were not repaid even over long periods of time.

Classical methodologies have addressed the mapping of the model elements to the *system* space (both problem and solution) quite well. It is generally recognized that there are a set of attributes of information systems that we must understand in order for use to effectively build a system. These include the elements discussed next.

Requirements

These are the attributes of the system that make it of value to the user:

- *Transforms* or functions; the actions performed by the system. These are the *data (or material or energy) changing* actions rather than the state changing actions.
- *Data/material/energy* consumed and produced by the system, including any intermediate data states (although these may be more a function of the design rather than requirements).
- *Sequencing* both for progressive data (material/energy) transformation and for other reasons, such as customer processing needs.
- *States*; the primary operational states of the system that represent the modalities of the system. Associated with these states are:
  - *Interrupts* or events that cause system state changes. These may be external or internal either from clock events or from completion of other state transitions or functions.
  - *Timing*, which may be linked to execution of functions (transforms) or transitions between states. Timing may be absolute or relative to other events.
  - *Multi-tasking*, which describes what different functions may or must be operating at the same time. This may also apply to states, depending on the level of abstraction and mechanism used to analyze or portray state behavior.
- *Data structures* for the data (and more rarely energy and material); there may be structural elements we must understand. These are almost invariably related to the inherent structure in the real world

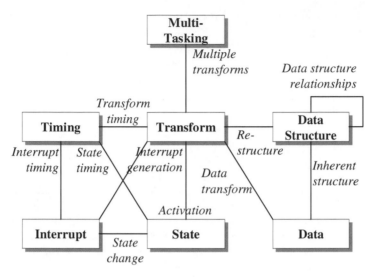

Exhibit 10. Generalized requirements meta-model.

that the system is somehow modeling (e.g., personnel records in an HR database will have the same structure as the data relating to the people whose data is being stored). This attribute is a complex one that includes physical structuring, data relationships, and, in object oriented systems, relationships that pertain to abstract properties of the data.

Exhibit 10 is a partial *meta-model* of a generalized requirements domain. Each of the model components is usually related to other model components. For instance, data may or may not be structured. One of the purposes of transforms (aka "functions" or even "processes") in systems is often to restructure data. Transforms invariably manipulate data, material, or energy, and may have timing requirements within which they have to work. The operational states of the system determine which transforms are operating at any time and these states are controlled by "interrupts" or events emanating from inside or outside the system. Internal interrupts are often generated by predicate transforms that recognize data conditions. The state changes themselves may be subject to timing considerations, and composites of functions may be required to operate concurrently with other functions; hence, the relationship with multi-tasking.

Each of these model components can be broken and analyzed in much more detail. For instance there are many kinds of data structuring involving data composition, inheritance of abstract properties, entities and relationships, etc. There may be linkages between the lower levels of granularity in the models. There may be both physical and logical relationships, cardinality, predicate logic and a number of other systems attributes. The

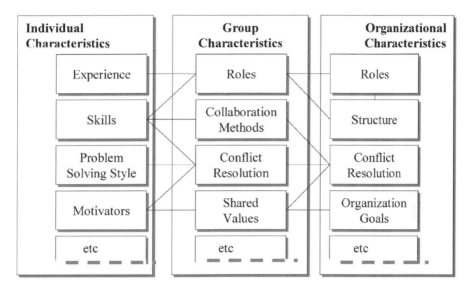

Exhibit 11. Project behavioral domain.

collection of these constitutes the "requirements" insofar as these define the purpose and operation of the required system.

Interfaces

In order for the system to function, the requisite interfaces must be established between the operational system defined in the requirements and the outside world. These interfaces have many of the characteristics of the *Requirements Domain.* They also include data and data structures, states, and functions. The nature of these system elements is usually more "physical," involving activities such as data transport and input editing.

Methods and Models

Development is more than models and syntax; it includes understanding and learning. Even more, it is cooperative understanding and learning. How the models get used and how people understand how to use them is probably more important than what the models are. Within each of the domains in Exhibit 3 there are a number of human behavioral models that operate. This is particularly true in the *Project Domain* (see Exhibit 11). Increasingly methodologists, practitioners, authors, and gurus of every stripe are looking at peoples' behaviors and interactions as critical determinants of productivity. Much of the work published under the rubric of Agile Methods addresses this area more than it does systems modeling graphical notational conventions. In looking at this area, these authors are acknowledging that cooperative behavior is one of the key elements of being able to successfully create systems.

The processes that operate in *this* domain represent the "organism" of the project. This differentiates it from the "mechanism" of projects and organizations. The organic components of projects are the people-based ones that operate on peoples' behavior rather than their tasks. For instance, as a project manager I might mechanistically assign roles to the people working for me. But will they perform those roles? Equally importantly, are the roles suitable for them and will they perform those roles well? Will they invest themselves in the work? Will they apply themselves? When they encounter problems of their own making will they own them and do what is necessary to improve? When they encounter problems not of their own making, will they just give up and blame the situation or will they endeavor to work around the obstacle? These are all aspects of the individual and collective ethic of the project and the organization. Personally, I have found that they are easily as important as the mechanics of the project. Yet as an industry we seem to spend more time working on the mechanistic components such as the modeling conventions used, the documentation targets, or the explicit role and responsibility assignments than we do the organic people elements of the business.

Of critical importance is the interrelationship between peoples' individual understanding of the models being used; their collective or group understanding of the model purpose, syntax, and content; and their combined abilities to integrate these to produce a relevant and usable populated model set.

It is here that things unravel. One person has a different idea than another of how a method should be used or even if a method should be used at all. The natural ambiguity of all language and all models means that different people understand the same thing somewhat differently; learning where the source of this difference lies and what it means and deciding between several choices and coming to a group consensus on what to do are skills that are not technical in nature and not usually taught in software engineering classes.

Minds

Project teams are made up of people. Not only do they come with their own proprietary thought processes and experience, they also come with a host of other characteristics: motivation, ethical basis, fortitude, helpfulness, resourcefulness, rapidity of thought, capacity to give and receive feedback, etc. These characteristics may be skills or they may be capabilities. These are not the same thing. Being helpful is an attitude. It may result in some physical assistance to a person, but helpfulness is not a fine motor skill. There are characteristics of people that are not intellectual skills. There are people who are skilled but not capable.

People are created differently and through application of their skills, through life experience, and through their inclinations, end up with different capabilities. But the source of the problem is not in differences. In fact, it is the differences rather than the similarities that make project teams effective. As Henry Ford once remarked, "Whenever two people always agree, one of them is unnecessary." People come in a range of abilities and temperaments. Some are literal information processors and highly detailed in focus while others are conceptual and "big-picture" thinkers. Some people are highly process oriented while others are mostly concerned with relationships. Given the same input, these two people may well process the information differently. They will almost certainly tackle the problem differently. The relationship-oriented person will usually collect together a group of people to tackle the problem, and will be highly involved in obtaining peoples' ideas and obtaining consensus on what to do. The process-oriented person will typically reach to what has worked in the past (the process) and attempt to apply that process.

Summary

Methods and models cannot be separated from the way that people think. More than anything else, software development is a thinking activity. As humans, we only think in terms of models. The constraints of those models assist us in the thinking activity, but also constrain us and may even predicate the result of our thinking by forcing an answer upon us. All of these elements, the methods we use and the models of our understanding that we create, including the code model, must conform to the requirements of the mind.

Chapter 6
The Advent of Agile

The old order changeth, yielding place to new

— Alfred Lord Tennyson
The Idylls of the King. The Passing of Arthur

We shall not cease from exploration
And the end of all our exploring
Will be to arrive where we started
And know the place for the first time.

— Thomas Stearns Eliot
"Little Gidding," pt. 5, Four Quartets

Plus ça change, plus c'est la même chose.

— Alphonse Karr
Les Guêpes, January 1849

It Has always Been Agile

It has always been Agile. Even back in the mythic days of Waterfall Models and go-to-less programming, when the world was procedural and structured, when it worked, it was also Agile. At least somewhat.

The reason is feedback.

If we look closely at the Waterfall Model (Exhibit 1), we notice that the "test stages" of Unit and System Test have feedback arrows. This implies that some attribute of the product is examined and, under certain circumstances, a corrective action is taken. The circumstances are, of course, the unearthing of a defect; the corrective action is the fixing of whatever caused the defect. It is rework — work being done again. But does this happen linearly as the model suggests, in that it only happens during a temporally contiguous "testing phase," and is the activity restricted to operating within this phase?

In any realistic project the answer to both of these questions is "no." Obviously, if the defect detected is a "requirements" defect — resulting from a lapse or misunderstanding of customer needs — then further "requirements" work is needed. Equally, if the defect detected is an architecture flaw, a detailed design error, or a coding problem, then the effort essentially must "return" to that phase. There are a couple of ways we could illustrate this in a graphical model of the life cycle. One is in Exhibit 2.

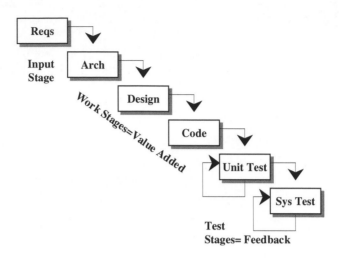

Exhibit 1. Waterfall life cycle model.

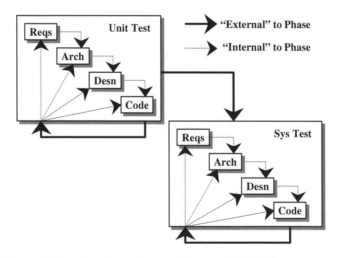

Exhibit 2. Waterfall feedback version 1 with embedded life cycles.

In this convention, a microcosm of the entire life cycle is "embedded" in each test phase. That is, once the defect is detected, a mini-requirements, architecture, design, or code phase is executed *within* the context of the testing activity. The information about the defect is passed back to this function, the corrective work is completed, and the defect is fixed. However, it is usually not enough simply to do the requirements work for a requirements defect; the change must also be factored through the design and coding phases to effectively function in the system as a whole. In the

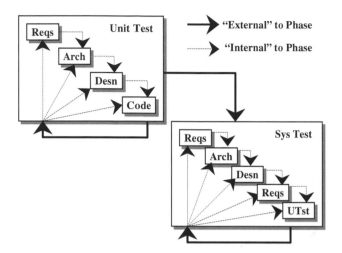

Exhibit 3. Waterfall feedback version 2.

system test phase, we could even make a case for retesting at the unit level; therefore, the system test phase would itself contain a recursive unit test mini-phase within it.

Test Phases with Embedded Life Cycles and Test Phases

This is shown in Exhibit 3. We could get even more complex and recursive if we considered that adjustments to the system as a result of detecting defects in system test would also require an embedded (repeat) system test within the system test correction phase. Of course, if we found defects during *that* phase, we would have to execute a system test correction phase within the system test correction phase. This not only becomes unnecessarily complex, it also becomes genuinely recursive. An alternative view of this is shown in Exhibit 4.

We can sidestep the embedded and recursive appearance of these cycles-within-cycles if we simply describe the activity in a more-linear model and "loop" through it multiple times.

Here the feedback cycles are shown as *external* to the phases. Each phase retains its "linearity," but is executed multiple times as defects are found and work is shipped back to be done.

Of course, these models are simply representations of a complex system and, like any life cycle model, cannot be taken as a literal and exact description of what actually happens in real life on real projects. The basic difference between these variations of the Waterfall Model has, in real life, less to do with the activity itself than with how the activity is managed. For instance, with separate groups tasked with each of the functions of requirements

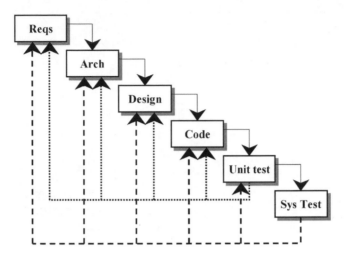

Exhibit 4. Waterfall life cycle model with external feedback.

design, etc., the model shown in Exhibit 4 is more "correct." When work is handed off to a testing group that is thereafter responsible for the product and everything that is done to it, then Exhibit 2 and Exhibit 3 are more "correct." In both cases, however, the following is true:

- Once the first pass of development is completed and the majority of the work is now in testing (i.e., under the control of some testing function or group), subsequent work is largely event-driven and depends on the kind of defect (event) that occurs and when it is detected.

- The length of time, resources required, and kind of work to be redone is a function of the kind of defect found, the work that has been done so far, and the maintainability of the existing system so far. For instance, certain kinds of foundation requirements defects and rework may require substantial redesign. However, if the system architecture has been suitably modularized and employs information-hiding techniques, the otherwise substantial redesign might actually be quite trivial.

The picture is further muddied by two things that almost always happen on projects.

The "Construct Phases" also Have Feedback

The term "construct phases" or "construction phases" of requirements, architecture, design, and code (i.e., everything up to the official start of testing) is a sop to the product view of software. While we commonly think of these phases as "building" the product and the test phases as verifying and validating it, in reality, as we have seen, both types of phases are really concerned with knowledge acquisition. The major difference between the phase types concerns the different kinds of knowledge being acquired, the source of that knowledge, and the processes used to discover and validate the knowledge. Another significant difference is in the target repository for the knowledge acquired. In the construct phases up to the activity of coding, the target is usually a paper document of some sort. In the construct phase of coding, the knowledge repository target is mostly the code itself, although it may include book-form documentation (which is sometimes embedded in the code, of course). While in the unit and system test phases *most* of the knowledge acquired is deposited in the executable, although some is put into the test cases, test scripts, in-code comments, and paper documentation. In all phases, additional project (nonfunctional system) knowledge is put into project planning and tracking systems and, of course, the software developers are busy storing experiential knowledge in their collective brains.

Most development organizations adopt some feedback mechanisms in the earlier phases: inspections, walk-throughs, even test case development, syntactic manipulation of semantic models, interactive development approaches, and prototype (executable and otherwise) development. The results of these activities are usually fed back into the primary knowledge repository, which is commonly a specification or design on paper, although other media such as change requests, action item lists, and test results are also used.

The fact that these phases have "feedback" further complicates the model. As with the variants of the Waterfall Test phases shown in Exhibit 2 through Exhibit 4, we can have either phase-external or phase-internal (your choice) feedback loops that also operate on an event-driven basis. And these can occur from each phase or sub-phase.

The Feedback Activities Generate Feedback Activities

It is very common that, in the process of applying a correction to a defect, other defects are found. So while we are in the middle of one feedback corrective cycle, we trigger another feedback corrective cycle (which, of course, might itself trigger yet another cycle, and so on). In fixing one thing we find something else that is wrong. This process is quite intrinsic to any knowledge-acquisition activity — one cycle gives the context for recognizing the next cycle, which gives us the information we need to recognize the next cycle, and so on.

This complex and highly recursive model is automatically constructed from the most basic linear Waterfall Model, once we introduce any feedback at all. The mere presence of any testing phases in the Waterfall Model means that *de facto* it is not, and never was, the strict linear model that its detractors criticize. It was, and is, still highly front-loaded. However. the Waterfall Model, when it worked, did so because the relative quantity of knowledge already known was large when compared to the quantity of knowledge discovered by *qualifying* the knowledge (proving that the known knowledge does indeed do the job). Making this already-known knowledge functionally executable was usually just a matter of implementing it and we did not tend to find much that was unexpected when we tested those kinds of systems. The reason is obvious in Orders of Ignorance terms: these systems did not contain much Second Order Ignorance. Nevertheless, the Waterfall was never a linear model. It could not be, *unless absolutely no new knowledge was ever found in testing*, in which case, there would be almost no need for testing at all.

To convert this model into the highly flexible life cycles being espoused today, we merely need to turn up the heat on the Waterfall Model: replace some 0OI and 1OI with 2OI, step on the market change rate accelerator, and change the underlying technology in the middle of the project.

In fact, we do not need to go that far. To convert an apparent Waterfall Zeppelin-type product-manufacturing mentality project into a flexible life cycle event-driven knowledge acquisition Jet Plane project, we merely need to dash through the requirements phase too quickly. Time pressure on the early phases will force the project to make assumptions about the requirements in order to "complete" the requirements document on time. The requirements document will then be incomplete, inconsistent, or just plain wrong. This will then lead to poor design decisions, and ensure the highly productive completion of code that does not work or if it works it does not do what anyone wants. This deferring of the requirements knowledge acquisition simply pushes into the testing phases where it will then occur *on an event-driven basis*. The ability to respond to knowledge discovery events is one of the primary characteristics of an Agile Method.

The Problems of "Big" Process

A number of major considerations have forced the software industry to start to move away from "big" or "heavyweight" processes in the last few years:

- *Unproven value.* Traditional "up-front" organizational processes requiring significant investment in analysis, process implementation, training, and application simply have not proven themselves sufficiently. Whether specific process implementations have or have not resulted in value addition to business practices is up for debate. What is quite clear is that large-scale process has not *proven* its worth sufficiently. Otherwise we would use a lot more of it.
- *Guaranteed cost.* The costs of developing and implementing large-scale processes are pretty easy to figure. The value is not. Given a

known cost and an unknown return, many companies opt for certain cost reduction over the uncertain value addition.

- *Required rate of development.* From the Zeppelin to the Jet Plane speeds, we no longer have the up-front time to create processes, particularly in a rapidly changing environment.

- *Rapidly changing business environment.* The change of business needs tends to invalidate older processes somewhat (due to increased 2OI).

- *Rapidly changing development environment.* The capabilities of development change even more quickly than the business environments, it seems. These changes have included the transition from centralized to distributed development; development across platforms, companies, people, and cultures; much greater application of commercial-off-the-shelf (COTS) and other package solutions; the enormous increase in capability of modern development environments, including object libraries, inclusive development platforms, virtual machines, and the explosion of programming languages.

These and other considerations have greatly accelerated both the required rate of development and speed at which development can be accomplished. Traditional process with its emphasis on careful pacing, adherence to plan, up-front analysis, and large-scale, phase-driven feedback loops has simply not been able to cope with the sheer rate of change; add to this a perennial tendency of the software process industry to attempt to reinvent itself every decade or so, plus a dose of faddism, and the death knell of process as it was done is sounding.

That said, there are still long-term projects that are not as susceptible to this accelerating change as more rapidly evolving environments such as Web-based business systems. For such projects, large-scale processes will still be seen to have value. Certain larger consulting assignments with an expected high turnover rate may also opt for heavyweight processes, provided the customer can be persuaded to pay for it. But even there, I expect that agility will creep in, simply because the larger planfull processes view change as bad and to be avoided when change is simply part of the business. Also, heavyweight processes encapsulate the manufacturing view of software more than anything, and before long that view will die out, to be replaced with the knowledge acquisition and knowledge storage medium focus that is the theme of this book. Ultimately, the large, organizationally focused, cold-blooded, and ponderous dinosaur processes will be replaced by compact, human-focused, warm, and Agile process frameworks. They will be focused around people, around customers, and around learning.

Agile Methods

Agile Methods are, as the name implies, flexible and adjustable. Describing the XP (Extreme Programming) variety of Agile Methods, Kent Beck says it is a "lightweight, efficient, low-risk, flexible, predictable, scientific, and fun way to develop software." The critical and defining attributes of Agile approaches are discussed next.

Change Is Expected

Probably more than any other criterion, this lies at the heart of what is increasingly coming under the rubric "Agile." Some proponents of Agile may even state that change is welcomed, although that tends to depend on the change. In fact, some of the primary differences between the Agile approaches are seen in how they address unexpected change. Significant scope change is simply part of the environment today. It cannot be avoided, and therefore legitimate processes should not try to avoid it. Associated with each change is, of course, new knowledge. The whole point of the change is that whatever it is, it is new and to some extent unexpected. Therefore, more than anything else, the Agile approaches are setting us up to expect the unexpected. In Orders of Ignorance terms, they are anticipating Second Order Ignorance. We have seen that it is 2OI that governs most of what we do, particularly in project estimation and scheduling. The Agile approaches simply acknowledge this fact and try to deal with it, rather than try to ignore it or avoid it.

Feedback Is Managed

The concept of development and feedback on development is carefully and organically managed. Even more critically, there is an expectation of significant amounts of feedback from activities already "completed." Feedback characteristics are:

- Short cycles of feedback within the project, so that not too much work is done before some method of determining the work's correctness is applied.
- Progress is test dependent, meaning that the progress of the project is a function of test completeness, rather than any "production" measure.

This varies significantly from classical waterfall projects where the expectation (if not the reality) was that most of the work was completion work, not feedback work.

Stepwise Development

The development does not proceed in one big unit, but is carefully directed in manageable and understandable increments, including:

- Development is incremental, both in the product and in its design (and even in requirements definition), building in small stages rather than monolithically. This often includes an evolutionary design approach rather than one of an early, predetermined design that is maintained through the whole life cycle.
- Development is flexible with respect to schedule, design, and functionality, and is especially responsive to the naturally changing business environment experienced by the customer.
- Each increment is "small," i.e., each executable component or set is a relatively simple component of functionality. Even if valuable functions cannot be delivered in small increments, *something* is delivered, which is then progressively upgraded to deliver real value to the customer within a short time.
- Each increment is "refactored," i.e., as new knowledge is obtained, effort is expended to ensure that the "old" knowledge representation continues to reasonably correspond to the total knowledge statement. This is often achieved by a regime of continuous integration, where the most recently developed pieces of the system are built back into the whole knowledge edifice, which is then regression tested to confirm its validity.

Human Factors

The development process is treated as a human activity rather than a mechanical activity. This includes techniques such as:

- Pair programming, probably the characteristic for which XP is most famous. The approach leverages the fact that an individual has no way to check whether a mistake has been made. It also uses the entirely human capability that, when explaining or discussing an issue with another person, we invariably process that information differently than when we sit alone, trying to solve the problem, and therefore we tend to see the problem and the solution differently.
- The use of metaphor to guide the understanding of the project. Long before the human race invented multi-media presentations, we passed on information through the medium of stories. Use of metaphoric constructs creates a shared story between people on the project and allows a level of identification with the concepts that copious lists of requirements cannot do.
- Collective ownership of the project and its outputs. While most articles on Agile methods still allude to products being produced, there is a strong emphasis on having all people take part in, own and manage all parts of the project.
- The system is not over-engineered, in that the simplest functional design is used that will fulfill the existing requirements at all times.

- A balanced work schedule is maintained. This has been bench-marked at a 40-hour work week (by Kent Beck). The implication is that, if the project requires more than this level of dedicated activity, it is probably using the wrong approach.
- Coding Standards are applied to ensure that shared code is maximally understood between team members.

Customer-Centric

Key perspectives on the Agile project are intentionally *customer focused*, i.e., there is a continuous and conscious attempt to take the customers' role and view the system from the customers' point of view, including:

- On-project customer resources, often including customer representation on the team itself
- Customer-focused project planning based on the delivery of value to the customer rather than on any internal development measures

As the Preacher in Ecclesiastes (1:9) points out, "there is nothing new under the sun." In many respects, successful projects in the old days of the Waterfall approach had many of the characteristics of the Agile projects: they viewed people as integral to the project; they were customer focused; they effectively responded to necessary changes when they occurred; they established metrics based on real value rather than artificial production of *something*; they built something that *worked*. Hence, they were successful.

Agile Is Event Driven

Even the modern models for software development are still models. They do not and cannot explicitly describe the detailed development activities, the true work products, many of which are brain resident and quite subtle. They cannot precisely replicate the real development phases or actual dependencies or types of knowledge. The more usable models are simply better approximations than given by the other models. They are still approximations because they are still models. The primary characteristic of Agile life cycle models is that they tend to be more event-driven than the product–production or manufacturing-influenced models. More correctly, they are driven more by what is actually learned than by what is expected to be learned. Agile projects are more responsive to what is really happening than what was expected to happen. The Zeppelin–Jet Plane metaphor is relevant — the behavior of the ballistic cannon shell at any point is almost entirely a function of the start conditions, and is quite predictable. The behavior of the missile is mostly a function of the behavior of the missile up to that point in time. Indeed, it might be almost entirely independent of the start conditions, in that two missiles with radically different start conditions could end up behaving almost the same, or two missiles with nearly identical start conditions might behave quite differently and end up at different end points. On Agile projects, the work being done at any point in time is a function of what has been learned through the project up until that point in time. This does include the starting points of the expected plan, early contracted deliverables, and probable design approach. But it also includes the reaction to changes in the expected plan, marketplace or customer-driven modifications to the requirements, the evolution of different design alternatives, and the ever-unfolding and continuous acquisition of knowledge that comes from building a system. In classical systems development, change is bad and must be avoided or controlled. In Agile development, change is considered inevitable and even valuable.

As mentioned previously, on traditional projects the only phase of software development that truly and intentionally lives by this principle is the activity of testing. While we can predict some testing activity before the project is started (although only at a conceptual or type level, such as "test all boundaries"), much of it must be based on what we find out in our requirements design and coding activities — through the agency of applying the test plan. In fact, it could be argued that *most* of the work we do in testing is a direct function of what we learn by doing the work in testing.

The Agile approach simply recognizes this, whereas the Waterfall and related approaches, entrenched as they are in the product–production paradigm do not. This is true even though, when examined closely, they *must* have taken it into account to be successful. The fact that the older life cycle management models and development processes are not sufficiently agile is one of the biggest causes of grief and failed expectations in software development. When we use models and mindsets that are rigid and deterministic to manage an activity that is fluid and variable, it is not surprising that people get disappointed.

The Agile approaches operate, at least implicitly, on the following assumptions:

- *Intrinsic Variability:* Things will change, deal with it.
- *Limits of Precognition:* We cannot know everything in advance.
- *Constructive Feedforward:* The act of trying to build something has the potential for changing key characteristics of what we are trying to build.
- *Contextual Positioning:* Sometimes we need to acquire some knowledge to know what other knowledge we need to acquire.
- *Constructive Positioning:* Sometimes we need to build things to find out how to build things.
- *Perspective Blindness:* One person looking at a problem cannot see what he or she cannot see.
- *Executable Validity:* Until we have made knowledge execute, we cannot assert we have developed executable knowledge.

- *Knowledge Discovery Is Anthropomorphic:* The discovery of knowledge is a human activity that is primarily a function of collective human thought processes and human understanding.
- *Knowledge Discovery Is a Function of our State of Mind:* It is compromised by people being tired, dispirited, and demotivated.
- *Knowledge Is Undividable:* Large collections of related knowledge cannot be fully understood by breaking them into pieces are parceling them out to different people.
- *Knowledge Irruption:* We can only expose knowledge in an environment that contains that knowledge (see The Dual Hypotheses of Knowledge Discovery in Chapter 3).
- *Knowledge Comparisons:* The only way to assert the validity of knowledge is to compare against another source of knowledge (see The Dual Hypotheses of Knowledge Discovery in Chapter 3).
- *Customer Arbitration:* The only and final arbiter of whether the executable knowledge is useful and valuable in allowing the customer to more effectively operate in the customer's environment is the customer executing that knowledge in the customer's environment.
- *Knowledge Structure Integrity:* It is necessary to maintain the structural integrity of the knowledge representation as new knowledge is discovered.
- *Occam's Design Razor:* The simplest design that suffices to provide the value to the customer is the best design to use.

There are a variety of so-called "Agile" methods, the foremost proponents of which have aligned themselves into the "Agile Alliance." The 17 authors* of the Agile Manifesto are a group of high-powered methodologists and practitioners (and skiers). They met at Snowbird Ski Resort in Utah in February 2001. One of the outcomes of this meeting was to change the group name of the methodologies developed and espoused by this group from the previous description of "lightweight" to "agile." The phrase "lightweight" was thought to connote lack of structure or attention to detail. People also thought it sounded somewhat ineffective, which was the direct opposite of the Agile Alliance proponents' experiences. This highly talented group with careers measuring significant percentages of the time software has been on the planet was, in many cases, refugees fleeing the methodology wars of times comprised. They had tried the "rigorous" methods and the paper-driven methods, they had used the introspective analytical methods, they had applied the proprietary methods, and the named methods, and the certified methods, and found them wanting. Their alliance was novel in other ways. Historically, methodologists and their ideas have seemed to be in contention, as if for one methodology to be "right" the other conventions must be

*Ken Beck, Mike Beedle, Arie van Bennekim, Alistair Cockburn, Ward Cunningham, Martin Fowler, James Greening, Jim Highsmith, Andrew Hunt, Ron Jefferies, Jon Kern, Brian Marick, Bob Martin, Steve Mellor, Ken Schwaber, Jeff Sutherland, and Dave Thomas.

"wrong." As we have seen, *all* methods involve the development of behavioral, systems, operational, etc., models of some type.

Extreme Programming (XP)

Although not the first of the Agile (lightweight) methods, Extreme Programming, usually known simply by its splendidly chosen acronym "XP," is arguably the most well known of the Agile approaches. Initially popularized by Kent Beck in his book *Extreme Programming Explained,** XP takes a minimalist approach, and has been shown to be effective, particularly on smaller teams. Detractors of Agile methods sometimes point to issues of scalability in the use of these approaches. They have a point, but it may be overplayed. Arguably *all* methods and models work "better" in the small. There is a very simple reason for this: the relatively lower complexity of smaller systems makes any method easier to use. The increasing reality of modern systems development is that it *is* being done faster and in smaller groups. Therefore, these methods must certainly fit the situation better than the previous inorganic approaches. That said, XP appears to suffer from scalability issues at least as much as most methods, simply because it eschews the layers of organizational overhead that are sometimes required to coordinate large enterprises.

The key elements of XP are discussed next.

The Planning Game

XP translates the activity of project (and therefore deliverable) planning into a "business game." First, by viewing it as some relatively objective intellectual exercise, some of the personalization and natural territorial behavior is lessened. When people are cooperatively making decisions about their workload, their responsibilities and, probably, activities that will result in reward or punishment, a number of emotions tend to reside quite close to the surface. These emotions may modify peoples' behavior and rarely result in higher levels of cooperative functioning. The two major constituencies are objectified into "Business" and "Development" rather than "us" and "them." The game is played with story cards on which small vignettes are written, describing the functions that would give value to the system. Stories are usually written by Business and their effort estimated by Development, but not always. Stories can be combined or divided. The stories are sorted by business value, and are further sorted by development risk (usually based on level of "estimatability" which is, of course, a function of the quantity of 2OI). Development gets to further adjust the prospective plan to be generated from the story cards by setting a development "velocity," which is basically a measure of the "effective" time available

*Beck, K., *Extreme Programming Explained: Embrace Change,* Addison-Wesley, Reading, MA, 1999.

within calendar time. Some project estimation and planning tools use a loading factor to calculate the same thing.

The story cards are used to create a project plan. Typically, the project plan consists of a series of iterations, each with a set of stories. One of the conventions of XP is that any iteration should be an end-to-end set of business functions, even if they are primitive. The idea is to deliver something to the customer that (1) really works and (2) provides some legitimate value. These are the Small Releases.

Small Releases

The continual release of functioning software in small increments is a feature of all Agile approaches at some level. Actually making the software work in the real environment does many things:

- It proves that the team can actually make something work.
- It may provide real value to the customer early on, helping to offset the cost of the project.
- Because the story cards were sorted by business priority, the tendency is to deliver the most valuable functions first and, as development progresses, pushes the same high priority functions through the most iterations, making them more likely to work properly.
- The activity of trying to make the functions actually work forces the team to discover and face the most difficult knowledge issues (2OI).

The Use of Metaphor

The "stories" mentioned earlier are good examples. All human intellectual processing is, at its basis, metaphorical. Studies have shown that good stories have a very high information density. We understand stories and analogies much better and more naturally than we understand other modalities. Before the human race invented PowerPoint presentations, we passed on vital information from generation to generation through stories. Our brains are wired to remember and respond to them. XP acknowledges and leverages this fact.

Simple Design

A tenet of XP is that the team should always use the simplest design that fulfills the *existing* requirements. It is easy to see where the potential issues could be with this approach — the project fails to anticipate obvious extensions to the system and it has to be radically redesigned. However, this "rule" preempts the more pernicious problem of the never-ending design and redesign Steven Jobs called "creeping elegance." If some design extension is needed, then a design extension story can be created, prioritized, and included in an iteration. In Orders of Ignorance terms, XP discourages unqualified prediction of 2OI.

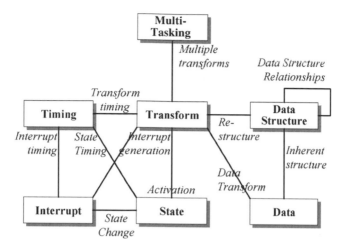

Exhibit 5. Generalized requirements meta-model.

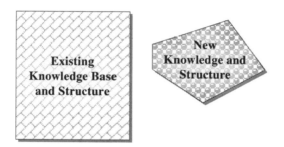

Exhibit 6. The application of new knowledge to existing structures.

Refactoring

This is arguably the most difficult part of XP. As new iterations progress, the currently existing knowledge representation must be refactored or restructured to maintain its legitimate representation of *all* the knowledge (both the previously factored knowledge and the knowledge incorporated in this iteration). The challenge of modifying the existing structure of a software system to cleanly represent the total knowledge base is the philosopher's store of software maintenance. This is a function that is not limited to software. In *The Structure of Scientific Revolutions*, Thomas Kuhn demonstrated that this difficulty pervades all disciplines, especially research science. The challenge is that the new knowledge structure usually somewhat contradicts the existing knowledge structure. This requires the structure to be deconstructed and reassembled. Various versions of this are shown in Exhibit 5 through Exhibit 10. For most software maintenance,

111

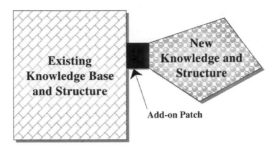

Exhibit 7. Nonintegration of new knowledge into existing structures.

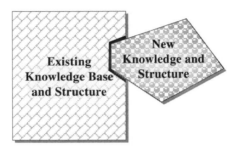

Exhibit 8. Partial assimilation of new knowledge to existing structures.

some shortcuts are made in integrating the new knowledge (Exhibit 6 through Exhibit 8) that end up compromising the whole structure. The most difficult is complete integration (Exhibit 10).

Testing

The difference between knowledge-in-brains, knowledge-in-books, and knowledge-in-software is that the knowledge-in-software objectively *executes*. Without testing the attribute of executability, we never know if the system will execute. XP specifies that the test cases are developed in advance of the code. This does several things — it encourages the developers to think also as testers, which gives them an alternative thinking modality. It forces them to ask, at least to some extent, if they *really* know what the system should do. Given that validating knowledge is always a comparison against another repository of knowledge (Hypothesis Two of the Dual Hypotheses in Chapter 1), they are already prepared with the "other repository." Interestingly, a common modification of the old Waterfall Model (called the "V-Shaped Waterfall") also recommended this approach. XP also encourages the capture of tests in an automated

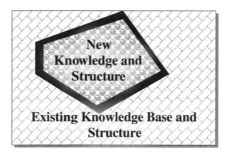

Exhibit 9. Embedding new knowledge into existing structures.

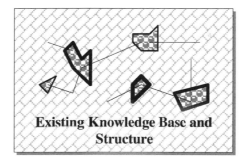

Exhibit 10. New knowledge fully integrated and refactored into existing structures.

medium, which is, of course, storing the testing knowledge in the fifth knowledge medium, which is what we should do all along.

Pair Programming

It is this characteristic for which XP is probably most famous. It is well known that we cannot see our own defects, because to us they do not *look* like defects. Joining two programmers at the hip and having them create together avoids the tunnel vision that creating causes. Pair programming also blows up the concept of "my" program, because it can be difficult even to spot "my" line in a program when pair programming is used. More than anything, pair programming collapses the feedback cycle on top of the construction cycle, so that very little work is considered complete before it is checked by at least one other set of eyes. Pair programming also scores in that most of us have a small set of preferred problem-solving approaches. If that approach does not seem to work, we tend to apply it again more forcefully, usually achieving the same results. The reason we have preferred approaches to solving problems is that (1) we may have an innate disposition toward them; (2) we are good at them; (3) being good at them, we tend to use them a lot; (4) because we use them a lot we get better at them, so we tend to use them more and get better at them. This is fine, unless the approach does not work. Under pressure, most of us will reflexively revert to the skill set that has been most successful for us in the past. Working closely with someone allows us access to *their* problem-solving style as well as our own. Finally, when we focus too much on a problem, we tend to lock in on one approach to solving it. Having to explain or discuss our reasoning with another helps to prevent this lock-in.

Collective Ownership

In addition to pair programming, XP encourages cooperative ownership of all work products including code. This means that anyone may change any code, although this may not occur practically, because the primary author(s) are usually the most qualified to change it. More than simply "who changes," cooperative ownership is an ethic of the team, in which everyone jointly shares in doing what is necessary to make the project work, and no one takes the position of "*my* end of the ship isn't sinking." Many traditional life cycle projects attempted this in the past through the agency of cooperative activities such as inspections and joint development sessions.

Continuous Integration

The very short cycles, iterative development, and constant refactoring result in a daily activity of integrating all the executable products through things such as daily builds and automated regression testing.

Intentionally Limited Work Week

This was specified by Kent Back as a 40-hour work week. Others have disagreed (see Code Science). This purpose is several-fold: to ensure a life–work balance as being more optimal than overworking, to "time-box" the process so that attention is paid to making the best decisions, and finally it adopts the view that if too much additional work is required, it is better to reconsider *how* the work is being done rather than simply to do more of it. This is a direct challenge to the manufacturing view of software.

On-Site Customer

XP attempts to break down the walls between the customer and the development group attempting to provide value. As well as the "Planning Game," XP calls for the close cooperation with the user/customer that can only be achieved by on-project representation from the customer domain. This has been a clarion call in software for as long as I have been in the business.

Coding Standards

XP also recommends adherence and adoption of cooperative coding standards. Given the ideal of anyone being able to go into any code, some kind of reasonable standards are essential.

Code Science

Code Science is a variant of XP developed at Geneer, a software engineering company based in Rosemont, Illinois, and is now actively practiced at a highly competent and innovative consulting company called AgileTek. It was a very successful approach and proved itself in the marketplace. Based largely on the precepts of XP, Code Science added, subtracted, and modified XP processes as follows:

- *Business Process Analysis.* XP, as well as many other methodologies, assumes that a legitimate source of business requirements is available. That is, the team has access to a customer constituency that has the answers to the questions the team will raise, but what happens if the customer does not know what he or she wants? Code Science adds a precursor step involving an analysis of the business environment to deal with this situation.
- *Delphi Estimation.* In addition to the Planning Game activities, a more-formal estimation using a Delphi (anonymous gathering of engineers' opinions on the minimum, most likely, and maximum estimates) approach. This approach allows not only estimation of mean, but also an approximation of variance, which can be factored into a calculation of perceived risk.
- *Modular Architecture.* XP has been accused of ignoring the up-front architecting of systems in favor of *ad hoc* development and continual refactoring through the development cycles. Code Science takes some of the essential design elements from more-classical development models to derive a base architecture that is likely to be more stable. This involves developing a componentized architecture that is resilient to all but major redesigns forced by significant business process changes.
- *Automated Contract and Regression Testing.* Code Science adds contract-based automated validation, particularly for regression testing, to the develop-and-test cycle of XP. This has the advantage of being customer-certified testing and can be used to assess progress on the project against the only truly legitimate measure: are we fulfilling the requirements for the customer?
- *Story Actors and Personified Requirements.* In addition to more-typical requirements-gathering modalities such as use cases, Code Science employs the idea of developing "personified requirements." These are requirements that are linked to a fictitious person (e.g., "Tom

115

the Tester") who uses, or specifies, or otherwise interacts with the requirements. This enhances the story and allows developers to interpolate and extrapolate the requirements ("What would *Tom the Tester* need under these circumstances?").

- *Wall GANTTs.* To use these, the project management system is located in the corridors of AgileTek's offices. Each project has its corridor and a Gantt chart is created for the project by hooking index cards over string that stretches the length of the corridor. Each index card represents a task and each of the parallel strings a project participant. Calendar dates are marked off along the wall. This "low-tech" project planning tool allows the team to visualize the whole project and physically congregate around the plan in a way that an automated tool does not allow. Each morning, the whole project team gathers in the corridor for a short stand-up meeting to discuss the status of the tasks. Generally, any task to the left of where you are standing should have been completed and any task to the right should be awaiting attention. The cards can be easily moved to reprioritize, and the highly visible plan acts as the center from which all work is tackled.

- *Automatic Document Generation.* Using HTML tags embedded in comments in source code allows the Doc-It tool to traverse the code directories and construct Web pages for all the source files containing all the comments. This relieves the developers of the mundane task of creating separate documentation. This is a good example of highly effective process from the perspective we have been discussing — the activity of creating readable versions of the code comments is a well-defined activity from which little can be learned. By automating it, the process is applied without anyone having to apply it.

Code Science also made other adjustments to XP, by relaxing the requirement for *all* code to be developed in pairs and allowing projects to work in excess of 40 hours per week, when the team thought it appropriate. Code Science also allowed modifications to the methodology for special situations where the flexibility of XP was not needed or there was a regulatory need (such as in developing under the supervision of a government body such as the FAA or the FDA).

Crystal Methods

Alistair Cockburn's delightful analogy of software development as a "cooperative game" is the cornerstone of Crystal Methods. Perhaps even more than other Agile approaches, Crystal Methods focuses on the human side of the activity of creating software, and is intentionally "process light." In fact, it is recommended that each project team create its own process or, more correctly, select and tailor its process from a set of methodology elements. The term "crystal" is a reference to the facets of a gemstone, each of which gives visibility into the same thing (the gemstone), but for which each view is different.

In his highly engaging book, *Agile Software Development,** Alistair Cockburn describes several flavors of Crystal. The approach can be modified by making the methodology "heavier" (higher intrinsic coordination, work product definition, supplementary documentation, and the other artifacts of defined methodologies). This is labeled by changing the "color" of the crystal. Crystal Clear is lighter than Crystal Orange, etc. The "darker" the color of the Crystal method used, the more expected and necessary method overhead we would see. The other crystal metaphor used is "hardness." "Harder" crystal levels connote systems whose intrinsic risk and cost of failure is high, with the highest cost being risk to human life. Avionics and medical systems will often be diamond hard. A Web-based retail business ordering system would be somewhat softer. Alistair Cockburn is quite forthright in assigning different levels or weights of processes to different types and sizes of projects. What might be suitable for one kind of project might be dangerous for another. Systems requiring a cast of thousands would not be well served by the lighter of the methods. Small colocated teams working on projects that are not life-critical are simply hindered by large analysis and paper-intensive methods while not balancing return in value for the effort expended to service such heavyweight processes.

Beause the cornerstone of Crystal Methods is flexibility of method, it is not as appropriate to list the characteristics of the method as it is for the other Agile approaches. Alistair Cockburn's describes two of the levels of Crystal methods in *Agile Software Development,* * the "lightest" of the methods is Crystal Clear.

Crystal Clear

All Crystal Methods share a common basis of principles that include:

- Being people (rather than process) centric, which means that processes (tools, work products, etc.) exist only to support human understanding capability
- Change tolerance, not only for externally driven changes (such as customer or business shifts), but also to recognize that each project is at least somewhat different from any other project and may require different processes
- Tunable process or rather intentionally tuned methodology and processes
- Intermediate work products can be reduced in number, size, and complexity as the code and testing products come online, and these products tend to provide a richer communication channel than secondary paper documents

*Cockburn, A., *Agile Software Development,* Addison-Wesley, Reading, MA, 2001.

- You need less control than you might think, especially when the project gains momentum
- Development is cyclical, learning from each cycle as well as producing products
- Regular delivery of working software with a suggested schedule of every 2 to 3 months for Crystal Clear
- Direct user/customer involvement on the project
- Low number of work products, certainly relative to more-heavy-weight methods, including (not necessarily in chronological order) use cases, screen drafts, common object models, design drafts, review schedule, release plan, executable code, migration code, test cases, and user manual; the emphasis is on usability. Crystal Clear (as other Crystal Methods) may also have discretionary work products as required or found useful by the team, including work product templates, coding standards, testing standards; documentation is expected, but its level and content is left to the choice of the team

In addition, Crystal Clear is intended for use on a small (e.g., around six people) colocated (everyone within hailing distance) project, working on a system on which neither very large sums of money nor peoples' lives will depend. It suggests:

- Low number of roles: sponsor, senior designer-programmer, designer-programmer, user
- Discretionary processes such as time-boxing and pair programming may be included as long as the team sees value in them

Scrum

Scrum, so named after the maul that is a feature of rugby football, was developed by Ken Schwaber and Jeff Sutherland, and is documented in the book *Agile Software Development with Scrum*.* Scrum cycles in 30-day "sprints," which are each a set of three components that plan, build, and monitor the development of a subset of the overall work. The three stages are called Pre-Sprint, Sprint, and Post-Sprint.

Pre-Sprint

The Pre-Sprint stage is a planning activity. A *Product Backlog* is the primary planning source. It may contain both user function and technology and architecture elements waiting to be completed by the team. The backlog list is "owned" by the Product Owner, who may be a person or a team representing the various customer constituencies (including technical staff, if necessary). The Product Owner reviews and prioritizes the subset of

*Schwaber, K., Beedle, M., and Martin, R.C., *Agile Software Development with Scrum,* Prentice Hall, Englewood Cliffs, NJ, 2001.

features in the Product Backlog to create the *Release Backlog*. This identifies the work the team will attempt for the next 30-day Sprint cycle. This list is used to plan the tasks for the development team. At the same time the Release Backlog is created, the team creates a *Sprint Goal*. This is best described as the business objective or the reason the next cycle will be worked. Adopting the Sprint Goal avoids having the team focus exclusively on the detailed tasks. It can also give some flexibility in working the plan — *"we didn't complete all the tasks but we did achieve the Sprint Goal."* More importantly, it keeps the team focused on the real task, which is to deliver something of value to the customer.

The Sprint

The scrum team members sign up for the tasks for the 30-day Sprint, and it is expected that the team will be largely self-managed. The primary management feature of the Sprint is the daily scrum meeting. This is a relatively informal planning and progress meeting that takes place every day at the same time. It should be short and to-the-point. It is attended by *everyone* involved, developers and users alike. The meeting is facilitated by a person called the *Scrum Master*. This person is in charge of the Sprint and functions, at least in part, to control changes. In general the 30-day Sprint cycle is closed to changes once the Release Backlog is agreed upon. This is an attempt to balance the need for continuous change in a continuously changing environment with the development team's need for *some* stability during development.

Post-Sprint

At the end of each 30-day cycle, the Post-Sprint meeting reviews accomplishments and shortfalls. It is also a meeting where the completed customer functionality can be presented. The end of this Post-Sprint meeting segues into the beginning of the next 30-day cycle.

Dynamic Systems Development Method (DSDM)

This approach evolved out of the Rapid Application Development (RAD) approaches of the 1990s. Popular in Europe, DSDM has evolved far enough to have a North American Consortium chartered with building and propagating the method. As the name implies, it is intended to be faster and more flexible than "traditional" methods, and its inclusion in the Agile family means that it is change capable, expecting and allowing for changes, rather than avoiding or fighting them. There are nine principles under which DSDM operates:

1. User/customer involvement is imperative.
2. Development (DSDM) teams are empowered, which implies that at least some of the decision making is devolved from management to the team itself.

3. Frequent delivery of product releases to the customer.
4. Value and acceptance is based on fitness for business use rather than a production metric.
5. Iterative development is necessary to converge on the best business solution.
6. Changes made during development can be reversed, if necessary.
7. Requirements are baselined at a high level, implying some degree of stabilization of requirements during development.
8. Testing is integrated throughout the life cycle rather than being a specific contiguous phase.
9. DSDM occurs in a collaborative environment between all stakeholders.

The DSDM approach has four "phases" (including a feasibility study), three of which are cyclical.

1. *Feasibility Study:* This may occur before the start of a project (if new) or between major cycles of development. Its purpose is the classic job of feasibility — to determine the major scope, and provide a high-level feasibility gate, so projects that are not valuable or not doable are not even started. It produces an initial list of prioritized requirements used in the *Functional Model* phase.
2. *Functional Modeling:* DSDM explicitly uses a prototyping approach, collecting, refining, and proving the requirements in (usually executable) prototypes rather than passive paper documents. This is done cyclically with embedded review cycles to check the prototype operation and output against expectations. "Successful" prototypes are used to drive the next phase.
3. *Design and Build:* The Design and Build phase, which may be significantly overlapped with the other phases, also uses prototyping as its primary activity. Prototypes may be built or extended from the Functional Modeling stage and can address any (prioritized) aspect of development: attributes, requirements, functions, interfaces, capacity, performance, etc. DSDM relies more heavily, or perhaps more specifically, on prototypes than do other approaches, with perhaps slightly lower expectations of full functionality from the code than is present with other code-driven approaches.
4. *Implementation:* The "final" stage operates on the output of the Design and Build prototypes and enhances them into fully functional components, including any additional services necessary to make the system operational.

DSDM applies many of the time-boxing approaches seen in other methods, but also has some interesting facets. Much of the "documentation" in DSDM is deemed to be in the prototypes themselves rather than in extra paper documentation. It also suggests some interesting roles over and above the traditional project manager and developer roles. There are user roles titled "visionary," "ambassador" and "advisor," with the visionary being responsible for the high-level business goals. The ambassador understands the business processes and the advisor interfaces with the development team to make day-to-day operational knowledge available.

Feature-Driven Development (FDD)

Feature-Driven Development (FDD) was developed by Jeff De Luca and Peter Coad at a project executed for a Singapore bank in the late 1990s, after a large consulting company had failed to deliver on the system, generating enormous quantities of documentation but no code. FDD has been documented in the book *A Practical Guide to Feature-Driven Development*.* FDD uses a five-step model with the expectation of change acceptance and flexibility of approach common to all Agile methods. FDD has a couple of other distinctive characteristics that make it of great interest: (1) it was one of the few approaches that was empirically designed in developing a large system, and shows some of the issues concerning the scalability of these approaches; and (2) it is not as code-centric as other methods, expecting some of the work to be done in modeling forms as well as code forms.

1. *Develop an Overall Model:* In this short phase (recommended at 10 percent of initial project effort), the "shape" of the system is modeled typically using a common modeling notational system. The challenge is avoiding the detail-driven descent into the depths of analysis. FDD expects that the necessary detail will be driven out by the later Feature development cycles. The purpose of this model is to provide macro guidance in the planning of the features and the integration of developed code.

2. *Build Features List:* In the second phase, the model and further customer input results in a comprehensive *Features List*. Typically, this approach is "top-down," based on decomposition of identifiable customer features. This is intended to compliment the more technically driven (and often more "bottom-up") approach used in the overall system object modeling. Feature scope is intentionally designed to require around 2 weeks of effort to resolve. If features appear to be bigger than this, they are decomposed.

3. *Plan by Feature:* The feature set is used by a development planning team to create the order and release cycles of the features. The usual-suspect characteristics are considered: inter-feature dependency, feature–architecture dependency, risk, resource balancing, and the like. Chief programmers run smaller teams and are typically responsible for major business activities. The responsibility for creating the

*Palmer, S.R. and Felsing, J.M., *A Practical Guide to Feature-Driven Development,* Prentice Hall PTR, New York, 2002.

necessary functioning classes and methods are given to developers. This creates a multi-level scheduling system with the Project Manager being responsible for the overall integration and the chief programmers managing their feature set.

4. *Design by Feature:* For each set of related business activities, the chief programmer develops design packages. These consist of the modeling components that will describe the objects to the point of transitioning the development activity into code form. Sequences and business level characteristics are developed cooperatively at the team level and the class and method development done by each class owner.

5. *Build by Feature:* Feature teams complete their assignments by implementing the classes and methods, writing and inspecting the code, unit testing, and integrating into the system-level (so far) build.

Lean Development

Lean Development (LD) originated as a management approach by Bob Charette, and the term itself is from the book *The Machine that Changed the World: The Story of Lean Production.** At its core, it views risk less as a challenge to be avoided or overcome (the classical risk management approach), but as a source of value. Note that this fits in with the Orders of Ignorance view of development, where the most risky area is 2OI, and the most valuable returns are in resolving 2OI. Bob Charette points out that merely attempting to accelerate development simply increases risk without equivalently increasing capability to deal with the risk. LD identifies four key factors and employs 12 abiding principles. The key success factors are:

1. Create visible customer value quickly
2. Build-in change-tolerance
3. Develop only necessary functionality
4. Be aggressive in setting and meeting goals

These factors are very similar to other Agile approaches, which is one of the reasons there is a convergence of ideas in this area (that, and the inspiring lack of territorial behavior on the part of their proponents). The 12 principles of LD are:

1. Satisfy the customer as the highest priority; not fulfill a plan, fill a document, placate a boss, or build some technically cool geegaw.
2. Provide best value for the money. Value is the difference between cost (to build, to buy, and to use — after compensating for defects) and value (the business value of the capabilities the system gives).

*Womack, J.P., *The Machine that Changed the World,* HarperCollins, New York, 1991.

3. Active customer participation as a real function of the development in that the customer representative is really committed in the decision making on the project and the consequences of those decisions.
4. Team effort in all aspects of development, including planning.
5. Accept change as being part of the business, anticipate what might occur (where cost effective), expect that it will occur, and deal with it when it does occur.
6. Develop domain solutions (again with the value proviso) rather than on-off solutions.
7. Complete rather than construct. Base design and build/buy decisions on the likelihood of completion (of customer value) rather than using construction metrics.
8. Pragmatic solution today rather than perfect solution tomorrow. Studies have shown that much of software functionality remains unused sometimes years after development. Driven by the first principle of customer value, the earlier application of some value is often more valuable than the later application of more value.
9. Minimize paperwork, overhead, extra stuff, excess communication by colocating teams and managing scope.
10. Need determines technology rather than using technology for its own sake. Pick a workable technology and use it rather than cycling trying to find the "best."
11. Growth is determined by more features, not more code. The size may be irrelevant. What is relevant is what (valued) capabilities the system provides.
12. Use lean development where lean development works best. While the business environment is becoming more changeable, and the need for Agile is growing, none of these approaches is (1) a silver bullet, (2) guaranteed to be 100 percent successful, (3) universally accepted in all companies, and (4) effortless. LD is a tool like other tools and, used intelligently, can work well.

Adaptive Software Development (ASD)

The Adaptive Software Development (ASD) technique was developed by Jim Highsmith and Sam Bayer in the early 1990s, and the book *Adaptive Software Development** was published in 2000. Like other Agile approaches, it is cyclical and acknowledges that changes will happen. ASD also acknowledges that "mistakes" happen naturally. In *Agile Software Ecosystems,*** Jim Highsmith writes that for some companies "…the idea that there is no way to *'do it right the first time'* remains foreign."*** Of course, the only way we could ever do it right the first time is if we knew exactly

---

* Highsmith, J. and Orr, K., *Adaptive Software Development: A Collaborative Approach to Managing Complex Systems,* Dorset House, New York, 2000.
** Highsmith, J., *Agile Software Ecosystems,* Addison-Wesley Professional, Reading, MA, 2002.
*** Page 311, italics mine.

what "right" is. In Orders of Ignorance terms, that would mean no 2OI. As we have seen, it is the increase in 2OI in systems that is causing much of our need to modify our development practices.

ASD uses a "change-oriented life cycle" that has three components:

1. Speculate or explore the options.
2. Collaborate cyclically using a variety of skills and team capabilities to "grow" the understanding of the system and its solution.
3. Learn, or perhaps more pointedly, usefully extract what has been learned to allow the knowledge to be used to create the system.

These components have sub-activities as described next.

Speculate

- Project initiation is done to set the primary goals and objectives of the entire project and to understand the constraints under which the project will operate. Initial scoping is done and the key risk areas are identified.
- Entire project time-box is set from the scope. It is implicit in ASD as it is in all Agile methods that estimates are estimates and will vary from actuals. Nevertheless, it is also known that people work best within known time parameters and that constraining projects to a generally expected timeframe helps greatly in focusing peoples' attentions and forcing legitimate and helpful prioritization of work.
- Decide number of iterations or subsets of the entire project. Like FDD, these should be deliverable features that can be used by the customer at the end of iteration. Iterations are themselves time-boxed with times ranging from 2 to 3 weeks, depending on the project. The time-boxing also allows the creation of a schedule for iteration.
- Identify theme or objective for iteration in a way similar to Scrum's "Sprint Goal." The theme is obviously closely linked to the feature set being worked.
- Assign features to iteration by cooperative effort between the customers and the developers.

These steps may be revisited several times before the team and the customers are satisfied with the result.

Collaborate

This is the phase where the bulk of the development work occurs. ASD is intended for environments where there will be concurrent development. It is highly cyclical and, while keeping an eye on the time-boxed clock, can be quite variable in formal process level and use of models and tools. The primary job of management in this phase is to continue to provide coordination capability to help ensure that things being learned on one sub-team are passed around and do not have to be relearned by the other teams.

Learn

The final "phase" terminates a set of collaboration cycles and its job is to intentionally capture what has been learned, both "positively" and "negatively" (i.e., what worked and what did not) in the previous cycles. As simple as this seems, it is a critical element to effective teams. It is well known that adults learn more from mistakes than from successes. Generally, if adults tackle something and are successful the first time out it is usually due to (1) skill and capability (we knew how to do it already or we very quickly figured out what to do, in which case we probably did not learn very much) or (2) we were really, really lucky, in which case we may come away with an inflated sense of our own competence. Establishing an environment that requires people to learn but punishes them for taking a wrong step is a recipe for paralysis. Jim Highsmith identifies four kinds of learning in this phase:

1. Quality as seen by the customer. This is to maintain the customer added-value focus that is a feature of Agile Methods and is, of course, the only legitimate measure of success.
2. Quality as seen by developers. This involves the assessment of "product quality" from a technical viewpoint. Examples of this include adherence to standards and conformance to architecture goals.
3. Performance management. This is a process assessment to look at what was learned by employing the processes used by the team.
4. Project status. As a precursor to planning the next iteration of the project, this is the jumping off point for building the next set of features.

Why Agile? Why Now?

The Agile movement is a welcome change from more than a decade of large organizational process. It has put some of the humanity back into what is inescapably a human activity. There is no doubt and little argument that the rate of change in systems development has accelerated, and that projects and organizations must learn to be both faster and more flexible in dealing with this reality.

When the outside world changes, our ability to fully provide a solution that will fit it is no longer a function only of our ability to understand the situation; it starts to become a function also of our ability to respond to these changes. Beyond a certain point (the "No Value Point" in Exhibit 11), the changes totally invalidate our view of the system. The level of "defects" — the functions or attributes of the system that are unknown to us and therefore do

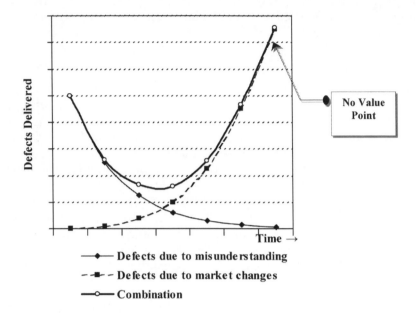

Exhibit 11. Defect/development time dependency.

not work — is the sum of the defects we create through poor understanding of the existing requirements (the requirements at the beginning of the project) *and* the "defects" caused by the fact that the need for what we have learned or built has changed.

Exhibit 12 shows that there is an optimal development time at the point where the sum of the two curves in minimal. In the Zeppelin days, the rate of defects due to changes was low, and the optimal development time was way off to the right.

What is happening in today's world is that the Rate of External Change curve is getting steeper and steeper (see Exhibit 13). This is causing the optimal development time point to do two things:

1. Time is decreasing. The points are moving to the left. We are seeing less and less time available to develop a system before outside circumstances render it useless.
2. Defects are increasing. The points are also moving up. This means that the intrinsic number of defects we would expect to see will increase, unless we do something about it.

Exhibit 14 shows this. Not only does the optimal point move in, it moves up. Unfortunately, we are limited in what we can do about the rate at which the outside world changes. The only thing we have control over is the rate at which we process the information (the "Defects due to misunderstanding

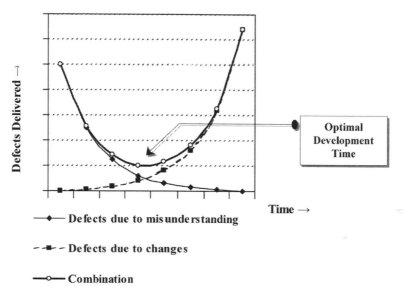

Exhibit 12. Optimal development time.

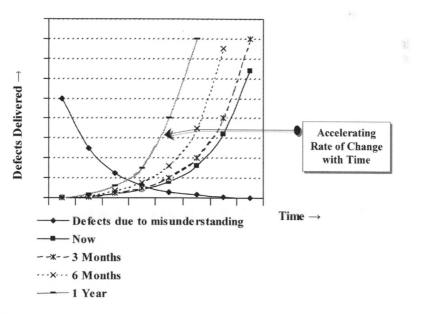

Exhibit 13. Accelerating rate of change.

existing requirements" in Exhibit 11). If we can get better at this, and accelerate our development capability, hopefully we can track this capability to match the rate of change in the outside world.

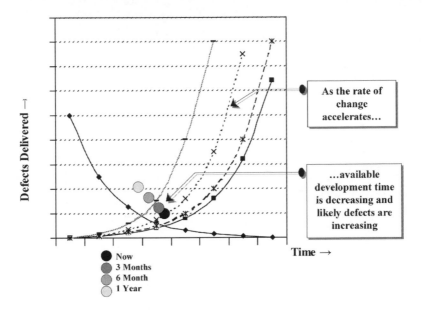

As the rate of change accelerates...

...available development time is decreasing and likely defects are increasing

Now
3 Months
6 Month
1 Year

Exhibit 14. Changing optimal development time.

Exhibit 15 shows the results of this. The optimal development time no longer rises. But it does continue to track inwards, representing the shorter and shorter timeframes available to us to develop systems. As the defects due to external changes start to predominate, it is obvious that our ability to react to those changes becomes much more important than our ability to analyze and understand in great detail any arbitrary set of requirements. While understanding these requirements is a good thing, it does not help us if, by the time we do understand them, they no longer apply. This is why the Agile approaches focus so strongly on intelligent and responsive reaction to changes. Due to these inexorable outside forces, we are, to some extent, getting more "out of control."

This reality has been a bit of a cold bath for many organizations. One of the major self-defining functions of management is to "be in control." When situations arise that cannot be controlled or when imposing control has a negative effect, management may panic. Some of the major movements in software development may have elements that indicate this kind of reaction:

- *Outsourcing.* While there are many reasons to outsource certain aspects of development, particularly in IT support areas where the skills are not considered to be core competencies of the business, there are companies who do, in fact, outsource their primary skills. This is invariably dressed up as a cost-saving measure, but sometimes it is simply an unconscious realization of a situation that management has not been able to control. Given the choice between

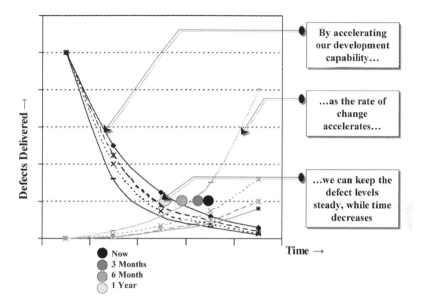

By accelerating our development capability...

...as the rate of change accelerates...

...we can keep the defect levels steady, while time decreases

Now
3 Months
6 Month
1 Year

Exhibit 15. Accelerating capability.

resigning from the control business and learning new patterns of behavior or simply abdicating the whole messy business and bringing in another set of management to offload the problem onto them, many businesses choose the latter. It then puts the client management staff in the role of customer rather than provider, which is much safer, more predictable in some ways, and more in line with the management's need for control.

- *Packages.* The theory is that perhaps a commercially developed package will solve all our problems. In general, what happens is *these* problems are replaced with *those* problems. The issue is still understanding the business need and how to satisfy it. Sometimes hiding significant amounts of the knowledge behind the walls of a package replaces easier-to-find knowledge (*"what is our business need?"*) with harder-to-find knowledge (*"how can we make this package do what we want?"*).

- *Process initiatives.* The large-scale process initiatives that many big companies have embraced have certainly addressed many glaring issues in process. Any company that neglects such core engineering business skills as configuration management and project planning have only themselves to blame for the self-inflicted pain they experience. Nonetheless, the large-scale investment in sometimes enormous process initiatives has other roots, I think. The concepts of "repeatability" and determinism are very seductive to management. They want to be assured that the decisions and commitments they make are good ones, ones they can keep. Coupled with the pervasive product and manufacturing view of software, I think there is a sneaking hope that somehow these process initiatives will make software development into a wholly predictable and mindless activity. Many of the templates, process models, and checks and balances are reminiscent of manufacturing. This approach is quite dangerous, as is any mechanism that tries to turn human activity into something mindless. The Agile movement is to be applauded to attempting to make development into more of a *mindful* process.

- *The never-ending search for a silver bullet.* The product view of software and the desire to be in control has also driven business to try to find the magic formula: the one process, language, methodology, tool, environment, consultant, or vendor that can make this complex and irritatingly inconclusive business into something easy and guaranteed.

For several years, I taught an executive seminar on software. This program was designed for senior executives of companies that had suddenly found themselves to be software companies. Businesses sometimes wake up and realize that the hardware component of their product line is being manufactured in China, and what *they* do for a living is create the software that goes into that product. It can be quite a shock to a company that views itself as being in the manufacturing business to find that it is really in the software business. After talking at length to such executives, I came away with the distinct impression that they believe, at a quite fundamental level, that software engineers know how to produce high-quality systems very quickly but for some reason, they just do not. This baffles the executives, and many search for the one process (or incentive or punishment or training class or tool or approach or language or whatever) that will make their people perform flawlessly. They do not fully understand that, for the most part, engineers do *not* know how to build the systems they are trying to build; it is their job is to *find out* how to build such systems.

There is no replacement for the intentional and deliberate facing of the realities of constructing software, which is that the organization and the people within it need to discover a quantity of knowledge that they do not have, and factor that knowledge into something that works.

While Agile is an overdue breath of fresh air in an otherwise stuffy, sterile, and mechanistic environment surrounded by walls of three-ring process manuals, it is no more a silver bullet than any other technique. In fact, there are a number of criticisms that can be leveled at these approaches. Common issues that have been raised are:

- Lack of scalability, which is probably not as big an issue as critics make out or, more reasonably, is not the fault of Agile. *All* methodologies have issues with scalability. The reason is simple: *we* have issues with scalability. Large, complex problems requiring the close cooperation and careful involvement of a lot of people are hard to solve. Having taught methodologies of many stripes to many engineers for many years, the number-one issue I hear is that the methods work very well on small simple problems and are very difficult on large, complex problems. This is just a function of our human ability to process large quantities of complex information. The problem is compounded by the fact that we are using models, and we either increase the model complexity to match the complexity of the problem, which makes the model harder to use, or we increase the difference between the model's representation of the problem and the problem itself, which results in solutions that work fine in the model, but not at all in real life.

- Lack of documentation is another problem some people have voiced. Proponents of Agile approaches will readily agree that there is a lot less paper documentation than with traditional system development cycles. In fact, that is touted as one of the benefits, and certainly helps to endear Agile approaches to many developers who tend to view documentation the way Superman views kryptonite. Some approaches volunteer that the documentation is in nontraditional forms. While this has echoes of the old apocryphal "self-documenting code," there is some validity in this, depending on what you need from the documentation (for an example, see AgileTek's *Code Science*). If you need simply to assure that the changes you have made to a product have not corrupted other aspects of that system, reading documentation is one way to gain that assurance. Having a trusted regression test suite that you can readily execute would be a much more efficient one, however. The challenge with documentation embedded in executables is that the structure of the executable is often contaminated with the legacy of the knowledge-discovery activity. That is, we build into our executables what we do not know at the moment we create them as well as what we do know (see Appendix B for a description of this). Of course, this occurs in other methods, and the careful consideration of where (in which medium) to put documentation is always important. Because the constraints of executability and understandability are often at loggerheads, we are often faced with a Solomon's choice of storing the knowledge in or very close to the executable or in some other place that is better formatted for understandability, but is more remote from where the knowledge actually works. Neither is a perfect solution.

- Repeatability. One of the benefits claimed for heavyweight process is that it engenders repeatability. Using the process, you can change the location, the people, the system, or even the customers, and still guarantee success. The criticism that Agile approaches might not do this as well is ill placed. Not only do most proponents of Agile freely acknowledge that there are types of systems development that are not suitable for the more radical Agile approaches, most of the Agile approaches are intrinsically flexible, with some of them having explicit phases where the method is tuned to the situation at hand. A careful examination of the repeatability of heavyweight methods will show that the repeatability generated is usually of low value. In software development, simply recreating exactly the same thing that we created before is not usually very helpful. Except, of course, insofar as it helps us avoid repeating the work we did to create the artifact in the first place or enables us to avoid the mistakes we made the first time around. That said, in software development, real value is not generated by creating old things, by successfully doing something we have successfully done already, it is by creating something we have never created before.

- Lack of control; again, often touted as a compelling advantage of Agile approaches (at least by the proponents of Agile approaches). To hide-bound controlling managers, Agile may look like anarchy. Here again we have to consider the type of system being built. There are systems for which Agile approaches are not helpful and may be harmful, and most authors on the subject are careful to emphasize this. Control works to direct something away from a less appropriate state to a more appropriate state. But this only works when we know what those states are and how to move between them. Control only works in situations where control works, and that does not describe many modern projects. Nevertheless, this "limitation" is one of the major challenges to the acceptance of Agile approaches, and is one of the reasons it tends to be more acceptable on projects where the perceived risks of being "out of control" are smaller. It is interesting to note that even small, simple systems may move outside of explicit control and predictability very quickly, especially where there are tight loops of feedback and feedforward. These tight loops are manifest features of modern development, and businesses have to accept that less control is possible.

- That said, there is a potential with Agile projects, as there is with straight prototyping projects, to simply "play." The lack of detailed accountability for tasks, product, and following process does provide the freedom to explore unexpected options but it can also give license to not deliver. Many of the Agile approaches lay a cornerstone of regular delivery of working software as the primary measure of progress. This focus, in the hands of a self-regulated team with a professional attitude, will help them avoid this pitfall.

Summary

The Agile approaches offer a welcome relief from process-in-the-large; they also help to countcract the desire to make software development a mindless, repetitive process. As their creators and proponents would happily acknowledge, they are no more silver bullets than any of the earlier attempts at codifying software development at either the mechanism or the organism levels. They do reassert the humanness of the business, and have shone a bright light on an oft-neglected aspect of building systems, which is the way that people work together.

Agile approaches, as evolutionary steps in our understanding of the fifth knowledge medium and what it takes to make it work, do run the risk of being labeled the next fad. Software always has a next big thing. There is always something that will solve all our problems and cure all ills, until it becomes unfashionable, of course, and is replaced by the next big thing. In my professional lifetime, it has been third-generation languages, databases, network databases, methodologies and other "structured stuff," CASE tools, application generators, end-user computing, 4GLs, 5GLs, VMs, models and other object-oriented stuff, dot-coms and other Internet stuff, patterns, and aspects. With each comes its allotment of hype, the honeymoon of application, the bingeing on books in the subject, and the hangover mornings when the industry wonders *what could we have been thinking?* But all ideas fit into their place in the scheme of things and all become valuable, although never infallible. Agile takes another step along the path, a big step in my mind, because it firmly reintroduces the concept of humans in the process of building software, but it is still only a step.

Another aspect of Agile that is refreshing is the degree to which proponents are willing to listen to each other and agree that, yes, your idea might work, even though it is not my idea. Perhaps it is a product of many of the leading lights in the Agile movement being refugees from the methodology wars of the past. Perhaps we are getting more open and tolerant. Whatever it is, the directing of energies toward bridging and building is a really good sign for this business.

Chapter 7
Agile and the Orders of Ignorance

This book has only one major purpose — to trigger the beginning of a new field of study: computer programming as a human activity.

— Gerald M. Weinberg
The Psychology of Computer Programming

This quotation is the first line of the first part of the first book I ever read on the subject of computer programming. It is from the Preface to Jerry Weinberg's book, *"The Psychology of Computer Programming."** The book was published in 1971, and I read it in 1972 shortly after the start of my career in software.

Talk about visionary. The study of software and systems development never quite coalesced into the study of programming as a human activity that Jerry envisaged, although he personally has been on this mission ever since. In 1972, structured stuff was yet to come, mainframes ruled the world, COBOL was king, there were no objects, a "software tool" was a compiler, and I was programming a mainframe computer in the north of England in an octal assembly language called PLAN. Much has happened since then but the concept of the book has stayed with me.

The Agile movement is all about regaining some of the software ground for humanity, to inject a shot of the oil of organism into the wheels of the software development mechanism. It has always been needed but this initiative has been made essential by the speed of the jet plane projects of today. The various Agile approaches accommodate or even embrace the change that is simply a part of the development landscape today. And that is very good.

Agile is also much about feedback, about evaluating ideas and making continuous minor adjustments to them in the same way a missile makes continuous adjustments to its trajectory to strike a moving target. Much of the interplay between Agile proponents and practitioners is devoted to this kind of feedback about the practices themselves: how do the processes work? How do the people work? What else could work? How much process is enough? How much is too much?

*Weinberg, G.M., *The Psychology of Computer Programming*, Dorset House, New York, 1971.

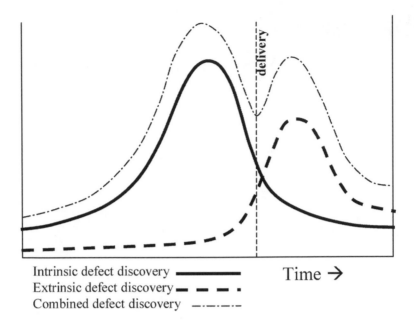

Intrinsic defect discovery ━━━━━━━
Extrinsic defect discovery ━ ━ ━ ▪
Combined defect discovery ─·─··─··

Time →

Exhibit 1. Intrinsic/extrinsic knowledge discovery.

Agile is all about cooperative human endeavors, and the net purpose of these activities is the accumulation and proof of a large variety of knowledge. How does Agile match up against the Orders of Ignorance and the Laws of Software Process?

Agile and the Orders of Ignorance

At one level, the Agile approaches admit that software development is in large part a discovery activity. It is expected that the time taken to create software will result in changes to what is expected, and it is also expected that the activity of creation will itself uncover things that are not known. These discoveries are always Second Order Ignorance things. Agile goes further by stating that only by building something that works can we uncover certain kinds of knowledge. This is manifestly true, especially for extrinsic knowledge (knowledge "outside" the software product).

In general, given a particular knowledge repository, there are two locations of knowledge that exist: extrinsic and intrinsic. Extrinsic knowledge is necessary knowledge that exists outside of the repository. Intrinsic knowledge is within the repository. Discovered defects are a good measure of rates of knowledge acquisition. A typical project defect discovery curve is shown in Exhibit 1.

For a software product, there are two things that may go wrong and cause defects to emerge. One is that the product is internally inconsistent: a table overflows, a variable is incorrectly updated, and a pointer is overwritten. The other thing that can go wrong is that the product is externally inconsistent, i.e., there is some operation, event, or expectation in the world outside the software that causes a conflict. These are "extrinsic" defects. The Dual Hypotheses of Knowledge Discovery state that we can only discover knowledge in an environment that contains that knowledge. Exhibit 1 shows this. The solid line represents the typical discovery of intrinsic defects in a cycle of development. Earlier stages tend to focus on capturing and codifying existing knowledge (0OI) and obtaining answers to known questions (1OI). As products become more populated with knowledge and the opportunity to really test that knowledge increases as the knowledge becomes more testable, we start to find out if we really did know what we thought we did. The defect rate climbs. It typically approaches a peak around middle system test, as we are testing large conglomerates of system functionality. It is also at this point that users have visibility into end-to-end processing which allows them to qualify the system's knowledge content. As the knowledge repository is updated by the 2OI→1OI, 0OI cycle described earlier, the defect detection rate goes down. However, as we transition the system from the relatively controlled environment of the lab or test system to the uncertain outside world, we start increasing the detection of rate of *extrinsic* defects. This is a separate curve that typically reaches its peak some short time after system delivery (the dotted line in Exhibit 1). No matter how good we are at detecting intrinsic defects, we cannot find many extrinsic defects until we send the system into the environment that will allow them to be exhibited.

Agile approaches explicitly acknowledge this by:

- Moving to executable knowledge (functioning code) faster
- Developing in cycles of much-smaller sets of components than full system size
- Developing, where possible, in end-to-end user functionality segments
- Having the user execute in the user's environment, preferably to actually do some of the work the system is intended to do
- Explicitly learning from this process, and applying the learning to the next cycle of development

This tends to compress the intrinsic/extrinsic defect discovery by not having to wait (and possibly predicate a lot of work) to find significant issues in the user's environment.

Consideration of the sources of the necessary knowledge when running Agile projects leads us to a few observations based on the Orders of Ignorance and the Laws of Software Process.

Increasing Opaqueness of Knowledge	0OI	0OI	Full Knowledge
		$1/_3$OI	Add Executing Knowledge
		$2/_3$OI	Minus Executing Knowledge
	1OI	1OI	Lack of Knowledge
		$1^1/_3$OI	Lack of Question Knowledge
		$1^2/_3$OI	Lack of Question Context
	2OI	2OI	Lack of Awareness
		$2^1/_3$OI	Non-culpable Lack of Awareness
		$2^2/_3$OI	Culpable Lack of Awareness
	3OI	3OI	Lack of Process
		$3^1/_3$OI	Unintentional Lack of Process
		$3^2/_3$OI	Intentional Lack of Process
		4OI	Meta-Ignorance

Exhibit 2. The spectrum of ignorance.

Before we explore the mapping of Agile approaches onto the Orders of Ignorance, we should examine and expand these to look at the components of the Orders of Ignorance.

Subdividing the Orders of Ignorance

Having used the Five Orders of Ignorance (Exhibit 2) for a number of years as a simple model for understanding the process of learning, it was pointed out to me that people may know something (have 0OI) yet not be able to use that knowledge for some reason other than lack of that knowledge. People may have ignorance (1OI or 2OI) and not care. Organizations may realize that their process is not effective (3OI) yet choose to do nothing about it. After some consideration, it seems that the "lower" four Orders of Ignorance needed to be subdivided if we want to fully explore and categorize how we acquire knowledge, use knowledge, unveil ignorance, and apply learning.

The Five Orders represent quantum levels of ignorance regarding the software development task at hand. While they are defined as discrete levels, in reality ignorance is more like a continuum. That is, our ignorance flows in a seamless range from fully factored, self-actualized, honest-to-goodness, provably correct knowledge through well-defined topical questions to large-scale contextual uncertainty to the vaguest of suspicions that maybe, just maybe, there is something here we do not know to the ultimate darkness of complete, sublime, and intentional ignorance.

We can divide each of the lower four levels into three sections, which have quite different characteristics.

Zeroth Order Ignorance (0OI): I have 0OI when I (provably) know something ... That is, I have the answer

The issue with 0OI is the word "provably." Unless I can prove that I know something, it is entirely possible that I do not. For example, suppose I happen to choose not to test a system because I think it works just fine — it would be very ambitious and more than a little foolish of me to claim that this system "works." Most software engineers would assert that unless you have tested code, you cannot assert that it actually works (i.e., you have correctly acquired the knowledge). In fact, most truly experienced and principled engineers would say that unless you have tested it, it *does not* work. The label "working" should be conferred on software only by observation of its performance in a test or in the field. In the software field, completely capturing all the knowledge necessary to prove something works involves interpreting, compiling, or otherwise making the knowledge executable. I will call this making-knowledge-executable activity "factoring" (the same word is used by a number of Agile authors to mean the restructuring of the executable knowledge representation to properly incorporate "new" knowledge. From a knowledge perspective, these two factorings are quite similar, although they operate on different knowledge). Factoring might involve simply invoking a piece of executable code, copying or including a piece of source code, and then compiling or even accessing a data table. The knowledge of how to "factor" the code is, of course, other knowledge, often with its own variables (such as compile parameters or start addresses). We can see that, even here, there are levels at which this knowledge may be available.

0OI — Fully Factored Knowledge: The Self-Actualized Answer. With "pure" 0OI (perhaps 0.0OI?), the answer is readily available in a fully factored mode. This means the knowledge is invokable by a very small piece of knowledge that is readily available and known to the invoker. This knowledge might be the function or object name, program offset, location, or another similar addressing mode. It also implies that the invoker knows the function performed by the piece of knowledge at some level, and knows that this function is the one needed. We know the name, we know what the function does, we know the result, we know the domain and context, so we know this is the "correct" function, and we have proved it works. So it is merely a matter of switching it on.

"Pure" 0OI means we have both the knowledge of the thing and the knowledge of factoring activity (how to make the thing work), both of which have been made executable. As an example we could point to a fully automated compile or install. Wholly automated regression tests are a good example of pure 0OI in operation. Pressing the power button on your TV is another example.

1/3OI — Applying the Factoring Knowledge: Switch It on. 1/3OI means that the answer is in a mode that needs to be factored in some way. For example, source code may need to be copied and compiled. Here we need slightly more knowledge than in the pure 0OI case. In order to gain access to the knowledge packaged in the artifact, we must supply *some* knowledge for the factoring. This knowledge could range from meager to quite extensive. To qualify for 0OI at all, of course, we must actually possess the factoring knowledge (otherwise it would be a "higher" form of ignorance). 1/3OI does require slightly more knowledge than the simple 0OI, which is why it is incremental to pure 0OI. Examples include a source code compile with "normal" compile parameters added, installation, or some executable with the target directory added. Switching on your TV and changing the channel to the one you want is the same thing.

2/3OI — Get the Factoring Knowledge: How to Switch It on. The answer is in a mode that must be factored but we have some questions regarding the factoring. This implies that there is some uncertainty (knowledge that must be gained) about factoring. Therefore this level is almost at 1OI (if the knowledge to be gained was about the system rather than about factoring, it would be 1OI). We might have full knowledge of the code product while still having some questions about how to make it active. We have to get the knowledge about the factoring activity before we can realize the knowledge in the product. For examples, porting operations often fall in this area; we know what to port, we know it works but there are a few things to find out about how to make it work in the target environment. From this it is evident that 2/3OI is pretty close to 1OI, which is, of course, why it is 2/3OI.

Hunting through a TV channel program listing to find the program you want before switching on your TV and changing the channel is an example of this.

First Order Ignorance (1OI): I have 1OI when I do not know something

To usefully assert that I do not know something, I must know that I do not know whatever it is (which is actually a kind of knowledge). This means I have the *question*. To end up with some software artifact that does actually work, I have to get my questions answered and factor them into the executable medium. There are two steps to this: resolving 1OI (getting the question answered), and factoring 0OI (making the knowledge I do have fully executable). In traditional life cycle terms these roughly correspond to the requirements-gathering/analysis phase (1OI) and the design/code phase (0OI).

1OI: We've Got the Question, Now Get the Answer: Just Gimme the Facts.

With "pure" 1OI, all aspects of the question are well known: I know the "who, what, where, when" of how to get an answer. The issue is simply an operational one of identifying and tracking down the "who," and getting my answer through an interview.

1.1/3OI: We've Got the Question but How to Get the Answer: Who to Ask?

The first increment at the 1OI level occurs when the basic question is known but key components of getting the question answered are not. An example might be not knowing the source of the answers (the "who"). Obviously, in this case there are two kinds of questions and two kinds of ignorance: I do not know the answer to my question and I do not know who knows the answer to my question. One is, of course, the subject and the other the process of resolving the subject. One is the knowledge I am seeking and the other is the knowledge of how to seek.

1.2/3OI: We've Kind of Got the Question but Where's the Ballpark? For the next increment, the general *type* of lack of knowledge is understood but not enough to formulate a strong question. This means that we cannot ask an explicit question (such as *"what is the layout of the message header?"*) because we do not have enough information about the context (we do not know message headers are needed). 1.2/3OI is exhibited when people ask what Jerry Weinberg called *context-free* questions,* such as *"what requirements do you have?"* This question acknowledges that the questioner knows the type of knowledge needed but not at a more-detailed or specific level sufficient to construct a localized question. Obviously, 1.2/3OI is very similar to 2OI, which is, of course, why it is 1.2/3OI.

Second Order Ignorance (2OI): I Have 2OI When I Don't Know That I Don't Know Something

Having Second Order Ignorance means my lack of knowledge extends into the context or domain of the knowledge I am seeking. Literally, I am not aware of the fact that I do not know something, which is why 2OI is characterized as "lack of awareness."

As we covered earlier, resolving 2OI in software development is usually where the bulk of our work lies. This is because of the rather obvious fact that the earlier (lower) Orders of Ignorance tend to be rather easy to resolve. As we dig into the finer gradations of 2OI, we find that they are a

---

*Weinberg, Gerald M. and Gause, Donald C., *Exploring Requirements: Quality before Design*, Dorset House, New York, 1989, p. 65.

little different than the subdivisions of 0OI or 1OI because they reference intent rather than knowledge quantity and quality.

2OI — General, Unintentional Lack of Awareness: Maybe We Don't Know. I have 2OI when I genuinely do not have *specific* awareness of my lack of knowledge. But I may well have a generalized awareness. One thing that differentiates experienced and inexperienced engineers is the presence or absence of this awareness. It may also be a function of other kinds of maturity conferred on us by living longer and experiencing more. Usually, hoary old engineers who have been around the block-structured program a few times tend to have a sneaking suspicion that they do not know as much as they need to. The older one gets, the more this sneaking suspicion seems to evolve into a cast-iron certainty. Newer engineers with more, shall we say, humid audio input devices, tend not to harbor such self-doubt — a condition that experience will correct in due course. It is in *intent* that we see the major difference between the incremental orders of 2OI.

2.1/3OI — Nonculpable Lack of Awareness: Blissful Ignorance. I have 2.1/3OI when I have ignorance but I am at least open to the idea that there are things that I do not know. Often this level of ignorance (vs. the more dangerous 2.2/3OI) is evident through the choice of process used. The difference between 2OI and 2.1/3OI is subtle but important. With straight 2OI, there is a general understanding that ignorance exists, with some expectation that steps will be taken to resolve whatever ignorance might surface. With 2.1/3OI, those steps simply are not being taken. However, this lapse in judgment is not intentional. It could be viewed as another dimension of ignorance (*"I don't know that I don't know enough to know what to do when I don't know something"*) but there has to be a limit to this logic stack. Suffice it to say that at the 2.1/3OI level none of the necessary steps are being taken to resolve the unknown unknowns. An example of this behavior is often evident in peoples' choice of testing methods. There are methods for testing software that are quite good and well proven, and are very likely to expose deficiencies (of certain types) in software. If, however, I do not know what these methods are, and do not know they exist and therefore cannot apply them, I have 2.1/3OI.

2.2/3OI — Culpable Lack of Awareness — Intentional Ignorance: The Ostrich. This level of ignorance might be typified as *"I don't know and I don't care."* It was a student tackling me on this point that made me think of subdividing the Orders of Ignorance in the first place. Up until that moment I did not know I had to subdivide the 0OI (and I guess I did not care enough to try). At 2OI, we expect effort to be made to resolve the ignorance. At 2.1/3OI, this effort is not being made. At the 2.2/3OI level, however, effort is actually being expended to *avoid* illuminating my ignorance. This level is arguably the most-destructive type of ignorance, because it is highly self-perpetuating. At least at 2OI and even at 2.1/3OI, there is a good chance that the system, a test result, a customer complaint, an accident, or life in general, will illuminate the foggy scene and expose my ignorance. At 2.2/3OI, I may intentionally choose to ignore the system or test or customer or life in general if it happens to highlight my lack of knowledge. Individuals operating at this level can perform some remarkable feats of self-deception to avoid recognizing any information that will contradict their belief in their own high order of knowledge.

Third Order Ignorance: Lack of Process

Third Order Ignorance is where we move into the process level. The definition of 3OI is "*I have 3OI when I don't know of a suitably effective way to find out that I don't know that I don't know something.*" Notice the supporting role of the various flavors of 2OI in this. The phrase "suitably effective" has to be included because there is a default 3OI process in software development, which is go ahead, build it and ship it. The customer will then surely inform us of all the things we did not know we did not know. We may choose, through the agency of 2.2/3OI, to ignore them but such lapses are still known as "defects." Good engineering practice does not have us build bridges or airplanes and then go figure out what we did not know when they break. Usually, we try to adopt some other process that is both more proactive and less dramatic.

3OI: General Lack of Process. This is the process equivalent of the 2OI level. The expectation is that we *want* to find a suitable process; we just have not done so yet. Interestingly, we could argue that for really truly 2OI, we *cannot* have a process because any well-defined process can only be created for things that we have done (the First Law of Software Process). What saves us in practice is that our ability to acquire different kinds of unknown knowledge tends to be similar across ranges of unknowns. Also the human brain, under the right circumstances, can perform remarkable feats of intuition to discover knowledge where its presence is completely unsuspected.

3.1/3OI: Unintentional Process Ignorance. This level is a little stronger than straight 3OI. It often involves a lack of process context awareness that is strongly coupled to 4OI; there is a general lack of reflection on the process activity and its effectiveness. This is quite common in my experience. Companies often carry on with the same "old" process in a situation where it no longer applies. Because we, as engineers, will often apply the same process irrespective of the knowledge needed, we can also be quite guilty of this level of ignorance.

3.2/3OI: Intentional Process Ignorance. This is simply the energetic version of 3.1/3OI. And it has parallels with 2.2/3OI, often caused by the same behavioral traits. At 3.1/3OI, we do not realize the unsuitability of our process but at 3.2/3OI we are actively denying it. We are expending energy to maintain the façade of effectiveness, perhaps in the face of stark evidence that the process does not work, is not telling us that there are things that we do not know, and is worthless. Of course, the primary reason for most people maintaining this position is the same as for 2.2/3OI — we do not like to be shown as being ignorant. Anthony Finkelstein, in his delightful spoof on process assessments (The Capability Immaturity Model or CiMM), described organizations that operated like this as being at the equivalent of SEI Level minus 2: Lunatic.*

Fourth Order Ignorance: Meta-Ignorance

The definition of 4OI is "*I have 4OI when I don't know about the Five Orders of Ignorance.*" 4OI is a meta level. It implies a certain degree of ignorance about ignorance. This is always a contextual issue. Many of the levels below contain strong elements of self-reference or recursiveness: We do not know what we do not know, e.g., we do not know of a process, presumably including a process to get a process. 4OI is not knowing about the subject of knowing. 4OI is the "highest" order of ignorance but it is not necessarily the most serious (personally, a good solid mixture of 2.2/3OI and 3.2/3OI does it for me). While not necessarily the most-critical order of ignorance in an operational sense, in some ways it may be the most significant over the long term. Possessing 4OI means that the premises of most of the lower orders of ignorance are simply not realized or not accepted. Like a hologram, 4OI is reflected in the "2/3" orders below. Any conscious intention not to accept that there are things or processes that are not known is *de facto* evidence of 4OI; either it is not like that or it is not important enough to change.

We could have subdivisions of 4OI but it is not really necessary and gets even more confusingly self-referential. Because 4OI is intrinsically recursive, subdivisions of this level are unnecessary or, more correctly, they are already there without having to be stated explicitly.

4OI is the simplest and the most complex of the levels. It stands on its own but it also includes all the other levels because if we truly have 4OI, we cannot really conceive of 0OI and its relatives.

A lot of things happen, most of them negative, when organizations have 4OI, including:

- Not recognizing that the true product is the knowledge contained in the software.
- Not treating software development as a knowledge-acquisition activity.

*Finkelstein, Anthony, *ACM Sigsoft Software Engineering Notes,* vol. 17, no 4, Oct. 1992.

- Not ensuring that the knowledge already obtained is available for reuse.
- Not managing the questions and context necessary to get the knowledge that is not available.
- Not recognizing when it does not know it does not have knowledge, and often acting (and making commitments) as if it does.
- Not establishing the necessary processes to ensure that it will recognize its ignorance and collect the correct knowledge.
- Not identifying that process deficiencies exist; therefore not taking steps to correct them.

We can see from this dive into further categorizing ignorance that the Agile approaches directly challenge some of these destructive behaviors. However, they also have the potential for being less efficient in other areas, particularly the lower Orders of Ignorance.

Agile and Zeroth Order Ignorance

Zeroth Order Ignorance is provably correct knowledge — things that we know work, that we have proven before, and we have available to us. They may be design patterns, knowledge of the user's environment or business practice, code fragments, or object libraries (with the knowledge of how to use them). 0OI is answers.

Interestingly, with their entirely legitimate focus on the discovery activities, Agile approaches may have some limitations with respect to 0OI (see Exhibit 3). The area where Agile tends to have most limitations is the lower Orders of Ignorance. The entirely appropriate focus on flexible feedback and knowledge discovery activities that is the hallmark of the Agile approaches seems to have led away from the application of *existing* knowledge. There are many assumptions made in Agile that are quite reasonable but should be recognized as being assumptions. It is in the application of existing knowledge that Agile approaches tend to be less explicit. The assumption is that if the knowledge is available it should be used. This is probably a reaction to traditional process. The purpose of most process is to ensure the efficient and uniform application of what is known. As described in the Laws of Software Process, process is at its best when it is fully factored and completely known. A good example of this might be the manufacture of small memory (DRAM) chips. Not only is this process very well defined, in many cases it is entirely automated. It has become so predictable that testing has often become statistical; merely testing samples of batches of chips and inferring the overall quality. While there are market price pressures for this reduction in testing, we could argue that testing is irrelevant if you do not find out anything new (of course, you could equally argue that if you do not test, then you certainly will not find anything new). Even in cases where the final product is tested, the aim of most automation

Exhibit 3. Agile and Zeroth Order Ignorance

Order of ignorance	Description	Knowledge need	Agile approach and issues	Agile focus
0OI	Full knowledge	A complete, fully factored, and context-aware repository system with the capability of updating as knowledge is discovered.	Most Agile approaches assume that this is simply available. Few of the processes discuss the presence or absence of suitable repositories. The human focus of Agile tends to rely on the knowledge in the brains of the people working on the project, and their ability to effectively retrieve and apply that knowledge. Much of the purpose of the highly cyclical process that all Agile approaches use is to "refresh" the knowledge but the implication is that this refresh occurs in the human brain and is captured in the code.	Very light
0.1/3OI	Add executing knowledge	The application of sufficient knowledge to allow the stored 0OI knowledge to become executable.	Again, the implication is that the developers know how to do this. That is, they possess the knowledge of executable factoring. In reality, much of this knowledge tends to reside in compile and execution scripts. Most Agile approaches do not specifically address the development of such scripts, although there is a general acceptance that it will happen and it is a good thing.	Very light
0.2/3OI	Discover executing knowledge	The discovery of the knowledge necessary to make the extant knowledge execute.	The cyclical nature of Agile can assist in this. It is entirely possible (although not specifically recommended in most cases) that an "executability" prototype cycle could be conducted. The purpose of this is to discover, not the knowledge of the system but the knowledge of how to make that knowledge execute. Such a prototype might be necessary if the team were using a new programming language. Again, most Agile approaches assume but do not prescribe that the team will do this if necessary.	Light

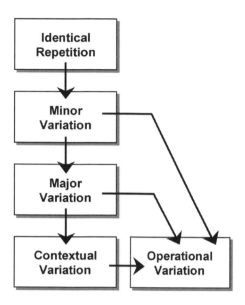

Exhibit 4. An evolution of knowledge storage.

processes is to develop a process that is so well defined that intermediate testing is unnecessary.

Where Agile has limitations is in the application of existing knowledge. To do this properly in software, *repositories* of knowledge must be present (Exhibit 4). Contextual access to these repositories must exist, access that allows people to identify and use the knowledge present in the way that they need to, to make that knowledge useful in the system they are building.

This propagation and refactoring of knowledge storage occurs reflexively in software development. As development knowledge is progressively obtained, it is commonly incorporated into executable form, sometimes with some quite-sophisticated interfacing, which progresses (though not linearly!) through several stages:

1. An activity is executed sufficient times to remove the unknowns. Once this activity has become definitive, it is captured in the executable process.
2. Very similar activities are recognized, and the similarities and differences between them recognized and abstracted into variables. Once that is done, significant and major changes are processed, with their (more complex and difficult) similarities and differences further abstracted.
3. As this is occurring, the developer recognizes the operational variation, which may or may not be related to the system functions.

147

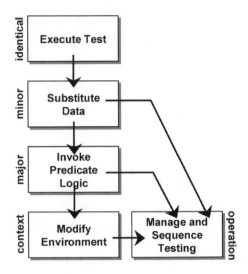

Exhibit 5. An example of evolutionary knowledge storage.

Gradually, all of these components are subsumed into an available and usually executable repository.

An example of testing may serve to explain this (see Exhibit 5).

Identical Repetition

When a developer is testing code fragments, the first tests are typically small, carefully crafted excursions into the system's functionality and behavior. Early testing is a high-discovery activity, for which explicit process is not very useful. As the artifact is debugged and the discovery activity lessens, simply running the test starts to become a chore. Less new knowledge is uncovered, and the activity of setting up and running and even checking the test results becomes tedious. Around this time, most developers start developing small scripts that execute and check the test. Because the tests are essentially the same every time, this frees up the developer's time to address other areas that are not so repetitive.

Minor Variation

In running these other tests, the developer starts to see the similarities and differences between them and the ones that have already been rendered automatic. If the differences are not very large, the developer will abstract key variables in the example and make a more-powerful version of the original script that allows the running of a range of functions, rather than just the original one. So the developer creates a single script that will run *this* or *that,* depending on some supplied parameter.

Major Variation

Of course, minor variations have a way of becoming larger and more complex. As these more-complex situations start to become well understood, the developer will often build into the execution script some of the predicate logic that operates in the functioning system. This logic usually operates on the variable data to set up different varieties of test. The script now becomes bigger and more complex. For example, not only will the system run a variety of data values present in transactions, it is also able to test a variety of transactions themselves.

Contextual Variation

This is a further extension of the major variation. Now significant operation components are modified, data is retrieved perhaps from "real" operational environments, and the system starts to function rather like the real thing. For large systems, this is the level that is usually called integrated system test. Now the script can run end-to-end processing, usually with the aid of operational variation scripts. We often see artifacts such as interpreted "testing languages" appearing, which control the functions being tested.

Operational Variation. This may operate concurrently with all but the lowest level of testing. As the tester progressively acquires and certifies the knowledge as being "correct," it is encapsulated into the executable scripts as described previously. As this happens, at the minor variation level, the developer/tester may notice that *this* script always follows *that* script. The solution is to create a script that manages the scripts and orders them in the correct sequence. As the test scripts themselves get cleverer, the "managing scripts" tend to keep pace. The operational script starts to include the predicate logic that will control the sequences of functions and the scripts start to interface with the environment in more and more clever ways as the knowledge of how that interaction should occur is obtained.

Before long, the developer has built *two* executable systems: the operational one that performs the functions required by the user, and the *test system* that proves that the operational system works. The operational system encapsulates the knowledge of the system necessary to make the system work for the user. The test environment encapsulates the knowledge of how to test this system.

There are a few interesting observations about the test system we can make:

- The test system tends to be *more complex* than the system being tested; it has to allow both the "normal" and "abnormal" processes, whereas the system itself should only consist of the "normal" processes.

- The test system is not a "deliverable" in the classic manufacturing sense, and therefore does not often get the same priority as the operational system.

- The "users" of the test system are developers and testers, although the beneficiaries are the end users and customers.

- Changes in the operational system must be continually reflected in the test system if it is to continue to be of use.

- It is possible to abstract attributes in the test system that are supersets of attributes in the operational systems, and to develop both reusable functions and a testing "language" that describes the operation of the attributes.

The system described here is cycling through the 3OI(2OI)→1OI,0OI cycle. The Agile approaches warmly embrace the discovery activities inherent in this but tend to downplay or ignore the target of these discovery activities. True, there is great emphasis on getting the knowledge into code as soon as possible, but where else? For example, what about the maintenance of production libraries and other resources of already obtained knowledge? The implication is that the cycles are necessary to allow the developers to acquire the knowledge if they do not have it already, although the brainstorm-code-test cycle. But what if they do not need to obtain it? What if others have already obtained this knowledge? How does the team obtain access to this already-known (although not by them personally) knowledge?

And, obviously, the other side of the coin: as the team is acquiring this knowledge, where are they putting it in their collective heads? One of the by-products of successful systems development is not only a bunch of useful knowledge in an executable system; it is also a bunch of useful and sometimes useless knowledge in the developers' heads. The question is, from an organizational perspective, are these the best and only places the knowledge should be retained? What will happen when the next team comes along and needs this knowledge? What if they cannot extract the essential knowledge from the code product (due to the pollution with the "what does not work knowledge" or "unknowledge," as described in Appendix B)? What if the people who have stored this knowledge in their brains are not available? What if they are available but they forgot?

It is this aspect of systems development that "traditional" process focuses on and Agile has tended to leave. It is here that the differences between traditional process and agile process may be useful and celebrated.

Agile and First Order Ignorance

It is within the range of First Order Ignorance that the concepts of Agile first start to appear (see Exhibit 6). Above all, software development is a discovery activity and, while Zeroth Order Ignorance is all about knowledge application, 1OI starts to address knowledge acquisition.

The role of traditional process has been to codify and make repeatable what is known. First Order Ignorance is on that boundary: there are things that are not known but that fact is understood. 1OI has been qualified earlier as having the question. But there are levels of question. It is possible to have the question but not know who to ask. That is, there is lack of knowledge about both the subject and how to get the answer to the subject. Agile approaches do not depart particularly from traditional approaches. Many of them suggest the use of checklists. None of them particularly decry the use of organizational charts, the definition and assignment of roles and responsibilities within organizations. The use of "expert lists" is recommended. The lower level of 1OI is not where Agile resides but it is not incompatible.

At the "higher" levels of 1OI, Agile starts to make its presence felt. This is because of the cyclical nature of the process. It is expected that things will be found that were not known at the start. At 1.1/3OI, the issue of resolving the key unknowns about the questions is left with many other issues that most Agile approaches do not particularly prescribe. Agile, correctly and appropriately, focuses more on the harder-to-find answers in the unexpected areas that are usually flushed out by activities such as testing. At 1.2/3OI, Agile starts to apply in the way it is intended. At this level, we (1) know we do not know something (because it is a flavor of 1OI), (2) may have a general domain where our lack of knowledge lies, but (3) do not know enough to formulate a specific question. Our questions will tend to be of the type-question form, such as *"what requirements do you have?"* Classical analytical techniques have used diagramming artifacts known as "context diagrams" to try to capture this level of knowledge but often the diagrams are so vague as to not be very useful; they contain generic functions (such as the "process transactions" mentioned earlier) and generic entities (such as "user") that neither illuminate nor classify. At this level, the need for flexibility to respond effectively to what is discovered and to learn from the results of the earlier cycle of the process become apparent. If we do not have a sufficiently contextual question that will give us a useful answer, what will give us a sufficiently contextual question? Can we operate on the context of the context? Can we deal with an instance and abstract the general? Can we use a metaphor that will bridge the understanding? Can we build something that someone will recognize as correct? Can we build something that someone will recognize as incorrect and be

Exhibit 6. Agile and First Order Ignorance

Order of ignorance	Description	Knowledge need	Agile approach and issues	Agile focus
1OI	Manifest lack of knowledge	Obtain the "who, what, where, and when" of obtaining the answer, and obtain it.	Agile approaches do not seriously differ from more-traditional approaches. Many Agile methods suggest or infer that keeping things such as checklists of questions is a good idea. Much of traditional process involves listing the steps necessary to resolve 1OI.	Light
1.1/3OI	Lack of question knowledge	Resolve key unknowns with regard to getting questions answered.	What if we know the question but do not know how to get the answer? The Agile approach does not rule out methodical analytical approaches to discovering new knowledge but it correctly implies that the "harder" knowledge to acquire often comes from execution in the target environment. Whereas traditional processes and artifacts such as org charts are heavy in the area of identifying who could or should be responsible for resolving issues, most Agile approaches tend to leave these issues in with other undifferentiated issues that must be resolved.	Moderate
1.2/3OI	Lack of question context	Resolve key context issues with regard to getting questions answered.	At this level, the lack of knowledge is known (otherwise it would be 2OI) but it is diffuse. It is generally understood that in certain areas there are things that must be found out but it is not known exactly what these are. It is here that the Agile ethic starts to kicks in. Exploratory development can occur in these areas. The focus on creating something executable forces the development of detailed questions and answers. The involvement of the user so common in Agile approaches ensures that the imperative of answering questions is maintained.	Moderate

able to identify the degree of incorrectness? Each of these leads us, like the missile making its adjustments as it rises, closer toward the target.

Agile and Second Order Ignorance

This is what Agile was made for and is, not surprisingly, where traditional process falls down. We start at 2OI (Exhibit 7), not knowing what we do not know. The challenge is to break into the cycle somehow.

The Agile approaches very strongly address all three 2OI levels. The discovery cycles and the focus on peer inspections, testing, and user execution all encourage and assist an environment in which discovery occurs. There is no expectation that the system will somehow magically work the first time. The approaches almost universally address both the culpable and nonculpable forms of 2OI. The close cooperation seen on Agile teams allows a sharing of perspectives that make it less likely that people will remain ignorant of their ignorance. There is also a strong theme of pursuing the unknown and asking the tough questions. Facing the reality of whether the system works, accepting that the system might work but that it is not what the user wants, and accepting that it might be what the user asked for but is not what he needs, are all manifestations of an environment that accepts discovery. Even those on a project team who would prefer to pretend that things are going better than they are and they know more than they really know, would find it much harder to maintain the pretense required of 2.2/3OI on an Agile team, even if the rest of the team would tolerate the pretense.

Agile and Third Order Ignorance

Agile approaches are processes in the general sense. They are mechanisms designed to help us build systems and so are themselves Third Order Ignorance processes (Exhibit 8). Therefore, much of the application of Agile at the 3OI level is *intrinsic* — it is the purpose of the Agile approach and the reason for its existence, rather than being a function of its operation or a result of its application.

The issue at the 3OI level is to somehow devise an efficient process for uncovering what is not known. We have seen that at a general level the activity of testing is one such process. At an equally general level in the area of life cycle management, the application of prototyping concepts is a 3OI process. One could state that with sound knowledge of Agile approaches and intelligent application to a given situation, the team would *never* have 3OI — the Agile approach correctly applied is the process that is the antidote for the "lack of process" that typifies 3OI. That would be ideal. Of course, there are gradations of process. I could state that I know that testing is a good 3OI process and assert I do not have 3OI (because I do know of a process). However, practically speaking, the issue is not

Exhibit 7. Agile and Second Order Ignorance

Order of ignorance	Description	Knowledge need	Agile approach and issues	Agile focus
2OI	Lack of awareness of ignorance	Discover what is unknown and unsuspected.	Agile comes into its own in 2OI, which is, as we have argued, where the real work lies. All the Agile approaches are founded on an expectation of discovery. This implies, even if it does not state, that the discovery is of things that are not known. The repetitive cycles of Agile are designed to efficiently flush out what is not known. The focus on peer inspection, user involvement, and execution testing (all very effective means of finding if something is "right") means most of the cycle is spent in this type of discovery activity.	Strong
2.1/3OI	Nonculpable lack of awareness	Discover that there are areas in which ignorance exists.	The ethos of Agile is to intentionally pursue areas where lack of knowledge may exist. In this the Agile approaches share with testing (as an activity) and intentional life cycles such as the risk-based spiral model a determination to shine a light where there are unknowns.	Strong
2.2/3OI	Culpable lack of awareness	Overcome the intentional lack of focus on discovery of new knowledge.	The human aspects of the Agile approaches refreshingly tackle this head-on. The approaches call for small teams of highly cooperative people. In some paradigms (XP), this level is brought to the line-by-line development of code by more than one person. All highly value information sharing, joint discovery, and validation of assumptions. These make it really difficult for recidivists to hide from the truth and most effective teams would not tolerate this behavior anyway.	Very strong

about testing as an approach, or even the principles of testing; the issue is to find out what I do not know that I do not know about *this particular system* in an efficient way. This might be a subtle point but it is critical. Generic

154

Exhibit 8. Agile and Third Order Ignorance

Order of ignorance	Description	Knowledge need	Agile approach and issues	Agile focus
3OI	Lack of process	Create, discover, evolve, or build an efficient process that will expose lack of knowledge for the system being developed.	This is what Agile is intended to be. The Agile practitioners who have been codifying and popularizing these practices have, through experience, tried to create a paradigm, a mindset, and (to some extent) a set of processes that will do this. They have realized that the business is one of *efficiently discovering what is not known,* and have tried to structure the work practices to fit that need.	Intrinsic
3.1/3OI	Unintentional process ignorance	Replace processes that are ineffective at exposing and resolving ignorance.	This is what Agile does. Most thoughtful proponents of Agile approaches freely admit there are situations where the Agile methods are not appropriate. But these situations are becoming less common as the pace of change accelerates. However, most Agile approaches address the organizational dimension much less than they do the smaller, intrinsically more-flexible team and project levels. There have been a number of reservations expressed about the scalability of these methods within a large organizational context.	Intrinsic at team level, light at org level
3.2/3OI	Intentional process ignorance	Counteract the desire to retain and continue to use processes that are ineffective or destructive in exposing and resolving ignorance.	The Agile approaches do address the issue of retention of "old" processes that do not work at an individual and team level. They bring to the software business a refreshing focus on human interaction. People are expected to work together, to coordinate, and to some extent sublimate, their individual working styles, and many of the anecdotes of the business show this happening on projects. What most Agile approaches do not address is moving the entrenched organizational process. There is an expectation that when organizations see the rightness of this approach, they will choose to change. It is unlikely to be this simple.	Intrinsic at team level, light at org level

test plans can only take us so far, and generic test plans will not tell us what we do not know about this system. Only well-executed and good test plans for this system will tell us about this system.

More than anything else, the Agile approach focuses on the activity of creating systems as one way of finding out what is not known. Many of the "processes" of Agile are meta-processes concerned with setting up a system (the project team) that is intrinsically flexible and can modify its behavior in real-time to meet changing conditions. Indeed, it expects to do that, and teaches a mindset that does not shrink from addressing the real problem. The Agile approaches are an intelligent, flexible, and human approach to the issue of 3OI.

Agile scores particularly high at 3.1/3OI and 3.2/3OI. These are the unintentional and intentional process ignorance degrees. When people operate at the 3OI level, they are either working with no process or an ineffective process (for the discovery of new knowledge, not necessarily the application of old knowledge). At 3.1/3OI and 3.2/3OI, these people are not just operating without this process; they are working against finding it. At 3.1/3OI, this resistance is unintentional; at 3.2/3OI it operates on purpose. Agile has many answers for this, the primary one being the structure and ethic of the project team. Few project teams applying Agile approaches as envisaged by the proponents would tolerate such a lackadaisical attitude as 3.1/3OI and none would allow the active resistance of 3.2/3OI. This is not to say that everyone will always agree with a given project's approach to tackling the problem and the solution. There will be, and should be, differing ideas about which way is best. Some of the Agile methods encourage this level of debate; Crystal, for instance, explicitly defines a process definition stage. What is not allowed is the unconditional support of ineffective processes. Indeed, it is as refugees from such behavior that some of the proponents and authors of Agile approaches came to codify these concepts.

There is one aspect of 3OI that bears discussing. As powerful as Agile approaches might be at the local team level, there remain questions about how they scale up, not simply in terms of system size, complexity, and failure tolerance but also in terms of organizational size. There are behaviors that organizations display and processes that they adopt that are often sub-optimal. Sometimes, large groups of people behave in ways that individuals and small groups would not and do not agree with. The Agile "movement" has not had a lot to say about this, perhaps leaving such macroscopic issues to Organization Development (OD) specialists and large-scale processes to the heavyweight methodologies that have the overhead to deal with this. In any attempt to propagate ideas, the behavior of the organizations that may support or work against these ideas has to be addressed at some point. Many, many battles have been fought over process, and it seems than many organizations have become converts at some level to ideas such as the SEI's CMM^{SM} and similar models. Of the detailed modeling conventions, few companies have expressed much interest at organizational levels. Similarly, in larger companies I have seen merely a mild interest in what Agile is. A major challenge for such companies will always be the apparent requirement for devolution of control to the team. Many large companies have a vested interest in what they consider to be maintaining tight control over the activities, budgets, assignments, and processes of the people working for them. To give up some of that control may not be easy.

Nevertheless, most of the literature on Agile has been directed at the smaller project; the intact, co-located team; and the single functional system. To make inroads into larger-scale enterprises, there are several issues that must be addressed:

- Scalability in system and team size, organizational size, and across multi-site, multi-generational, and possibly multi-company development.
- Resistance to new ideas within the vested interests in the company.
- Change management to overcome the resistance, and implement and propagate the ideas.
- Standard Operating Procedures. What happens when the Agile approach seems to go contrary to the organizational processes developed in the hard-fought process wars?
- Process champions and owners in some companies have established their positions supporting large-scale concepts such as SEI. Their reaction and support may be vital in the effectiveness and certainly the acceptability of these ideas.

These are issues that all process initiatives have faced in the past and have addressed or ignored. The organizational imperatives are one of the most important factors to consider, if Agile is to make inroads into either the process-free ad hoc shops or the monolithic hide-bound organizations.

Agile and the Fourth Order of Ignorance

This is the "last" Order of Ignorance, and it is also the first, because it rather defines the acceptance of all the other Orders of Ignorance. What does Agile have to say about it? (See Exhibit 9.)

There is no doubt that historical, "traditional" software processes have been blatant copies of manufacturing. Very few, if any, process manuals I have ever read (including a couple I wrote myself) even mentioned the people involved, or that people were involved. It was as if these processes were somehow executed in a vacuum — the process was defined and it executed and the resulting system rolled off the assembly line. Where the work was done — the processor — was never mentioned. Such processes view

Exhibit 9. Agile and the Fourth Order of Ignorance

Order of ignorance	Description	Knowledge need	Agile approach and issues	Agile focus
4OI	Meta-ignorance	To transition the entire focus of the business from a product production paradigm to one of knowledge acquisition, management, and application	This mindset seems implicit in the concepts and certainly the application of Agile approaches but there are a few drawbacks. The primary one (to my mind) is the almost total focus on code as the primary knowledge repository, and the intense concentration on the coding activity as a primary vehicle for exposing ignorance. The code is very important and obviously must work at some point but this approach may not deal most effectively with the storage and accessibility of knowledge, especially at an organizational level. Paradoxically, while Agile approaches directly confront the critically important issues of knowledge acquisition and human interaction, the concentration on the code product may also detract from it, by re-emphasizing product at the expense of knowledge.	Ambiguous

people as simply some set of interchangeable parts that you plugged in whenever you needed to do some work; and indeed, that was the model as viewed by many companies. The Agile approaches have firmly put people back into the picture. They use people-oriented devices such as metaphor and close teamwork, and pair programming and stories to allow people to effectively process the information given to them. Agile has helped reassert software development as a human activity.

They have equally firmly held that software and systems development is, in the greater part, a knowledge-discovery and acquisition activity. They tacitly allow that it is *unknown knowledge* that determines our fate, rather than the correct application of what we already do know. The rapid cycles encourage "controlled failure" that allows us to learn and to check what we have learned against the real world and real users doing real tasks.

However, nowhere in the Agile literature have I come across an unqualified assertion that the job is to learn. Most Agile approaches focus on the

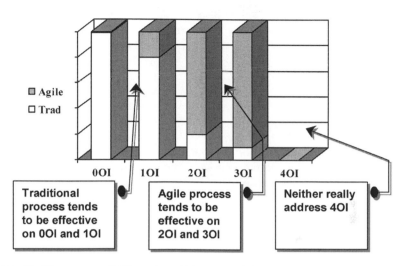

Exhibit 10. The compatibility of traditional and Agile process.

production of code, and I feel there might be an unfortunate side effect of this. Code is important but only code *that works.* As mentioned in earlier chapters, it is very easy to produce code. It is quite easy to produce code that does *something.* It is even easy to produce code that kind of does what is needed under certain controlled circumstances. But it is hard to produce code that really works in the field to provide value to a customer. The customer does not buy the code but buys what the code does or what the code allows him or her to do. Given a few not unreasonable conditions, it might be possible to produce code very, very quickly — if we have the knowledge base available. It might even be possible to extend this knowledge base rather quickly — if we have the knowledge base available in the right form.

The Agile fixation on code is understandable but it may further encourage the view that software is a product to be produced, and the knowledge that goes into the software product has little purpose other than to go into the software product — that software product, that time.

This is the view that indicates 4OI, and Agile seems to be somewhat ambiguous about it (see Exhibit 10). On one hand, it firmly states that the job is to acquire the knowledge necessary to make the system work for the user; on the other hand, it does not say much about the storage and care of that knowledge beyond cramming it into a piece of code and into someone's head.

Summary

A quick look at where traditional process and Agile process operate against the Orders of Ignorance shows that they seem to be reciprocal.

Traditional process is good at and is set up to store and apply known knowledge. It is poor at deviating from that. It does not assist much in the acquisition of new knowledge and, under certain circumstances, may even work against it. Traditional works at 0OI and 1OI levels.

Agile process is good at discovering new knowledge. It is an intrinsically flexible process model that places a premium on dynamic adjustment based on what is being learned and then cycling through the discovery process, getting closer and closer to the optimal answer. Agile processes do not much address the application of "old" knowledge, usually assuming that if the knowledge is available it will be used, and that if a previous process worked and the situation has not changed much, the same process will be applied again until there is evidence that it does not work and there is something to learn. Agile processes work at 2OI and 3OI levels.

It would seem that some compromise based on selecting the process by Order of Ignorance might be in order. This makes sense. There are processes that are good for applying what we know and processes that are good for discovering what we do not know. These processes are rarely similar. The fact that one approach works well for one system but then does not work well in another situation does not mean it is a bad process, it means it is an unsuitable process for that situation.

Neither traditional process, nor most Agile approaches seem to explicitly accept the true purpose of software development and focus their attention on supporting that process. The Agile approach is much closer than the classical models to the real situation but still does not overtly address what will be the key to software development in the future.

And that is the alignment of the organization with the activity of learning and the development of knowledge storage, refactoring, and retrieval systems. When these are coupled with the deterministic processes operating at the 0OI and 1OI levels and with the human-oriented Agile processes operating at the 2OI and 3OI levels, organizations will be able to achieve unimaginable levels of productivity.

There will be organization structures, executable and storage systems, alignment of knowledge capture, and development with company strategy. There will be radically different development modalities and metaphors, coupled with locked-down-tight support processes that are invariable. There will be models and meta-models of the customer's system and the customer's domain. There will be executable models of the project domain and organizational decision making. In the middle will be the people, just as Jerry Weinberg envisaged. The activity of developing systems will be seen as being a truly and wholly human activity. The stage will be set for one of the most-radical advances in human society that has ever occurred.

Chapter 8
The Future of Software Development

THE TIMELESS WAY
It is a process which brings order out of nothing but ourselves;
It cannot be attained but it will happen of its own accord,
If we will only let it.

— **Christopher Alexander**
Preface to Chapter 1, *The Timeless Way of Building**

Where do we go from here? In the last 30 years the software business has grown from an offshoot of the payroll department (the origin of many IT groups), or a sideline of the manufacturing engineering group, to the central mechanism for designing, acquiring, building, selling, and distributing almost everything that we make or use. In the early 1980s, after I had moved to the United States, I remember diligently searching out the one bookstore in the Chicago area that was bold enough to carry books on software development.** A quick look in any major bookstore will show how that particular situation has changed. It used to be that one developer could expect to be conversant with all aspects of developing systems, from the business environment to systems analysis, through the programming of the system to the punching of the tape loop that controlled the chain printer feed. Now the software business has fragmented and specialized in a way that makes the medical profession look like a convention of generalists.

Where will the profession go from here? As Woody Allen once remarked, the only thing I cannot accurately predict is the future. With that caveat, we can use the conceptual basis of this book to venture where the business of software might take us in the immediate future.

*Alexander, C., *The Timeless Way of Building,* Oxford University Press, Oxford, 1979.
**It was Books and Bytes on Ogden Avenue in Naperville, Illinois. It was still there at the time of writing this book.

The Execution of Knowledge

For the moment, we are restricted to the five knowledge-storage media of DNA, brains, hardware, books, and software. Perhaps another knowledge medium will come along but it is not clear what that might be. It is clear that more and more of our present-day knowledge will be inexorably transferred into the medium of software, simply because there it is both controllable and executable. The Knowledge Management movement will see a migration to the software medium. Many of the books on knowledge management allude to this movement* but consider that software resident knowledge is limited to the relatively arcane areas of expert systems, "case-based reasoning," and neural networks. These are types of knowledge-in-software but there are many other kinds. Anytime we use a digital instructional format to control a machine, we are encoding and encapsulating our knowledge in a software form. The idea that knowledge on a Web page constitutes knowledge-in-software fails the litmus test of executability. If the storage medium for the knowledge is passive and needs to be read for any action to be taken on it, it is essentially a book, no matter what format it is in. True, the end result of the calculation of a spreadsheet must usually be read by a human but the processing execution of the data has been done in the software of the spreadsheet.

The potentiality of knowledge-in-software is not in its storage but in what Don Tapscott called knowledge deployment.** In the same way that our use of hardware as represented by the stone tools we created gave us control over our environment in the Paleolithic era, and books revolutionized our management of knowledge in the 15th century, software will revolutionize the present-day society and for the same reason — it will make certain kinds of knowledge usable. Ultimately, I believe all knowledge of the human race will be transcribed into some software form. What some of it will look like in that form is hard to imagine, and knowledge that is relatively fact free (such as propositions in ethics) might hold out for a long time before suitable software forms are found. Many of the obvious ones have already been covered: simple and repetitive mathematical constructs such as payroll calculations; machine control from very simple actions to very high degrees of sophistication; and complex management of processes such as chemical diffusion and pharmaceuticals have all given way to the onslaught of software. It is likely that even the book form of knowledge which is currently captured through (although not in) a software medium, may give way as interactive authoring packages start to work with the human creating the written word. We already have the barest beginnings with certain syntax checkers and authoring templates. Ultimately, all knowledge will

*For instance, see *Working Knowledge: How Organizations Manage What They Know,* by Thomas Davenport and Laurence Prusak, Harvard Business School Press, Cambridge, MA, 1997, p. 126.
**In *Growing Up Digital: The Rise of the Net Generation,* Tapscott, D., McGraw-Hill Trade, New York, 1999, p. 216, the term was borrowed from the Alliance for Converging Technologies.

have its analogue in the executable software form, even if versions remain in passive book form and in peoples' brains. And we will increasingly see the knowledge-in-software form as being the most valuable. Sam Palmisano, the CEO of IBM, asked what is left after we have automated the back office, reengineered our business functions, and outsourced noncore business activities. He answered his own question by noting that the job will be to get all the automated systems working together to respond quickly and flexibly to the changing world.* This means that all the critical business knowledge and the knowledge of how to leverage that critical business knowledge are being moved into software systems. As we get more and more knowledge into an executable form, the challenges will be

1. Creating new and different knowledge
2. Creating new and different combinations of old knowledge
3. Integrating old and new knowledge
4. Creating knowledge management structures that coordinate the knowledge across businesses, enterprises, domains, and societies

This last point may prove to be critical, because it represents the management of the knowledge of knowledge.

One of the essential aspects of being able to create or to prepare for a future is to visualize it. Building on the thesis of software as a knowledge medium and plotting the trends in the evolution of software development, there is no doubt that the business of software will change radically within the next few years. These changes will be disruptive and liberating. They will be painful and energizing. They are as inevitable as the sea of changes in society caused by Johann Gutenberg's invention, and for the same reason — they will liberate knowledge and capability in a way unimaginable when this medium was invented 50 years ago.

And it will begin with the business of software.

The Demise of "Software Engineering"

Viewing software as a knowledge medium strongly implies that the very concept of "software engineering" is flawed. It was a necessary step, especially in the early explosive-growth days of the software business. But if software is simply a knowledge medium, then "software engineering" would be knowledge about software as an entity. This is rather self-referential. It implies knowledge about the knowledge medium, in much the same way that an English major might have knowledge about the intricacies of the English language. The primary issue, of course, is not the medium but what knowledge is stored in the medium. Increasingly, it is the domain knowledge that is important, not the knowledge of how to transcribe the domain knowledge into an executable form or knowledge about the

Information Week, January 2003, p. 18.

medium. Indeed, in many IT areas this transcription has already been done, as in the case of commercial off-the-shelf (COTS) or package software. Few IT professionals these days find themselves coding their own solution to problems, and fewer will do so in the future. Perhaps one could argue that certain types of software, such as operating systems, will require "knowledge of software" as opposed to knowledge of the domain, but even there one could construct an argument that for an operating system the domain is the processor and the execution environment. Perhaps the only true "software engineering" would be the construction of languages but, as we shall see, even this is suspect.

The original focus on software engineering came about as a historical fact related to the relative quantities of knowledge required to program a computer to perform a task. In the early days, to require a machine to multiply two numbers together required very little knowledge of the domain (numbers and multiplication) and a lot of knowledge of the computer (how to input data, load registers, invoke op codes (in assembly language) or other commands, store values in memory, and output results. For example, to this day some assembly languages* for small microprocessors do not have a MULTiply or equivalent command, and the activity of "multiply" must be crafted by a combination of add (or shift, depending on the algorithm) and "test carry" commands. For large numbers and situations where arithmetic product overflow must be dealt with, this can become a nontrivial task. In such machines the ratio of domain knowledge to "software" knowledge was low. Clearly, in modern development this ratio has switched to the extent that in some environments, the developers neither have nor need any knowledge of how the machine actually performs the work. They only need to know the domain in sufficient detail and be able to transcribe that understanding into the tool set that contains the knowledge. Because these tool sets are becoming very powerful, certainly when compared to a 6802 Assembler, the "software" knowledge necessary to make the tool set work is becoming minimal.

Exhibit 1 and Exhibit 2 illustrate this. The "quantity" of software knowledge (i.e., knowledge about software) has probably been rising slowly over the years; but its nature is changing significantly. Whereas the knowledge used to be of the processor, and the operation of registers and accumulators, the "software knowledge" is now of the format of SAP R/3 tables and the like. Both are forms of programming instructions, in that they instruct the machine, but their target is quite different. The assembly language maps onto the operation of an electrical circuit or a piece of silicon, and the SAP table maps onto a business function. While it is very difficult to empirically measure the "quantity" of knowledge in an Assembly language instruction vs. an SAP table entry (for reasons discussed earlier), intuitively one could

*For example, the Motorola MC6802 8-bit Assembler.

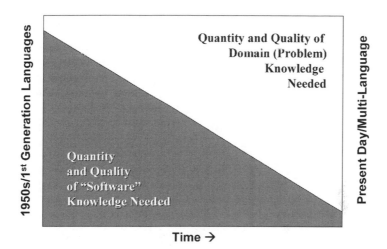

Exhibit 1. The changing ratio of software/domain knowledge.

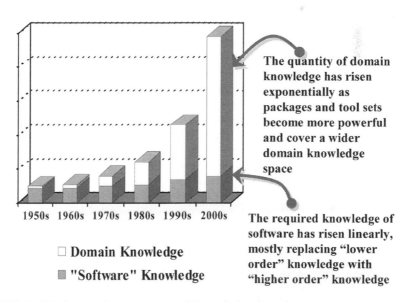

The quantity of domain knowledge has risen exponentially as packages and tool sets become more powerful and cover a wider domain knowledge space

The required knowledge of software has risen linearly, mostly replacing "lower order" knowledge with "higher order" knowledge

□ Domain Knowledge

▩ "Software" Knowledge

Exhibit 2. The increasing quantity of knowledge in software.

assert that from a human perspective, they are probably not that different. That is, the human activity of effectively creating a line of assembly language instruction or a table entry are similar in scope. It certainly is unlikely that the difference in effort is in orders of magnitude. What each line actually does, of course, may well be of several orders of magnitude difference. The reason that statements in the higher-level language do more than statements in the assembly language is that the higher-level language primitives contain more knowledge than the assembly language. Therefore, the program statement executes more knowledge. It does not require more knowledge to push a button to switch on a robotic assembly machine than it does to effectively use a hand axe. What the robotic assembly machine does is much more complex than what the hand axe does but the knowledge necessary to initiate it is not that much different.

We are moving into an era where the knowledge present in the tools is enormous, the tools are becoming more domain-specific (of which, more later), and the knowledge of the software is becoming less and less. The end result of this will be the disappearance of the concept of the "software engineer" as it has been known historically. If we are engineering the structure of the software, such a person might be better called a "knowledge engineer" or a "domain engineer." As more and more "software knowledge" is encapsulated into software artifacts, the need to know the traditional disciplines of software engineering will vanish and will be replaced by knowledge of the domain and knowledge of the domain language constructed to operate on that domain. Indeed, while a debate continues over the need or validity of certifying and licensing software engineers, the job may well morph into something else and make the debate irrelevant.

Likely, there will always be people we will call software engineers, and they will be able to trace their lineage from the machine coders, assembly language hacks, structure people, and OO implementers of the past. However, they will function quite differently. Even those people tasked with creating the "primitives" of software construction will routinely employ tool sets that remove them substantially from the grind of rehashing the details of the environment in which they work. The knowledge of the environment will be replaced by the knowledge of the tool set.

The End of Code

Code as we usually think of it is a sequential procedural model that intrinsically implements only two obvious relationships (next–prior). True, with various devices, such as naming conventions and suffixes, we can create other kinds of links embedded in the code but it still remains a sequential model that intrinsically has some severe limitations (see Chapter 5). Knowledge is rarely linear and sequential. Knowledge is also rarely generic, although it usually shares common abstract properties with other knowledge. Given the changes described here, it is fairly certain that the future will go, not to the generic code languages but to the application-specific packages.

The problem with most coding languages is that they are domain non-specific. We can use C++ to write a payroll system and write a machine control function. The language neither knows nor cares which you are writing (with the exception, of course, of the data typing enforced by the object classes and methods used, and the presence or absence of specific function libraries). Because the language has no insight into what you are doing, it cannot help you do it. Packages such as SAP do not have this limitation. They "know," within quite a narrow range, what you are trying to do, and can be very helpful in directing you. We could write a device driver or a paper report using an assembly language. Crystal Reports™* is very good at writing reports but could not be used for creating a device driver. This apparent "limitation" of the Crystal Reports language is, of course, nothing of the sort because we would never consider trying to use the tool to write a device driver in the first place. Because Crystal Reports is highly conversant within the domain of report writing (read: contains a lot of knowledge of the activity of report writing), it is able to both recognize what we are trying to do and greatly assist us in it. Domain nonspecific languages do not.

One of the reasons for the present-day proliferation of languages is that each language carries with it a certain degree of domain specificness. Even the most domain-free languages tend to have some bias toward a flavor of processing — assembly languages map closely to the processor, HTML maps closely to the physical nature of the screen presentation of text, many scripting languages are designed for string and regular expression manipulation, etc. These languages tend to attract their quota of adherents who can become quite vocal in their support of their version of the one true language. The reason for the certain degree of chauvinism that seems to accompany the enthusiasm is that through repeated use the language becomes peoples' way of thinking. Naturally, because they have started to think using the language constructs and structure, they tend to be highly effective using it, and the language seems very logical to them. Some of the brightest minds of the 20th century such as Minsky,** Bohm and Peat,*** and Weiner**** have shown just how dependent the view of the problem is on the language we use to express it. But it seems that along with the facility comes a certain amount of tunnel vision on the subject. That said, one of the realities of many current projects is that they are routinely programmed in a variety of programming languages and approaches. This

*A product of the Crystal Decisions Company.
**For instance the "interpreted operation" in Matter, Mind, and Models, by Marvin Minsky, *Proc. Int. Fed. Inf. Process. Cong.,* 1965, vol. 1, pp. 45–49.
***In *Science, Order, and Creativity,* by David Bohm and David F. Peat, Bantam Books, New York, 1987.
****Weiner observed that learning in humans is a function of language in *Cybernetics, or Control and Communication in the Animal and the Machine,* MIT Press, Cambridge, Massachusetts, 1948/1961.

requires that developers are competent in a range of languages and learn to apply them where they are best suited. Along with the demise of software engineering as a discrete discipline it is possible that the concept of the one, universal, all-purpose programming language will join Esperanto on the dusty shelf of language history. More likely, we will keep a few relatively domain-free languages around for those tasks that cut across diverse domains and for which it is not efficient to create specific syntax.

We are seeing, particularly in the IT world, that we use generic languages to build systems from scratch less and less. The movement seems to be relentlessly toward more domain-specific applications. Text editor-based HTML sprouts functional wizards that evolve into specific HTML editors, which give way to Web page designing packages, which become functional development packages that use the Web page designing packages. A variety of development packages spring up for the different uses we have for them. The packages incorporate wizards that supply much of the context for creating the system until, if the developer has even an inkling of what needs to be created, he or she can create it. Coding purists may scoff at this "script kiddie" approach, with some justification, but there is no denying the effectiveness and popularity of the trend.

There is no reason to believe that this trend will not continue. The reason is simple: if we use a generic language it does not know what we are trying to do and cannot help us do it. More pointedly, we must provide almost all the knowledge that will be present in the system we are creating, because there is little knowledge above basic manipulation functions embedded in the generic language. If we have to provide all the knowledge, we must either already have it (be experienced coders in both the language and the domain) or we must get it. If we must get it, we will take more time building the system, which is the same as saying we will be less efficient. Even if we already have the knowledge, there will be Second Order Ignorance things we do not know, and generic languages will still not help much.*

So the future development environment will consist of a large toolbox of packages and domain-specific languages, most of which will not be in the traditional command-line format. They will be managed inside a multi-domain-aware environment and will employ meta-languages and tools to address the issues that are not covered by the domain-specific tools and languages. They will not look much like the code we know today.

*However, we can also make the case that higher-order languages are predominantly 0OI and 1OI devices, and the resolution of 2OI is best done in a language that makes few assumptions. We can see this when we attempt to use languages outside of their domain. We can spend weeks trying to figure out *if* the language can do the job at all. The development of meta-languages will probably alleviate this.

The Death of CASE, the Death of Method

To some extent, Computer Aided Software Engineering (CASE) tools have been a disappointment. The reason is quite simple. Many CASE tools are simply passive drawing tools that do not encapsulate any knowledge and do not make knowledge executable. In the extreme case, the tool only allows us to draw a picture of the system and then look at it. This is not software, it is a book, and a fairly primitive one at that. Practitioners and organizations have become wary of the impressive claims of the capability of these tools made by their vendors. In many organizations I have interactions with, even if the tools are present they are not much used. The reason is that the value realized by using the tools is not enough to offset the effort of learning and using the tools. In knowledge terms, we need more knowledge to use the tools than the tools give us.

Similar to methodologies, there are great benefits to adopting an effective framework for describing and understanding the domain (although the tools suffer from the same problems as the methods in that they tend to be highly domain nonspecific). It is important to note that these tools are intentionally domain specific, primarily for market-driven reasons.

Additionally, the application of the methods and the tools may lead to a sequence of discoveries that tends to work against the use of the method and tool:

- *Tool Artifact.* The constraints of the method and tool syntax force an artifact or unwanted complexity on the problem that is not there. You may hear people say, "I know what the problem is, I'm having trouble describing it in the tool." In many situations, the use of the method and tool make the job harder and take longer than not using it, without a concomitant payback across time or across the organization. In the extreme case, the method and tool may force a completely wrong answer, although this is usually due to the use of an inappropriate approach or an inappropriate tool for the particular problem at hand.

- *Increasing Scope.* The use of both tools and methods tends to draw out Second Order Ignorance. This is actually their primary function but what appears to be happening, from the perspective of project management, is that the work is expanding rather than contracting. It is not expanding, of course. What is happening is that the use of the tool and methods is exposing the true scope of the task by unearthing 2OI and converting it into 1OI (questions) or 0OI (answers). Because the method and tool do not contain the answer, their use usually drives out 2OI in the form of questions. This makes it appear as if the workload is getting bigger. The apparent increase of work and scope can sometimes spook people and, when coupled

169

with the first point, may result in a project abruptly abandoning the tool, blaming it and the process for causing the additional work.

- *Domain Nonspecific.* This is the most significant and most legitimate criticism of these tools and methods. The methods and tools are domain nonspecific, just like generic coding languages. This means that neither the method nor the CASE tool knows what you are trying to do with it. The only constraint checking most tools and most methods perform is some simple syntax. Examples of these syntax checks include checks that only certain kinds of connections can be made to certain kinds of icons, that arcs or connectors must terminate somewhere, data items must have names, and relationships are defined to have a certain cardinality, etc. These checks are against the generic syntax conventions of the method and tool, not against the domain the contents of the tool represent. What does not happen is that the tool checks that the right number of the correct kinds of connections are made between the most appropriately-named entities under the logical conditions that would pertain in the real world. Most software tools cannot perform that kind of validation because they are not connected to the real world. What is also not shown is what happens when these things do not align, when the relationships do not have the correct cardinality, or the arcs are not attached to a node. The reason the method and the tools do not show these things is that the method and the tool are not close enough analogues of the real-world situation. To be so, they would have to become domain specific. There are many reasons why methodologists intentionally create domain-nonspecific methods, and tool sellers sell domain-nonspecific tools. For the methodologist, it is simply easier to create generic, all-encompassing methods that generally describe systems behavior. For the tool-maker, the reason is more obvious — the market for a generalized tool is much larger than for a specialized one. In both cases, the method and the tool are some distance removed from the problem. This distance must be made up by the practitioner, and that means extra work. The effort of refactoring of the knowledge into the method and tool syntax, the confusing variance between the problem and the problem representation in the CASE tool, and simply the extra effort and cost required to learn the tool itself all work against the adoption and continued use of the tools

- *Nonexecutable.* Methods have never billed themselves as being "executable;" it is understood that they are frameworks of thought with which to limit, constrain, and control the problem analysis and solution design activity. The tools, however, have some expectation of executability, because they are nominally software entities. However, most CASE tools have fallen far short of their promise in this. They may generate structures from CASE-resident structures, they may be able to duplicate and load data relationships such as class definitions in a compilable environment. They may even be able to perform an isomorphic transformation of logic into an executable code form. In almost all cases, the tools are merely doing a 1:1 translation, "copying" the structure or the logic, with only a slight translation between languages. They do not add anything or provide additional capability or insights. In many cases the tools can only translate relatively simple logic from a graph form to a command-line form, and complex or incomplete logic is beyond them. Therefore, the tools end up being good at doing things that are easy to do anyway. Because the tools only perform isomorphic transformations, all the work must have already been done. That is, all the knowledge must have been acquired and inserted into the tool for the tool to do the work.* The tools are performing at best a simple translation activity that is easy, if tedious, to do manually. The biggest problem with the tools, after the issue of their being domain neutral, is that they only act as a passive repository of the knowledge. They are, in effect, complicated books. Electronic books to be sure, but books nevertheless. The models stored in these tools merely describe the knowledge they contain; they cannot evaluate it, they do not validate it, and they do not execute it. This is why, when time on projects gets short, the use of these tools gets cut. For the same reason that other nonexecutable knowledge repositories are often short-changed, tools and methods are routinely abandoned when time is of the essence. The reason is obvious — the job of software engineering is to acquire knowledge and store it in an executable form. When push comes to shove, activities that do not store the knowledge in an executable form (writing requirements specifications, documenting design and code) tend to be left in the dust of code writing. As ineffective as any gallop to create code can often be, one can see the logic — if something has to go, it cannot be the executable code, because that is the system. So it is going to be the nonexecutable something. This issue of nonexecutability is one of the most-significant drawbacks in traditional CASE tools, and the one area where they have least lived up to their promise.

Perhaps predicting the death of method and of CASE is a little extreme. There are many vested interests in both and they will probably continue in some form for a while. Also, today's CASE tools will probably evolve into the meta CASE tools, to be discussed later. It is in these tools that the future

---

*In their book, *Exploring Requirements: Quality before Design* (Dorset House, New York, 1989), Jerry Weinberg and Don Gause describe the "guaranteed cockroach killer," consisting of two pieces of wood. The instructions for use consisted of (1) place cockroach on block A, (2) hit cockroach with block B. The knowledge is the cockroach and the CASE tools are the blocks. Once you can isolate the knowledge, the rest is easy.

of tool-based development lies. The tools that do flourish will be the ones that shake off the constraints listed here. They will be programmable, domain specific, and, above all, executable.

The Incubator of Knowledge Engineering

If software engineering as a discipline is to disappear or evolve into something else, what would it be? At the risk of applying a rather-overused phrase and concept, I would suggest that it will become knowledge engineering. That is what it has been all along, of course. It is just that the primary knowledge that needed to be engineered was how the computer worked and how the programming language could make it work; hence, "software engineering." With that effort behind us, we will start to look to the real nature of the knowledge that we are trying to make executable. The study of knowledge — epistemology — is a rich and complex subject. Many attempts have been made to classify and categorize knowledge. Without getting too metaphysical, many authors acknowledge the anthropomorphic nature of knowledge. There does not seem to be anything that resembles "empirical knowledge," it is all a result of the human constructs we build to understand the world around us. Ludwig von Bertalanffy noted that "all scientific constructs are models representing certain aspects or perspectives of reality."* Our systems understanding is defined and constrained by the mental, paper-, tool-, or code-based models we build and the rules these models impose on us; and the paper-, tool-, and code-based models are simply analogues of the mental models we construct to understand things. We get to choose the models and the rules that govern them. When we understand things we are both constructing the model and its rules and populating the models with data that fits or sometimes does not fit, those rules. The models themselves are a mapping onto some observed or expected set of events, entities, objects, rules, functions, etc. in the "real world." We consciously or unconsciously select the rules of the models as conventions to assist us in understanding the behavior of the real world and the real world surrogate of the system. Given this, we can state a few requirements of a knowledge engineering system.

Model Based

The development process of the future will be "model based." In the software world this usually means graphical models, typically in the form of a directed graph, because for some reason code and text are not usually

---

*von Bertalanffy's seminal and somewhat forgotten book (*General Systems Theory*, George Braziller, New York, 1969, p. 94), does a very good job of synthesizing the commonality of all systems: biological, economic, scientific, and political. While von Bertalanffy did not discuss computer systems and barely mentioned computers at all, the ideas apply to such systems. But even with such a sound construction of a theory of all systems, von Bertalanffy comes to the conclusion that they are (1) not empirical, (2) understood by humans in terms of their models, and (3) subject to human-constructed models.

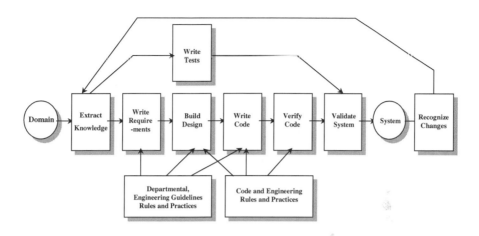

Exhibit 3. The traditional view of process.

considered to be "models," even though they manifestly are. However, there is no reason to exclude linear text-based models — provided the system being modeled fits the physical characteristics of single tasking, sequential, linear processes. That the future software development process will be model based is a given, because all thought is "model based." However, the clear understanding of what that means will become a key element in future development paradigms, and the selection or construction of the model components and language will become a key part of building systems.

Anthropomorphic Models

It is a little-explored aspect of software development, Jerry Weinberg notwithstanding, but all models are developed by humans for humans. There is considerable evidence that humans respond to certain model types better than others. Our conventions in writing — the division of language into characters, words, and sentences, and their linear relationship with each other — arise largely because that is how certain parts of our brains work. Spoken speech does not have the same divisions and punctuation between words and sentences as written speech, simply because the parts of the brain that process audio input do not have that requirement for understanding. This means that while we cannot effectively read an undifferentiated string of letters, we can hear and understand an uninterrupted stream of words. The most effective models will not only be based on the needs of the domain, more importantly they will be based on the needs of the people creating and using the models.

It is quite strange that our traditional life cycle models (see Exhibit 3) completely and utterly ignore the only place where the work is done. The

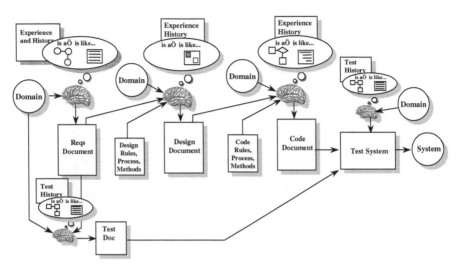

Exhibit 4. The true development life cycle.

"stages" of traditional life cycles are nothing of the sort; they are simply collections of repositories for knowledge of different types. There may be some commonality of function and some temporal congruence in the functions at each stage (e.g., similar work is done in obtaining systems requirements and the work is done around the same time). However, the true location of the work is not in the requirements document as shown by the life cycle models; it is in the collective brains of the people analyzing the environment and whatever prior knowledge repositories exist (see Exhibit 4). The operations conducted on the information obtained are not abstract manipulations of some calculus or independent transforms applied to some model syntax; they are thought processes operating in peoples' heads. The prototypical, object-oriented relationships of "is a…" and "is like…" are not constructs of some convention-based modeling method that happens to work better than the more-traditional procedural processes; they are fundamental understanding functions of the human brain. The logical application of this realization in the future is that software development starts to use and apply the concepts of human information processing and cognitive reason in the construction of our model types. Perhaps the day will come when each software project will employ a cognitive psychologist to assist the team in developing its human understanding processes.

Programmable Interface

The syntax, appearance, components, rules, methods, and most other aspects of the models we use must be programmable. That is, while there

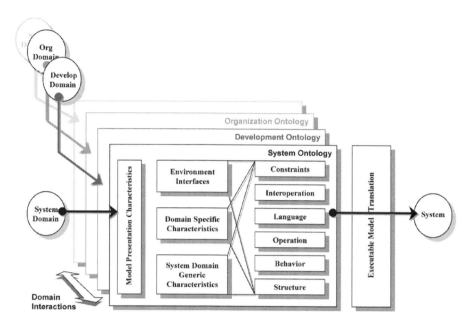

Exhibit 5. Development programmable tool set components.

may be some stable set of primitives, perhaps devoted to instantiating different types of models, the models we use will be designed for the specific use to which we put them. This will mean that developers will not tend to use or accept generic model types but to some extent create their own specifically for the job at hand. This might sound like extra work and a step away from the move toward "standardization," but even a casual look at the nature of the work we do currently shows that we routinely create our own languages, models, and programmable environments. We create them to do just the work we need to do. The test script scenario described in Chapter 7 is an example. The minor, major, and contextual variations of the script contain variables that represent the scope of function in that activity. They are not generic; they are extremely specific to the task at hand, and it is this that makes the script valuable. The Operational Variation level of script contains the knowledge of the operational environment (rather than the function) in which the script is being executed. Again, it is not generalized except insofar as the environment needs to be generalized.

For most scripts, the "modeling" language is some form of command line but it does not need to be. It could equally be graphical (see Exhibit 5) or tabular (as in SAP programming, for example). This presentation interface, as in the testing process example, usually comes about as an accident of design — the first reasonably viable format that someone comes up with is the one that is used. We could certainly do a better job of crafting the interface that encapsulates the knowledge we are executing. By designing modeling conventions that are adapted to our thought processes, we can create more consistent interfaces than we do currently. In the general state, we will be able to design whatever kind of model we wish, with whatever kind of user interface is most appropriate.

Variable Rule Based

Within the programmable executable models we will need the capability of embedding predicate logic. This logic will operate at several levels, depending on the purpose of the model. For systems models, the logic will represent systems conditions. This will be the functional equivalent of the decision tables and other predicate logic devices we routinely capture and put down in text form in requirements and design documents. For environment models, the logic will determine process operations. For management models, the logic will operate on resource and project metrics, and may result in processing the typical decision logic that managers use to make the decisions that control their projects.* Coupled with executability capacity (see the following section), this will allow the models to execute in simulation or code construction modes.

Executable

More than any other characteristic, the most valuable and inevitable one will be that our understanding tools will also become executable. In most cases today, only the code form of our knowledge representation will actually execute its knowledge. Certainly most requirements and design documents do not "execute" in any real sense. Even designs in CASE tools do not usually "run." Perhaps we could make a case that the test data view of the system executes in a fashion but few of our knowledge repositories, apart from the code actually run. The passive knowledge repositories of feasibility documents, statements of work, contract books, requirements documents, architectural and detailed designs, and even down to program specifications do not execute the knowledge they contain; they merely describe it. The knowledge contained in them is not manifest; it is motionless. The only way the knowledge can be used is by transporting it into a human brain through the processes of reading and understanding. In the future, most if not all of our primary knowledge representations will —

---

*Some years ago, I started to create a model-based logic engine that would answer the question posed by Brooks' Law (from *The Mythical Man Month,* Frederick P. Brooks, Addison Wesley, New York, 1975, p. 25). The question is, "if I have a project that is running late, should I add people to it to speed it up?" The answer is, "it depends." If the project can be usefully partitioned into chunks that can be separated and given to the newcomers, if the newcomers are knowledgeable and experienced, if there is more-mundane work that can be given to them that will free up my present developers for more-valuable work, the answer is "yes." More commonly, the addition of people will require that my current staff take time away from being productive to instruct the newcomers, resulting in a net drop in productivity. Hence, Brooks' Law: *adding manpower to a late project makes it later.*

must — execute. To understand the system we wish to build and document our understanding, we will create domain-specific models that will also run. In addition to their ability to create native code that will execute, the models themselves may actually execute in the target environment. Perhaps the models will simulate execution, or they may calculate what would happen during or after execution, or they will schedule execution. They may install themselves, interact with the development or management environment, or do any number of things but they will do *something*. Again, using the simple example of the test script, we see that the script is a representation of our knowledge about how to test the system that runs. It does not describe the knowledge of testing, it does not explain how to execute a test — it executes the test. We could certainly take the knowledge that is present in the test script and write a narrative test procedure that would tell the reader how to run a test but it would be wholly passive and much-less valuable. We see this progressive transitioning of knowledge into executability happening all about us in a variety of systems: test scripts become test systems, simple configuration management check-in-check-out procedures become complex change-set managers, installation manuals become installation scripts which become installation and remote maintenance systems, passive Web pages give way to active server pages that recognize the user and act accordingly. It is quite obvious why we do this — it is our job. The software developer's profession is the acquisition of knowledge and its translation into an executable form. As the Third Law of Software Process wryly states, what we need to do is to apply this principle to itself and make the knowledge of making knowledge executable itself executable (see Exhibit 6).

The developers, process engineers, managers, or users of the future will interact with the executable models in a fundamentally different way than we do today, although the interfaces may look similar to today's CASE tools. These developers will interact with the executable knowledge repositories to explore and discover new combinations of knowledge primitives and constructs, all the while testing their assumptions and the viability of their new ideas by running them against the executing knowledge store.

Translatable

The future models must be translatable from one model type to another. This means that requirements models will be transitioned into design models, which will be able to create native code. For some situations, the "native code" will be other models. More often, the models will be translated through a rule set into a more-suitable (for execution purposes) language. The rule sets for translation between models will themselves be executable models that map the relationships between the model components.

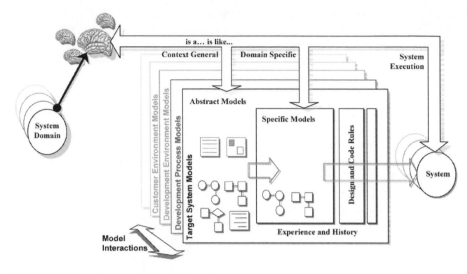

Exhibit 6. Domain modeling life cycle.

In some cases the models will be converted from one model format into another. This will rarely be an isomorphic translation, which tends to be of low value, because by definition nothing is added or removed from the knowledge. There will be some of these transformations, for instance, to resolve certain kinds of tool performance issues. An example might be generating compilable source code from an icon-based model — the executable icon-based model would almost certainly be an interpreted system, which will tend to run slowly. Converting the interpreted icons and relations into compilable source code, which is then compiled into a processor-based language, almost always produces a faster-running system.* More commonly, a model will be used to develop the basis for the next stage in development and provide the foundation for the addition of more knowledge. This will be particularly true of requirements model →design model translations. The equation will be requirements model knowledge + (design constraints + design options + execution support requirements) = design model knowledge. Similarly, design and "code" models will be used as a foundation for testing models. It is important to note that, as clever as these models might get, they cannot generate the new knowledge. That must be done by a human. Undoubtedly, the machine will be able to present choices, and certainly it will assist in manipulating the knowledge

---

*Everything has a price. The speed improvement generated by an interpreted language → compiled language is paid for in several ways. First, someone has to write the translator; next, there may be artifact (unexpected and unwanted feature and function changes) introduced by the translator, so it ends up not really being an isomorphic translation. Finally, depending on the logical languages on either side of the translation, it may not be possible to provide an exact 1:1 mapping.

to the point where the human can assert its correctness or otherwise (that will be the primary function of these tools); but for the foreseeable future, the tools will not be able to assert that something is correct knowledge without the human intervention.

On the support side, there will be close linkage between "standards" models and the product and process models, with the application models inheriting their characteristics from the standards models. For management, the linkage will be between the system's models (the classical models containing the knowledge of the product under development) and the resource and planning models. For the environment, such as network management, the linkage will be between the resource and system models and the environment models that control the networks, workstations, and tool sets.

Domain Specific

Another key difference between the development environment of the future and today's approaches will be that the tools and methods will become domain specific. As we have seen earlier, the advantage of a domain-nonspecific method, tool, or language was clear when the bulk of the knowledge to be gained was of software and software engineering. Perhaps more correctly, the domain-nonspecific tools of language and operating system were actually domain-specific tools targeting the domain where most knowledge had to be gained, which was in the software and processor environments. Whichever way we look at it, this generated a need for people to be trained in these generic methods, tools, and languages. These modalities then became the way that these people thought and processed information and a feedback dependency was set up. Even today, in the area of package implementation, we can see this cycle being broken. Packages are rarely domain nonspecific.* As model-based development takes hold, it may start being domain independent, as it is today with languages such as UML. But this will inevitably submit to the low-value proposition and the need to increase the value of using the tools, and these models will be become domain specific over time.

We see this in other disciplines to some extent. The notational system and rules for electrical engineering are quite different from the rules and notation used for chemical engineering, and we would never consider using electrical circuit notation to describe chemical activity. While these domains are further apart than many software domains, the different business domains will create notational systems that specifically address their

---

*We could argue that report-writing packages are domain nonspecific, because we can use them to write reports for any type of business domain. The packages are, of course, specific to the activity or domain of constructing reports, which is why they are very efficient in that area and very inefficient in any other area.

needs. We will have notational systems and models for different types of business systems and different types of engineering systems. These models will contain the characteristic primitives of that domain along with the rules and logic inherent in the domain. Not only will these models contain the components of the functions and objects and states domains, they will also contain the important collections of these components that characterize the domains.

Object Oriented

There is no doubt these models will be object oriented in the general sense that the models will be defined at different levels of abstraction and levels will "inherit" their characteristics from their owning levels. This is the only logical way to organize such models without resulting in excessive duplication.* When the technology catches up, these inheritance relationships will be resolved dynamically and under the control of decision logic based on the environment of the model. This is the only way in which we will avoid large-scale redundancy and duplication.

Domain Variable

The models will each represent the domain appropriate for the system, project, environment, and organization involved. The key characteristics of these domains will be abstracted into the models. Similar domains will be created by using the object inheritance from high-order abstractions of the domains.

Domain Interdependent

In real life, domains are not independent. In fact, even within systems, many of our boundaries are simply conventions that we define to allow us to better manage the scope of what we do. The real world is a highly interconnected Web of systems and objects. As has been noted earlier, we cannot really separate the process of creating a system from the system being created. Equally, we cannot entirely separate the system from the people creating the system and the organization and environment in which these people work. There are literally thousands of domains and factors that interact in the creation of systems. As we become more mature at the business of software, we will start to manipulate and manage these domains interdependently.

Model Interdependent

We will map these domains onto executable models in our integrated tool set. These models will have connections that map key characteristics of models to their dependent models. The "standards" models will have

---

*Of course, the "usability" of object-oriented approaches is primarily a function of their usability for the human activity of learning and thinking.

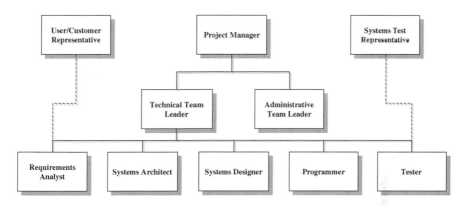

Exhibit 7. Typical traditional project team.

templates of processes and deliverables that the process and systems models inherit. The management and environment models will be linked to the systems models to control the population of the models and the creation of the knowledge artifacts. As these artifacts are developed, their status will be reported back to the management models that will maintain an overall view of the project. Larger, more-comprehensive models will roll up individual projects to provide enterprise-level views of the development.

Meta-Models and Meta-Languages

The higher levels of abstraction and the need for integration between models will result in the development of meta-models (models that define and control the behavior of models) and meta-languages (languages that allow the control and interoperability of other languages). Meta-models are already present in some meta-tools such as Honeywell's DOME tool,* and define the format of the models defined by the meta-model. At this level, much of the work starts to look ontological (the relationships of being) and linguistic (the meaning of words and other communications elements).

A Radically Different Project Setup

The traditional project team (Exhibit 7) owes as much to the army as it does to the needs of software development. The project manager occupies the role that a captain plays in the army to convey the orders from above and pass back information on the status of the project, being the bearer of

*Obtainable for free download from http://www.htc.honeywell.com. Solidus DOME (Domain Modeling Environment) is a good example of the kind of tools that will populate the landscape within a few years. DOME was created when its developers, after many years of creating different software tools targeted at different domains, stopped to consider what they would build if they considered software tool building a domain in its own right. Much of DOME is actually written in DOME.

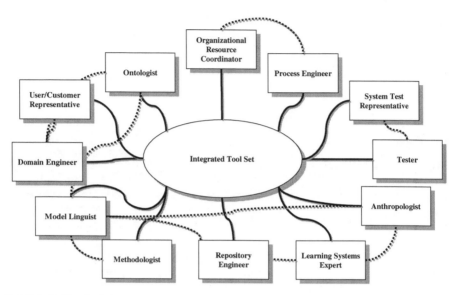

Exhibit 8. Typical future project team.

the overall project and organizational strategy. The classical team leader is the sergeant responsible for making sure that the work is actually done on the shop floor. Other roles are based on loose sets of functional skills and experience. None of the roles particularly addresses the activity of learning or acquiring knowledge. Few of the processes that these people employ address such considerations. Along with the fairly strict hierarchy of such projects goes a stratification of function. In many cases, the manager is not expected to be highly technical. In some cases, it is even acceptable that the manager has little understanding of what is actually done on the project. These are similar silos of skills within the project.

To effectively manage software development as a knowledge-acquisition activity means that this project structure must be seriously overhauled. The roles of projects in the future will likely be radically different (see Exhibit 8) and focused on the human activity of learning and the model-based activity of storing, codifying, structuring, modifying, and making available the knowledge already learned. The wider perspective of the acquisition of knowledge in a business and organizational setting, supported by the suitable domain models, will result in an organizational structure that little resembles the project of today.

Some of the typical roles will be:

- *Organizational Resource Coordinator.* This is the closest person to a classical project manager. Collections of functions or systems undertaken by an organization will probably still require a single point of contact, if not a single point of responsibility, to which the organization can look for accountability and status. This person will be in charge of the management aspects of the model tool set.

- *Process Engineer.* A role that is currently used extensively in many companies. The difference with today's project team is that this person will be responsible for creating the executable model process elements that the people on the project use. This cannot be done in isolation, and there must be close cooperation between the project and the process engineer. Probably, process engineers across the company will be associated in communities of practice to share ideas across what remains of organizational boundaries, perhaps under the guidance of a controlling body. In more-loosely-ordered companies, this body may be a cross-functional Software Engineering Process Group (SEPG). In some companies, there may be defined organizational elements controlling the software process and the process tool set. However it is organized, these people will act like the Process Focus elements at Level 3 of the SEI CMM model. The executable model components they create will be the "process assets" defined by the Process Definition process area of the CMM.
- *Ontologist.* This is a very different role than any envisaged today. The projects that create systems within an organization using processes, tools, and languages are themselves systems operating on systems within systems. The ontological point of view addresses the essential knowledge of these systems. While this seems rather abstract and philosophical, it is actually at the core of systems representation and therefore at the core of any knowledge representation we may use — the ontology of a system is how we think about it, including representational modalities and structures (both internal to ourselves, and external in the executable models). While this is a new branch of what software engineering is becoming, it will likely become a critical one as the characteristics of semantic models grow in complexity across the traditional domain boundaries. There are a couple of likely subsets of ontology that will be evident.
- *Model Linguist.* The syntax and semantics of the models we create and the meta-models that govern their behavior will require analysis in the context of peoples' understanding of the models. That is, the model linguist will focus on the mapping of the model onto peoples' understanding modalities. The model syntax will likely include much of what we consider modeling today (icons, directed graphs, etc.) but may also include more esoteric modalities such as stories, games, and other cooperative behaviors.
- *Methodologist.* This is a role we have today, and one that will continue. Closely coupled with the ontologist approach and the model linguist, the methodologist will be mostly concerned with the overall model structure that best represents the domains in question. This

person may operate somewhat in the abstract mode of methodologists today (at the meta-model and higher levels of domain abstraction) but will also operate closely with the Domain Engineer to create methods that work, not just abstractly across wide domain spaces but also specifically for the task at hand. This person will also be responsible for the creation of the executable model types populated by the project as it acquires the necessary knowledge to provide the system to the user.

- *Domain Engineer.* Will occupy the role that the traditional analyst does today. In fact, many successful analysts take exactly this view. The Domain Engineer will interact closely with the User Representative, and in some cases they may be the same person (i.e., the User will interact with the Integrated Tool Set to create combinations of system components that will perform the functions needed). The knowledge area will usually be wider than the typical systems analysis done today, although there is a possibility that domain engineering will become highly specialized and domain engineers might operate in quite narrow areas of specialty rather like, for instance, network capacity engineers work today. The Domain Engineer and the User Representative are primarily responsible for populating the knowledge repository for the systems knowledge. Other disciplines (such as the Process Engineer) might be considered Domain Engineers for their particular domain, which in fact they are.

- *User/Customer Representative.* This role will probably never go away. All the evidence is that successful projects require close participation with someone who is not only knowledgeable in the customer's business but also represents the customer's business. This person will work closely with the Domain Engineer and may be the same person in some cases. As the systems being built and the domain become more and more inseparable, this is likely to become the norm.

- *Repository Engineer.* This role is a significant extension of the software configuration management engineer of today. The repository will not take care of itself, and considerable effort may be needed to maintain it both physically and logically. The Domain Engineer and User Representatives will be primarily responsible for maintaining the external logical integrity (i.e., mapping onto the domain). The Methodologist and Ontologist will primarily be responsible for the internal logical integrity of the repository (the internal syntactic and semantic consistency of the contents of the repository) integrity. The Repository Engineer will be responsible for the physical integrity of the system. Additionally, structural changes made by the Ontologist, Methodologist, or Methods Linguist roles to support the scope and structure changes identified by the Domain Engineer will have to be actioned in the tool set. This role may be spread among these people (or their roles devolved into the Repository Engineer) but someone will have to be in charge of maintaining the integrity of the repository.

- *Anthropologist.* Some companies have already invested in establishing this role. The development of software will continue to be a human cooperative effort for as far as we can predict. The job of this role will be to work on people working together. One of the biggest challenges to developing cooperative ontologies and mental models is that peoples' mental processes are different. Much of the writing on Agile Methods addresses what is needed to get people working together at both conceptual (mental model) and operational (cooperative behavior) levels. This will be the job of the Anthropologist, although it is unlikely that this title will be used.

- *Tester.* This role will, along with the User/Customer Representative, be the most unchanged, although the practicalities of executing the role will be drastically revised. The reason for the relative lack of change, I think, is that the role of testing is the one aspect of software development that really has matured to the point where it truly operates as a knowledge-acquisition process. The testing will operate more on the concepts of the system as demonstrated by the executable models than on the final executing system, but the principle will be the same. Certain kinds of testing will largely disappear, or more correctly will be taken over by the domain constraint checking done within the tool set. It is likely that testing will become considerably more subtle than it is today. For instance, it is possible that the Tester will be responsible for constructing an alternative execution structure to the primary systems representation. With a very rich tool set that is both executable and domain specific, it might be possible for the Tester to create test systems from the sets of executable model components also used to create the system itself. It might be possible to test systems against alternative combinations of their own primitives to find out the similarity/difference in execution. This may go some way toward the paradox of testing that occurs when the system and the test suite are constructed from the same source of information. My guess is that the tester will continue to be not accorded the level of respect due the position. Some things will not change.

- *System Test Representative.* The necessity to integrate the systems and testing activities will require an organizational-level test coordination in much the same way that the resource management will require a point of contact through the Organizational Resource Coordinator. This will be further evidence of the continued importance of testing in software development. It is possible that the System Test Representative will have a set of testing tools quite independent of the development and local Tester. Already in highly integrated

185

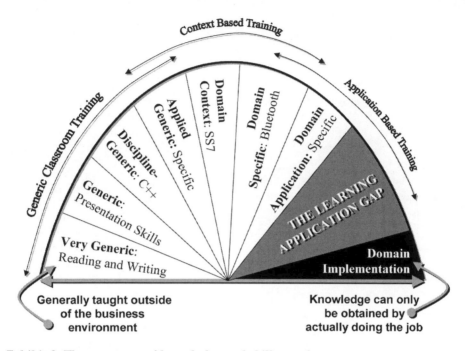

Exhibit 9. The spectrum of knowledge and skill transfer.

systems, we are seeing radically different testing needs at an inter-system level than at the system level. As systems become ever more-highly integrated, this role will undoubtedly grow.

- *Learning Systems Expert.* I left this to last in the list of possible roles for the project of the future because in many ways it is the most important. The reason is simple. Learning is the parallel activities of knowledge acquisition and knowledge integration. It is not the manufacturing of a product. It is not even the application of what is already known. Learning is the discovery of what is not known and the integration of this new knowledge into the body of existing knowledge, with all the paradoxes and restructuring that usually accompanies knowledge addition. This is also the nature of software development.

It is axiomatic that the only thing that can learn, in the sense we usually mean it, is a human brain. And the only thing that can learn a lot of integrated information is a collection of reasonably integrated human brains. The ontology, methodology, linguistics, models, tools, and languages are simply structures we use and places that people put the knowledge they are acquiring and integrating (Exhibit 9). The anthropological viewpoint is the same from the human side of the equation. In essence, it is all learning. Without the learning there is nothing. The systems, tools, and models cannot learn by themselves any more than a requirements document can write itself. Indeed, the purpose of many of the other roles is simply to establish a reasonably effective and efficient learning environment. In association with the tools and methods, there must be attention to the learning activity itself. This learning will operate across a wide spectrum.

This learning activity is so important, that in the organization of the future it will not only become the key component of successful projects, in far-sighted organizations it will become the purpose of the organization. Many people have predicted this, from Peter Senge* to Peter Drucker;** what they did not predict was the medium in which the results of the learning would be deposited.

Software Development as an Educational Activity

There are two primary outputs of a software development project: knowledge stored in software and knowledge stored in peoples' heads. We could also include knowledge stored in documentation but in order for such to actually do anything, it must be transferred back into someone's brain. Although the primary output of the project is the knowledge stored in the software system we ship to the customer, before that knowledge gets into the software it must first get into someone's head. When we consider the implications of knowledge acquisition at the core of systems development, it leads us to the realization that the creation of software is in large part an educational activity. Perhaps this is not so apparent now, because much of what we do in building systems is to apply our existing knowledge repetitively. One of the reasons experienced developers are so sought-after is that they have already learned what they need to know to build certain kinds of systems. Therefore, they can be "more productive" than others who have not yet learned what they need to learn to build systems. But what if we could construct systems that stored and made available all the learning that had taken place to date? What if the existing knowledge was available to all?

We have been seeing the trends in this direction for a number of years. Companies routinely specified, designed, and created their own payroll systems 20 or 30 years ago. Each company, each project, each person had to learn what it takes to build a payroll system. Presumably experienced payroll systems developers were in high demand. We do not do this any more. Those companies that have not outsourced their payroll systems in their entirety tend to use packages — encapsulated knowledge of payroll that is now available to anyone. As foundation class libraries become more

*The Fifth Discipline, Peter M. Senge, Doubleday, New York, 1990.
**Post Capitalist Society, Peter F. Drucker, Harper Collins, New York, 1993.

common, this availability of existing knowledge is increasing.* There is absolutely no reason to believe that this will not continue and even accelerate. So what will happen when most, if not all, of the existing knowledge is available and does not need to be relearned by each person, project, and organization tackling a task for the first time?

At that point the job will become true discovery. The only real work will be the uncovering, deduction, development, or combination of wholly new knowledge constructs. We will spend less and less time on 0OI and 1OI activities, because the processes that employ the known knowledge will be automated and integrated to a very high degree. The developers will spend their time in the 2OI and 3OI areas. This will be learning of a very high degree. It will resemble research more than education. The truly valuable activities will be the ones that uncover the really new and wholly original ideas and make them work.

At this point, we will be presented with a paradox. The development activity will have become an almost 100 percent learning function. But it will be learning of a different sort than we are used to. Most learning paradigms involve three entities: the teacher or teacher surrogate, the knowledge to be learned, and the student. The learning activity involves transporting the knowledge from the teacher (or teaching system) to the student in an efficient way. Good teachers learn to recognize the learning modalities of the students and can modify the teaching process to optimize the learning. But what happens when the teacher does not know? What happens when we do not have the knowledge already so we cannot convey it in a teaching mode? What happens to the processes of teaching and learning under these circumstances?

The most apt description of what must occur to learn effectively is "efficient discovery." The process of learning something that is not yet known can be done efficiently or inefficiently. Each of our life cycle models attempts to be based on this approach. The Waterfall life cycle philosophy is that the most efficient approach is to fully qualify the "what" of the system (the requirements) before we start to learn the "how" of the system. The Agile approach is that you cannot learn certain things about a system until you implement it, so the act of implementing is the most efficient learning mode. In the life cycles of the future there will be two key considerations in learning:

1. How do we train people?
2. How do we most efficiently learn what is needed for this system?

These considerations are not fundamentally different from today, but how we approach them will be radically changed. In many ways we use the

---

*Although as we have seen, at the present much of the learning is occurring not in the target systems domain but in learning the language, prepackaged functions, and object libraries.

process of building systems as one of our primary teaching methods. The problems with this are obvious:

- While people are learning by building systems, they are also building their lack of knowledge into the system they are building.
- The learning process is quite unstructured, often requiring people to learn the same lessons several times until they are able to recognize the commonality of the problems.
- If one person learns something, that knowledge is rarely available to others who have to go through their own unique learning curve on the very same type of problem.
- As people rise through the ranks of development expertise, they are often promoted to levels where they no longer need to use the knowledge they have learned earlier.
- They are, of course, replaced with a new generation of developers who have to undergo the same learning cycle, with all its inefficiencies and negative results on product quality.

When software development is seen as the discovery-and-learning activity that it is, this will have to change. Indeed, this cycle of learning is so inefficient that it is already changing in the areas where we have the capability, with some of the lessons being embedded in packages, languages, libraries, and wizards. The project of the future will approach these issues quite differently.

How Do We Train People?

Exhibit 9 shows a spectrum of learning targets and potential modalities that best address the targets. There are many problems with how we train people today, especially in the traditional classroom setting. Typical training courses tend to:

- Be theoretical
- Be generic and wide ranging
- Not apply to specific issues
- Deal with concepts rather than practicalities
- Leave the application to the student

This leaves a gap between the training event and application of what is learned to do the job.

It is common for engineers to ace a class on software methodology, to fully understand the principles being taught, and to perfectly solve all the classroom problems, yet be quite unable to apply the same principles in their job. They are usually left completely on their own to somehow make the transition from the classroom theory to the workplace application. Given that the application of learning is the primary goal of business learning, it is clearly failing in its mandate.

Levels of Learning

There are degrees of "specificness" of any learning activity that range from very generic to very specific. We can stratify these into overlapping levels of learning:

- Very generic learning programs cover basic human skills that are needed and used across wide ranges of human activity. An example is the ability to read and write. This kind of learning usually occurs in schools and is expected to be basic skills of most employees.
- Generic skills are those skills which are usable across a wide range of domains. These may or may not be learned as a job-based activity. An example of this kind of learning is training and experience in presentation skills.
- Discipline generic skills are those which generically apply across a discipline An example of this is generalized programming language training as in teaching C++ or Perl, for example. This kind of learning occurs both in specialized schools and in the context of business training. Usually, it is expected that full facility in the language is obtained through use in a real application environment.
- Applied generic skills are taught as modified by the framework in operation in the business. Typical examples of this include, for example, SEI CMM assessment process training targeted at the way that assessments are done in a particular company. Because these programs are becoming specific to a way of doing business, they are not usually taught in a scholastic environment but are developed for a particular business.
- Domain context skills are generalized engineering knowledge that is applied across a specific engineering domain. An example is teaching someone ITU's Signaling System Seven (SS7 or C7) global standard for telecommunications. It includes generalized elements of telecommunications and processor intercommunication loosely based on ISO's Open Systems Interconnect (OSI). However, it also contains much of the design of systems that conform to this protocol.
- Domain-specific skills involve learning the modification of a generalized domain that is used in a particular area of implementation. An example is learning the Bluetooth wireless technology as it applies to Ericsson or Motorola platforms, for example. Such learning is necessarily quite close to the application area where it is used, and is almost always developed by practitioners.
- Domain application learning is close to the domain-specific learning except it includes very specific implementations. Here the learning operates on the actual project and product.
- Domain implementation is the most detailed level of learning. It occurs while actually doing the job. This is the resolution of 2OI and 1OI necessary to complete the project. It is not training as much as

doing. This kind of learning cannot be removed from where the learning occurs, although sometimes the lessons learned can be abstracted into the earlier levels of learning.

These levels overlap. Some of the levels would not be taught in a business context (e.g., very generic). Others are commonly taught in discipline schools (e.g., in college engineering curricula) or are developed external to the business. As the learning becomes more and more specific, the involvement of the business in the creation and delivery of the learning must increase, because the content largely references knowledge that is present only in the business.

At the most detailed level, there is only one place that this learning can occur — on the specific project solving the specific problem in building the specific product.

How Do We Learn Most Efficiently for this System?

Plaguing most learning activities is the Learning Application Gap. This is the difference between what is taught and what must be learned to actually do the job. In many classroom-based learning processes the gap is very wide.* One of the challenges facing the project of the future will be to narrow this Learning Application Gap. It can never be closed for the same reason we can never be sure we do not have Second Order Ignorance. But because most of the effort on a project is this learning, and in the future it may be all of the effort and all of the value, we must do things to make the learning more effective.

If we look at the widest ends of the learning spectrum we can see some of the choices. On the left-hand side are the generic learning levels. These are the general life skills and highly abstracted engineering skills. These will probably continue to be taught generically. We would never consider putting illiterate persons on a development project, expecting them to learn to read and write on the project — this would be way too inefficient. Equally, we could not conceive of developing classroom training for very specific implementations for several reasons: very few people would need to know that particular level of detail; the level of detail would mask some of the generalized concepts that people could reuse elsewhere; we do not have access to what we need to know to create the learning experience — if we did, we would have already learned whatever it was and would not need to have the learning experience at all.

---

*This has been my experience in nearly 15 years of training software engineers. I have likened most methodology training to teaching people the rules of chess, and the real-world application of the methodology to playing a good game of chess. Knowing the rules of chess is not the same thing as knowing how to play chess. It is what mathematicians call a "necessary but not sufficient condition."

In the middle of the spectrum the picture is cloudier. Presently, much professional systems development learning operates at too high a level. There are several reasons for this. The primary reason is that it is easier and cheaper to create generic training than it is to create specific training. To make any educational experience domain specific, the educational experience designer must have that domain experience and knowledge. The more domain specific the learning, the less applicable the learning will be across wider ranges of audiences. Simple economics as applied to most educational establishments both within businesses and in schools dictate that courses are more cost effective if more people can benefit from them. The project of the future must address this issue, particularly around the Learning Application Gap. If the only truly- and immediately-effective training is training that can be applied to specific domain environments, that is where the learning must occur. Currently, much learning occurs offline. This means people do the work over here but go to training over there. When learning is the job, this cannot continue.

In the project of the future, the executable models that encapsulate the acquired knowledge being created by the project will also become the learning environment. Higher levels of model abstraction will have "learning modalities" associated with them. These could well be methods defined for abstract classes of objects that control their creation in a learning or demonstration mode. We see some capability in today's packages, where key elements or procedures can be "walked through" to teach people how to use them. Usually this capability is separated from the actual operation but sometimes it is not. Sometimes the "show me" operation actually does the work that it is trying to teach the person to do. Of course, like any process, this can only be done for things we know how to do. But this capability would extend the purpose of the systems we are building to include some of the knowledge of how to build them. Tools and models will have "learning modes" built into them.

So much for teaching people what we already know how to do. Extending this idea further, what about the things we do not know how to do? We cannot create a training program for 2OI by definition. We would not know what to include in the training program. What these executable models could do is create a learning environment in which experiments could be conducted to uncover 2OI. That is, as we build the system, it would inherit (from the process and project domains; see Exhibit 3 in Chapter 5) tools such as prototyping shells and testing harnesses. These would allow the developer to experiment with different solutions and different combinations of executable elements, run them, and even conduct some evaluation of the results to determine which works best. This basic cycle actually occurs today, especially in high maturity organizations effectively using Agile approaches — the developers quickly put together feasibility prototypes, run them, modify them, learn from them, modify them again, measure results, and circle closer and closer to an optimal solution. People work this way because (1) its is an effective and efficient way of working and (2) we now have the computing horsepower and tool sets locally available to do it. As the tool sets become more powerful, more executable, and more domain specific, this will become the way we learn and the way we build systems.

The executable domain-specific system models, with their varying levels of abstraction, coupled with the executable process and project and management environments will provide almost all of the learning environment necessary. Probably there will be some core generic functions that continue to be taught generically but they will quickly give way to this graduated learning modality based on live interaction with the domain systems.

At this point, the activities of learning, learning how to build the system, and building the system become inseparable. They always were but our social and business structures kept them separated. Anyone who has ever taken part in a worthwhile project will confess that it was a learning experience. If we analyze what we learned and when on such a project, we see that the generic learning we possessed coming into the project merely provided the context in which what we learned on the project was assimilated. It also allowed us to absorb generic skills (such as basic programming language capability) without having it complicated and involved with the activity of learning the domain of application. Beyond that, what we really learned was learned on the job. The most visceral education and the only source of wisdom occurs while actually attempting to do the job. The training can prepare us by allowing us to be in the most receptive mode but the only learning occurs at the point of discovery.

Controlled Failure

Adults learn primarily from failure. If we are successful at something it is either due to skill or blind luck. If we already have the skill, we do not learn anything. For jobs of a reasonable complexity, we are unlikely to be lucky enough to produce the right answer right away. We usually acquire the knowledge by trying our best and finding that it is not good enough. In the right environment, we are encouraged to change our approach, our methods or process, and our thinking to attempt to arrive at a more-optimal solution. Often, the second, third, or fourth attempt also "fails." But in the right environment each of them is a step toward a better result. And in each step we learn. Each step is a "failure" if we take the perspective of creating a product but it can be a success if we view it from the point of view of knowledge acquisition. The challenge is to make this failure more controlled.

Presently, we learn most on the project. The trouble is, we tend to capture our misunderstandings into the product along with our understandings. It is to remove some of these that the Agile approaches recommend a "refactoring" activity. Currently, software projects are somewhat uncontrolled failures that result in uncontrolled learning activities. This must change. As the executable mode tool set becomes more comprehensive, integrated, and domain specific, it can become a place where "failure" can by tried and tested. Requirements models of flow charts can be made to "flow" to see what happens. Design models can execute, use resources, interact with other systems, interact with their environment, in simulated ways or in real, live execution ways. From these interactions, we can learn.

As we play with the systems and reconfigure them, add functions, change interfaces, devise and execute tests, the systems we are interacting with can learn from us. Such systems would be the brainy descendents of our primitive configuration management systems, managing not just the physical existence of the software artifacts but also their relationships with other artifacts in the domain, in other domains, in the project, and in the development environment. As we learn something, these systems will snapshot it. They will catalog it and store it. They will maintain the relationships of the artifact with all the other artifacts with which it has associations, the symbiosis of human learning and machine storage of knowledge to radically change what we currently know as software engineering.

The Project

Brandon was late to work that day. Traffic was getting so bad, despite the ubiquitous telecommuting. There were always so many people who lived over here but needed to be over there. Of course, if they lived over there, then they would need to be over here, Brandon mused to himself. The team would complain good naturedly about physically coming into work. But he could not. Brandon had called the meeting.

Yan-Ping met Mayank on the stairs up to the office on the second floor. "Hi, Mayank, what's up? Looks like The Shrink brought in everybody." Brandon's nickname within the project was "The Shrink." But Brandon was not a psychiatrist, he was a psychologist and anthropologist by training. Brandon used to joke, "I did my Masters studying the behavior of children and that prepared me for Kdev." Kdev or "knowledge development" was what the "devvers" on the project did. Years ago, it might have been called software engineering, and they might have been called software engineers but nobody uses the word "software" much any more, not since *everything* was software.

Maria, Hafsa, Jill, and Praveen were already in the media room where the meeting was to take place when Yan-Ping and Mayank walked in. They spent a few minutes catching up on each others' news as they waited for everyone to arrive. Praveen was the resource coordinator. He had been in early this morning, choosing to work at the office rather than from home. It had been a busy morning.

Praveen's Morning

After getting his early morning tea, Praveen went through the complicated process of logging in and authorizing his session on the system. There were many levels to 'rizing, as it was known, and it never seemed to get simpler. "The price we pay for global systems." Praveen sighed as the thumbprint reader scanned the prints on his right hand. Passed. Next he peered through the eyepiece for the retina scan, and entered his password and his cert code from the cert chip in his watch.

So much security, he thought, just to prove I'm me.

The snoop test scanned the machine and environment for agents and devices that might capture keystrokes or screenshots. Clean.

The machine knew his routine and had brought up his assignment screen. He navigated through a complex three-dimensional maze of images and icons. Of course it was not complex to Praveen, because he had designed it. Well, borrowed it anyway. He zeroed in on the project status elements. Somewhere in cyberspace there was the project. Probably all over cyberspace. Nobody really knew where anything was kept anymore. Not that it mattered. "Hey, I don't know where I keep my knowledge of squash," Mayank had said the other day between breaks in a game. "It's not necessary as long as I can retrieve enough of it to beat you, Praveen!" he laughed. Mayank and Praveen regularly played squash once a week, and Praveen was looking for Mayank's profile.

Praveen parked the project view on one side of the screen and brought up Mayank's profile. At the highest level, it was an icon derived from the Devanagari script character *ma*. This was Mayank's mark. Praveen moused over the icon and it expanded; he rotated the pointer with a practiced flip of his wrist and the scene rotated. Mayank's calendar opened up. Praveen could see Mayank's progress on his current task, a set of logic elements to calculate network load balancing. Punching down, Praveen could see the test metrics looked very favorable. He did not quite understand what they meant but then he did not need to. It was not his job. Mayank had set the autotester running overnight and the comparator seemed to indicate the logic configuration was at least as good as any other available system of this type for which they had data. The performance improvement curve over the last few releases also matched the optimal spec.

Mayank's good, Praveen thought, not for the first time. He's nearly done, time to give him some more.

On the project side, Praveen flicked his wrist to bring up the domain view of the project, and searched for the network loading and logic optimizing domains — these were Mayank's strong suit. Clicking one of the task icons brought up the database. The model seemed rather unfinished, and a trial run showed gaps.

Well, this should keep him busy, thought Praveen as he steered the icon representing this chunk of work over Mayank's *ma* and dropped it. He added a little annotation and a greeting to welcome Mayank to his new work.

Mayank's Morning

Truth to tell, Mayank had forgotten the meeting until he logged in. Luckily, he was a early riser. Once the machine started and he was rized domain, he navigated to his domain. The autotester had configured correctly. Good. The results looked good. Time to go to press. He collected the task elements with the task net icon and dropped the whole lot on the complete stack. Either the whole set would go on to Hafsa or perhaps Praveen would reassign, depending on the configuration.

But I'm done for now, he thought with a sense of satisfaction. Mayank liked to get things completed. He flipped back into the project maze and started navigating across the work products and models. He found a part of Yan-Ping's remote setup procedure and tried to follow the model. It was an unusual model. Yan-Ping and Maria had devised a notation system that added elements at varying distances from system factors. The distances seemed to mean something. Mayank navigated to the meta-model to inspect the rules. A few minutes of looking at the rules clarified some aspects and confused him about others. He made a note to ask them about it.

Probably one of Maria's brainchildren, he thought. Maria was the company's Ontologist and Methodologist or "methontologist" as she liked to call herself. It was her job to work with the devvers to create the model syntax they used to do their jobs.

Some ontologists are standards freaks, thought Mayank, and they always want to have you conform to some standard notational system.

Maria was not one of these. She had thought up some pretty wild model types in her time. Sometimes they were hard to understand and difficult to use. But sometimes they took your thoughts down a really different path than the one normally traveled.

Mayank's musings were interrupted by the appearance of a new icon on the screen and in his calendar.

"Oops, The Shrink's called a meeting this morning. I forgot. And what is this?" he peered at the screen "Praveen's up early this morning, he's already given me more work." Mayank clicked on the icon and many things happened.

The icon on Mayank's screen was "sent" to him by Praveen dropping the task on Mayank's *ma* icon. Mayank's icon keyed into the structure in the Resource and Environment repository or repos, as it was called. This structure represented Mayank. In a way, it was an analogue of the man. There were elements in the model (the "standard" model for devvers this time, not one of Maria's inventions — this had been mostly created at U.S.C.) that represented most of the key attributes of Mayank — his expertise areas, his authorizations, his addresses, and access modes. These matched the nature of the task allocated to him by Praveen's wrist flick; otherwise, warnings would have flashed that he was not "eligible" for the task. The task itself mostly pointed to a collection of interacting models in the Product and System Models repos. These models mostly inherited their formats from the Standards and Process Models repos. Different types of systems had different types of models. What you could do with the knowledge was pretty well defined by the SPM repos models. Well, until Maria got hold of them anyway.

Mayank clicked on the task and it expanded. Mayank's tool set was quite different from Praveen's and he chose not to use too many tweaks. Half of the project would have been able to use Mayank's tool set without changes. Some people liked to create their own but Mayank did not see the need.

"Just as easy to train yourself to a standard," he had asserted in one of his occasional debates with Hafsa.

Hafsa was the project tester and a fan of customizing everything. Merely clicking on the icon did not activate it for work but did let Mayank browse it: mostly standard models, functional, object, and state. The state models had a specific methods set that pointed to another timing model that Mayank had helped design. This allowed very-large-scale calculations of average switching time and throughput on the system while it was still in a design stage.

Saves lots of time, thought Mayank, a sight better than finding out by building it anyway.

He had been thinking of some improvements to the model just the other day. There were situations they had found where the behavior predicted by the model did not match what they built. They were a special set of conditions, and Mayank thought the model could be adjusted to allow for them. As he scanned the rest of the model set, he could see it was quite incomplete.

Lots of work to be done here, he thought as he clicked open the notation from Praveen. It read "Lots of work to be done here. Have a nice day. P." Funny guy. Mayank accepted the work by dragging the icon over to his stack. He closed down his session and made ready to go to work, leaving the system to set him up for the work. As Mayank was driving to work, the system integrated the working models by moving them into Mayank's protected area in the Project Model repos. It stamped all the model components with his authorization and locked out the originals, creating a separate revision for any changes that might be needed elsewhere in the change set. The model elements already populated in the Product and System Model repos were scanned and compared with the project templates from the Standards and Process Models repos. The closest match found generated a task set and populated Mayank's calendar with it. Now he had a plan. The system models were matched up against Mayank's tool set requirements. There were no adjustments necessary, one of the advantages of "going standard" that Mayank would usually wave in Hafsa's face during their regular but good-natured disagreements. Hafsa had his own way of doing things.

Hafsa's Morning

Hafsa had not gotten up as early as the others. He had remembered the meeting but had decided he needed to work the test plan a little before leaving. He had spent a long time yesterday hunting for the right test cases. These search engines still need work, he thought. Sometime in the night an idea had come to him and was still with him when he woke up. He wanted to try it before his busy day pushed the idea way. Bringing up the function, he stared at it for awhile. Unlike most of the work products, this was a command-line model, what would have been called "code" a few years ago. It was a little different from code he had seen before, because whoever had created the model had included the capability of having tabular code and sets of commands arranged in tables. He checked the records and saw that this model type was developed by Maria's predecessor.

Well, if we can't integrate the model type, perhaps we should reconsider it, he thought.

He could create tests for most of the code with a couple of clicks. They were standard predicate-based control statements. The interfaces to the routine were all domain-generated and the domain library would create both test cases and test profiles. He had just needed to run them and run the profile analysis. About 90 percent of the issues would be flagged by the analysis. He had data to show this. But these tables...

The code was dotted throughout with tables. Most were two or three columns but he found a couple at four and five. He also found references within the columns to other columns. And he had not been able to find suitable test frameworks for it. The author had included a primitive train and Hafsa executed it. A "train" was a method associated with a model component whose purpose was to assist someone in learning what the model did. In the olden days, it would have been called "documentation" and it would have been totally passive. Someone had described this to Hafsa.

"You have to read it, right, that I understand." Hafsa had been puzzled by the explanation. "But what does it do?" When it was explained that the documentation did not actually do anything, Hafsa was baffled why anyone would include such a low-value artifact at all. This train was quite crude but it did work. It ran through the syntax. Hafsa stopped a few times and ran it backwards to make sure he knew what it was doing. Each table, it seemed, ran more or less independently. The "code" ran consecutively until it hit a table; then, depending on the system conditions, one or all of the table columns would run concurrently. They were complicated by having some capability of interacting between columns. Hafsa was not sure under what circumstances a column would wait to synchronize or carry on without sync-ing. He had had an idea in the night to convert some of the model predicates and retry the search. This time he struck gold. A test harness for a very similar system popped up. Unfortunately, its syntax and semantic was quite different. But it was a start. He parceled up the ideas and dropped them on the Methodologist stack. This would be a good one for Maria.

Maria's Morning

Maria was actually on her way to work when the pager announced the message. She scanned the message quickly while at a stop light. From Hafsa. It looked interesting. She had not actually seen the code/table model. Well, not exactly; she'd played around with something similar a while ago but thought some extensions to existing models would do the job just as well. With a few minutes before the meeting, she opened her toolkit, which was radically different from any other on the project, including the self-designed tool she called her meta-meta-analyzer-analyzer. This was her pet project, and the tool attempted to walk through models and meta-models and abstract their meta characteristics (using a notational system Maria had devised) to allow a comparison between knowledge domains. It was a work-in-progress but sometimes it drove out unexpected ideas. The name, she had said, was not technically correct.

"I shouldn't strictly call it a meta-meta-analyzer-analyzer," she had explained to a baffled Praveen a few days earlier. "It's not linear meta-meta, it's more like embedded or hologrammatic. Perhaps I should call it a me(meta-analyzer)ta-analyzer? Anyway, it's more like meta(meta)→meta."

Sometimes Maria just lost people. There were not many methontologists around, which was probably a good thing, Praveen thought privately.

Before leaving for the meeting, Maria made a note to discuss meta-meta with the repos engineer, Jill. She dropped the note as she signed off and headed for the meeting.

Jill's Morning

"You have to have one of the most thankless tasks, Jill," commented Praveen as they met up in the hallway and walked together to the media room. "How do you keep track of everything? I mean, I just have my resource section and sometimes I think that's too complicated. You've got the whole thing. How do you do it?"

Jill thought for a moment before replying. She usually thought carefully before doing anything. She needed to. As the repos engineer, she was responsible for managing the entire repository for the project. She also had to act as liaison with other company repos engineers to ensure the project data meshed with the rest of the company. It was a complex and detailed job. Luckily, Jill was a very detailed person. "It can be a challenge, I admit," she said. "It seems as soon as I get everything all neatly tied up, Maria or Hafsa or somebody changes things around. The good news is that many of the areas, yours for instance, are really well defined, standardized. and static."

To Jill's mind. static was a good thing. However, she realized that the dynamic nature of the knowledge they were working with was just the nature of the job and without changes to manage, she would not have a job. Praveen's area was indeed static. The resource management models and tool set were as standardized as any. Project management was one of the first areas to be computerized years ago. It was funny though, thought Jill, how we still need people to work these systems. You can have the best management model in the world, and you still need a good manager to interpret it, and sometimes overrule it too. Sometimes Jill wondered if they would ever get resource management fully automated. Probably not as long as it requires people, she thought.

Jill was responsible for literally thousands of interacting models, each of which could be in dozens of versions of design, and each design containing hundreds of variations of knowledge stored in them. Luckily, she thought, I do not have to understand the content or maintain the knowledge base. That is the job of the Ontologist and the Domain Engineers. However, she knew all of them and interacted very closely with them all day. It was amazing how many things people could do to the models that would cause them to disconnect. If the truth were known, the disconnects caused by model changes were one of the sources of greatest information generation on the project, something that Jill suspected but had never tracked. Her role, an extension of the old responsibility of software configuration management, was often considered a secondary and support role on the project.

The Meeting

"Hey, thanks for coming in," said Brandon to the assembled team. "Before I start, I'd like to introduce John." He waved his hand toward a tall, sandy-haired man standing at the back of the room. "John is our Learning Engineer."

A murmur spread around the room. The job of Learning Engineer had never been filled on this project, and only one other project in the whole company had one. Among the more-technical people and domain engineers, it was considered a bit of a fad.

"Just more searching for a silver bullet," Maria had shared with Praveen when they had talked about the concept a few weeks earlier. "It's not like it's one of the really important roles on a project," she said.

"Not like an Ontologist, you mean?" asked Praveen with a slight smile, "or even a Methontologist?" Praveen was unfailingly polite, and it was hard sometimes to see when he was joking.

It seemed to pass by Maria. "Right," she said, "or even an ancient role like project manager." She said it with an entirely straight face. "But it seems like one of those touchy-feely things that our resident Shrink would dream up."

Brandon was actually well respected on the team, and had done much to help the team gel into its present level of high performance, as anyone would admit. They still poked fun at him, and Brandon understood fully that the kidding was part of the role. But he also recognized that some elements were missing.

"This hasn't exactly been a secret," said Brandon, "John and I and Yan-Ping have been working together for several weeks. I know some of you are a little skeptical of the concept of a 'Learning Engineer,' so I wanted to demonstrate why I think we need John's expertise."

Brandon flashed up some animations on the media wall. "I'm running some snapshots of the system repos over the last couple of months." A huge spiderweb of models appeared on the wall and started changing, growing in some areas, and shrinking in others. "At the same time, I'm showing discovery metrics against inter-model disconnects. You'll recognize some of these, eh, Jill?" A chart started growing in one pane as the models changed and changed again. "As you can see, there is a direct correlation between these discoveries and disconnects." The graph was quite explicit.

"Okay, I see the relationship," said Praveen, "but what does that mean? He added hastily, "I mean, in words I can understand," because it looked like Maria was about to offer an explanation.

"Can I suggest we ask the learning expert? John?" Brandon gestured for John to step forward.

"What it means in simple English," said John, smiling at Praveen's exaggerated look of relief, "is that the team is learning some of the most important lessons and getting some of its most critical data by generating domain views that conflict."

"Is that bad?" asked Jill. "I mean, I know better than anyone how much pain the model disconnects are but at least we're finding the stuff."

"No, it's not bad," said John, stressing the last word, "but it's also not very efficient. If it weren't for your efforts, Jill, there would be a lot more wheel spinning. I also have some data that indicate it's getting worse."

"That's the way it feels to me," said Jill. "I talked to Brandon about it a while ago."

"Which is why I collected this data and invited John along," said Brandon. "This is a very high functioning team but I've been observing some issues with communication and coordination of peoples' mental models." There was a very slight groan from a few people. When Brandon mentioned "mental models," it usually meant that some psychological testing was about to happen. But not this time.

"We've gone a long way toward learning to work very efficiently together," said Brandon, "but it may be too slow, and perhaps we can learn faster. John and I and Yan-Ping have developed something that we're going to work together on over the next two weeks." He clicked the mouse and a new pane opened on the media wall. A big one. In it were pictures of the project team, all of them. "Welcome to your virtual selves," said Brandon "and your virtual team." People stared at each other around the room.

"This is a project simulator," Brandon continued into the slightly stunned silence. "We have programmed it with you." He waved his hand across the room. "The avatars in the simulation have been set up to make decisions as you would make them based on what I know about you, which, as you know, is quite a lot. Yan-Ping in his role as Process Engineer has programmed the simulator to duplicate our processes in microcosm, and John has programmed in a series of situations that resemble challenges we have faced and will face. We're going to play project."

"Cool" said someone into the silence.

"Why?" said Maria. "What will we get out of this?"

"Controlled failure," said John. "We will play this game and see what we learn. If we make 'mistakes,' we can go back and try something else. We can't do that in real life. Well, not without costing the company a lot of money. The simulation isn't you. It's not the real world. It's not as complex nor as rich. But it'll help us see how we can change and then let us practice it before we do it for real. Well, actually, while we do it for real."

"Who knows?" said Brandon, "perhaps we can get 50 to 70 percent of the learning out on the simulator? John is confident that processing our issues and decisions in a radically different way will let us see different solutions and ways of working. It's not unlike Maria building different model modalities for you."

"It kind of looks like a game," said John, "but it's not. It's just like the real thing. It's all about learning."

Summary

The project described in this chapter is obviously fictitious but it follows the precepts we have laid down. The technologies described are already available at a foundation level. Many projects have managers and team leaders who act as psychologists. Configuration management systems for complex projects in high maturity organizations are able to control very complex scenarios and allow rich and detailed management of sets of work products. Engineers routinely create their own tool sets for the specific needs that their jobs present. In highly coherent teams, these tool sets are shared and combined to create powerful automated tools that span functions and domains within the project. Any engineer worth his or her salt researches what is available before creating additional work products. Good teams constantly look at how they work, where they are spending time, making mistakes, and learning. They strive to optimize that learning. They work to accelerate it where they can, to minimize rework, to practice in the small before they have to commit to the work that they will deliver to the customer.

Perhaps the greatest change is not in the tools and processes or in the roles and methods; it is in the shared understanding of the core purpose of the team. This future will come for the simple reason that it must. The purpose of software is to store knowledge and the purpose of those who create knowledge is to acquire the knowledge that is to be stored. Everything else in the business is secondary. The individuals, teams, companies, and societies that are first to realize this and act on it will so utterly revolutionize the business that the effect on human society cannot be easily predicted. As with any leap forward, the risks and the spoils will go to those who accept the challenge of the fifth medium of knowledge.

Appendix A
The Five Knowledge Storage Media

A man must carry knowledge with him,
If he would bring home knowledge.

— **Samuel Johnson**
Boswell's Life of Johnson

Knowledge

What is "knowledge?"

All natural language is imprecise.* While there are some advantages to this imprecision, it does sometimes cause difficulty in defining and sharing our understanding of things. The ambiguity of language is a natural result of language evolution and different domains of use. Even words that are quite well defined and generally accepted may have several distinct meanings, as any dictionary will attest. Most languages have the capacity to infer additional meaning in words by their context (the meaning of the words surrounding them) or by their order. In the spoken word, a lot of the meaning is carried by the tone by which the word is spoken. Sometimes words have specific meanings to specific groups of people, and the different groups' interpretations may vary. Sometimes the same word spoken by one person means something quite different if spoken by someone else.

The word "knowledge" is one such word; it is a broad word with many meanings. It is used extensively in this book, and I would like to clear up an issue that has prompted some discussion. Epistemology — the study and science of knowledge — is large, complex, and highly recursive, and a general review of the subject is beyond the scope of this book. People have classified knowledge into taxonomies and hierarchies. One taxonomy** has "knowledge" divided into:

*Noam Chomsky, in *Powers and Prospects* (South End Press, Boston, 1996), stated that two people are no more likely to share a "common language" than they are to share a common surface area.
**Russell Ackoff, one of the founders of the concept of Systems Thinking, developed a similar taxonomy. His divisions were Data, Information, Knowledge, Understanding, and Wisdom. See Ackoff, R., *Ackoff's Best: His Classic Writings on Management*, Jossey-Bass, San Francisco, 1999.

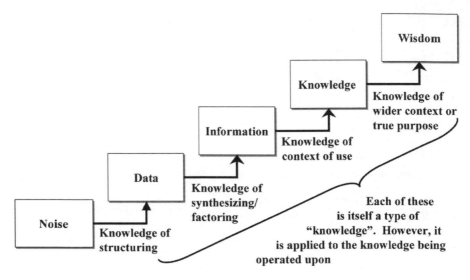

Exhibit 1. A hierarchy of knowledge.

- Noise
- Data
- Information
- Knowledge
- Wisdom

This classification, which can be a useful one in context, is highly Information Technology oriented (see Exhibit 1). Noise is undifferentiated input. Structuring noise to some extent, e.g., by defining and labeling elements of it, produces data. Synthesizing data by manipulating it in some arithmetic or logical way, such as by adding data items together, produces information. Understanding the information in some context of use provides knowledge, and using that knowledge in a wider context — in an appropriately useful way — exhibits wisdom.

There is a surrounding shell of knowledge that is not explicit, but is strongly implied in this hierarchy: just *how* does one "structure" noise to create data? Specifically what kind of factoring transforms data into information or defines the acceptable and appropriate use that turns information into knowledge? Obviously, the answers to these questions imply that we obtain additional knowledge; I (or something) must "know" how to perform this structuring activity. Equally, any synthesis I apply to data to make it into information requires the knowledge of how to perform that synthesis. At the "higher" levels, I not only have to know how to structure things, I need to know *why* and in what context to perform these operations. These are all more varieties of "knowledge." In this book I have cut through this confusing situation, bypass the taxonomy issue almost entirely, and simply describe all of the above as "knowledge."

Knowledge, therefore, may be knowledge embedded in a relatively undifferentiated form, as in noise or data, although the implication will always be that, in order to actually use the knowledge, there must exist a way to process the noise to produce something more useful. There is an even stronger assumption that, if it is *classified* as knowledge, someone or something actually does process the noise. Equally, the knowledge may be moderately processed, highly processed contextual, or it may be knowledge of the knowledge-processing operation. For my purposes it is all knowledge. As to wisdom, while we could discuss it at length and we could apply our atomist and taxonomist tools to piece it apart, I do not think it would clarify the situation much and I think other sources are more qualified to do this than I.

Another issue I wish to clarify is that of the presence or absence of a "knower." Can we have knowledge without someone, specifically a person, knowing? I believe the answer is both yes and no. The source of these contradictory answers lies in the creation of knowledge, which I will argue does require a "knower," and the storage and use of knowledge, which I think does not. Ultimately, I believe that, at an entirely practical level, only a human can qualify something as *being* knowledge. As far as I am aware, machines have no opinion on the matter. Only humans can ultimately determine "correctness" and that, whatever an artifact might be, it is not truly "knowledge" by my definition until a human validates ("knows") it.

This is certainly true in a practical sense when we consider, for instance, the testing of a computer system. Once a human has passed judgment on the operation of the program and labeled it "correct" (it contains the necessary knowledge), machines can certainly *store* and *execute* it thereafter. Simply put, in this world-view, machines may store and execute knowledge, but they cannot create it.

A final issue that may confront readers is the recursive nature of knowledge* of any description. Self-reference and its associated recursion seem to be innate characteristics of knowledge and are the direct cause of a number of the apparent paradoxes that occur in software development, in much the same way that self-referential logic is the source of paradoxical statements (such as *"everything I say is a lie"*). Recursive logic obeys significantly different rules than "traditional" logic** and exploring its intricacies is itself a rewarding occupation. We will content ourselves here with noting the paradoxes as they occur.

*For a complex but satisfying discussion on this, I would suggest Maturana, H.R. and Varela, F.J., *The Tree of Knowledge,* Shambala, Boston, 1987.
**Hofstadter, D.J. and Goedel Escher, B., *An Eternal Golden Braid.*

Perhaps readers will have their own views of what is and is not knowledge. I have to use *some* word to describe the subject of this book, and the word "knowledge" is the closest one I can find to the meaning I intend.

A Brief History of Knowledge Storage

DNA

We do not know how it started. There is spectroscopic evidence of the presence of free radical and small molecules of carbon, hydrogen, oxygen, nitrogen, and silicon — the elements that make up organic materials and, ultimately, life — that float in the spaces between planets and between stars. These particles are certainly widely spaced, but then space itself is wide, and the catchment area swept out by our solar system and our planet is large. In the approximately 4.55 billion years our planet has existed, it would have swept up substantial amounts of these atomic and molecular building blocks. Perhaps it originally came from space?

Stanley Miller's 1953 experiments at the University of Chicago* using a soup of hydrogen, ammonia, methane, and water vapor subjected to electrical discharges showed the potential for the creation of at least the amino acids that are the components of proteins. These electrical discharges are presumed similar to those that happened in the violent storms that shook our planet around 4 billion years ago, and may have provided the basis for life. This much we know. The next steps, the development of amino acids into proteins and then into RNA, are highly conjectural. In a mechanism that is not at all well understood, the amino acids probably developed into nucleotides, and possibly through pseudo-cellular structures into structures akin to what we label as ribonucleic acid (RNA). At some point these proto-RNA structures became capable of copying themselves, of replicating at least portions of their chemical structure. The steps after this are better known, and some, such as the evolution of RNA structures, have been demonstrated in the laboratory (see Exhibit 2).**

The development from unstructured strands of chemicals into cell structures is another blank spot in our understanding, but at around this time, the chemical machinery was set up that would allow the input of information from the "outside." Conditions external to these chemical strings could now have an effect on the content, chemical structure, or ordering of chemical structures, of that string; and with the string's ability to replicate itself, that "information" would be transported through time, and from one string to another.

*Craig, H., Miller, S.L., and Wasserburg, G.J., Eds., *Isotopic and Cosmic Chemistry,* North Holland, Amsterdam, 1963.
**Bishop, D.H.L, Claybrook, J.R., and Spiegelman, S., Electrophoretic separation of viral nucleic acids on polyacrimide gels, *J. Mol. Biol.,* 26: 373-87 1967.

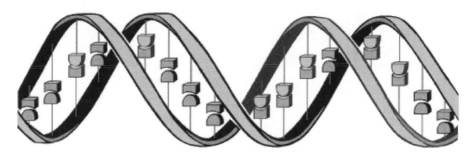

Exhibit 2. DNA.

This development proceeded through many other stages: mitochondrial cords, and the wrapping of RNA into double strands of DNA; the development of archeobacteria, single- and multi-celled organisms; through the selective differentiation of cell types into species; then further differentiation into both the speciation we see today and the variation of cell design and function within animals and plants. With this mechanism the first knowledge storage was achieved.

DNA was the first knowledge medium.

When a wildebeest calf is born on the grasslands of northern South Africa, it is able to stand and run away from predators within a few minutes of birth. How does it "know" how to do that? Where is the knowledge of running away stored? How does it "know" that a hyena is dangerous? How does it "know" that its mother is nurturing? How did this knowledge originate and where is it kept?

As humans, we have many degrees of behavioral freedom, but we cannot consciously control much of what we do. Our endocrine and our circulatory systems work without our having to learn how to work them. Where in the human body is the set of instructions for an endocrine system? How do those instructions get into the body?

The answer is that this information is stored in the DNA of each of these animals. Through mechanisms that are probably very complex and are certainly not well understood, the "knowledge" of certain kinds of operations — running away, the production of insulin, the recognition of predators, the recognition and response to nurturing parents — are encoded into chemical strands in the genetic coding of the creature and passed from generation to generation. Because this information is "learned" by the species, it does not have to be "learned" by individuals.

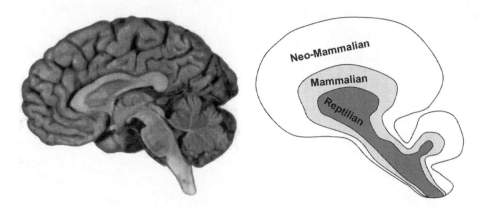

Exhibit 3. Brain. Copyright © Wellcome Department of Imaging Neuroscience, University College, London, England. Used with permission.

Brains

Between eight and five million years ago, it is widely believed, the first recognizable ancestors of present-day humans evolved.* It is as if nature used the human race to conduct an experiment. Certain clusters of nerve cells clumped together in ways that had not perhaps occurred before. All nerve cells have some information retention capability; it is part of their function. However, our Australopithecine ancestors were probably some of the first to possess a set of nerve cells with significantly different capabilities; they could learn substantial and useful behavioral modalities and adjust and optimize their actions based on that learning. While all animals have some capacity to learn, most of them have little ability to adjust their behavior over anything other than a very narrow range. The human brain seems to be significantly different in this function and capability. It can store knowledge, then erase it, then add it again, build on it, extrapolate from it, and interpolate within it. It can develop concepts that do not exist in the "outside world," it can create and store knowledge that does not otherwise exist and has no recognizable analogue in the outside world. The human body has a lot of instinctual operations, such as the functioning of the pancreas, but relatively little instinctual (DNA stored) behavior. For the most part, humans learn their behavior. It gives us a tremendous range of operations, but the price we pay for this is a long lead-time. It takes us a long time to grow up and become fully functional, to separate from our parents and become self-sufficient. The advantage is we can live almost anywhere. The human race can survive in the Sahara Desert and at the North Pole, when it has stored the appropriate knowledge in its brains.

The brain was the second knowledge medium (see Exhibit 3).

*See Gould, S.J., *The Structure of Evolutionary Theory,* Harvard University Press, Boston, 2002.

Hardware

Man has been called *"tool maker."* That was the name (Homo Habilis) given to the fossil discovered, along with deposits of primitive stone tools, by Louis Leakey at the Olduvai Gorge in Tanzania in 1960.* Humans and tools get along well, and for good reason. There are many things our bodies cannot do. For instance, our hands are not suitable for cutting things. They are not sharp enough or strong enough; our nails are weak and blunt. Our arms are short and the muscles weak, at least compared to some other predators. Some of the earliest tools created by people were hand-axes, rough pieces of stone chipped and chiseled to hold an edge that could compensate for the weakness of our hands. A primitive hand axe is made from a rock but it is not a rock. The true value of a hand axe, of any tool, is the skill with which it was made and its appropriateness for the use to which it is put. A rock is just a rock. A good hand axe has been selected from the right material for the job. It must hold an edge and be sturdy. Slate and shale can be very sharp, but are brittle; granite is tough, but will not take an edge. Flint, on the other hand, is hard, sharp, and durable. Once selected, the rock is then chiseled and flaked to just the right angle for the work it will perform — fine edge for slicing, broad edge for chopping. The heel of the tool must fit in the hand; it must not be too big, or too small, too wide or too thin. The real value of the hand axe as a tool is not in its material, but in the knowledge that went into its making.

Hardware was the third knowledge medium (see Exhibit 4).

We do not usually think of hardware, tools, and machines as being "knowledge storage" devices, but they are. Every tool contains the knowledge of its use. Humans are not good at repetitively measuring distances, so we have learned to mark a "standard" distance on a ruler, and use the information stored on the ruler to ensure accurate measurements again and again. If the quality of the ruler's markings is poor, then its use as a measuring device and its value as a tool are equally poor. In World War II, the Norden Bombsight (see Exhibit 5) was instrumental in greatly improving the accuracy of gravity bombs dropped from great heights. It was reportedly capable of dropping a bomb within a radius of 100 feet from a height of 4 miles. The bombsight was an analogue computer that retained in its design the knowledge of the relationship between the altitude of the plane, air speed, wind speed and direction, angle of drift, and a number of other factors. The device was also an automatic pilot of sorts and could compensate for plane pitch and roll. The value of such a device obviously was in how closely the designers could make the system an analogue of the real plane, air, and target environment. The value was in the knowledge that went into the device. The quality of the knowledge that went into the Norden Bombsight was a significant improvement over the extant knowl-

*Pickford, M., *Louis S.B. Leakey: Beyond the Evidence,* Janus Books, 1998.

The difference in the quality of knowledge used to make these artifacts 696,000 years apart is quite evident

| Acheulean Hand Axe Olduvai Gorge, Tanzania approx 700,000 years old | Clovis Point Spear Head North America approx 11,000 years old | Axe Head 1st Dynasty China approx 4,000 years old |

Exhibit 4. Hand axes.

Exhibit 5. Norden Bombsight. Copyright © Mike Zierdt. Photo used with permission.

edge in the earlier bombsight developed by Elmer Sperry. It was also much better than attempting to place the same knowledge in each and every bombardier's brain.

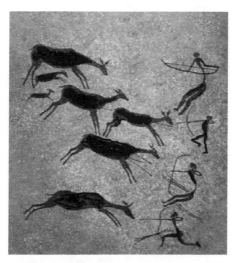

Exhibit 6. Cave paintings, the original "hard copy."

Books

People have been marking objects to retain images and information for a very long time. Archaeologists have uncovered artifacts whose purpose seems to have been to store a visual image of some sort (as opposed to performing a physical function) that are tens of thousands of years old. Many of these artifacts were fetishes or objects of worship. Nevertheless, their purpose was to "store" some image in a relatively permanent state for viewing later. The famous "Venus of Willendorf" is dated to about 30000 B.C.E. The cave paintings at Lascaux in France (see Exhibit 6) date from around 28000 B.C.E. These would probably not qualify in most peoples' minds as "books," although the Lascaux paintings could perhaps be considered one of the first true "hard copies." More information-rich media started to appear in the Middle East with Sumerian clay tablets inscribed with cuneiform script at around 3500 B.C.E. The earliest of these tablets seems to have been the equivalent of "bills of lading" recording shipping transactions. Around 2500 B.C.E., tribes in Western Asia started using animal skins, and Egyptians started using papyrus to record their thoughts, instructions, transactions, and laws. This object became known as the book.

The book is the fourth knowledge storage medium.

Software

While, generically, books were invented around 5000 years ago, they had little impact on the human race until the development and popularization of moveable type books in the fifteenth century. The bootstrap of freely available books, containing useful information requiring higher literacy to

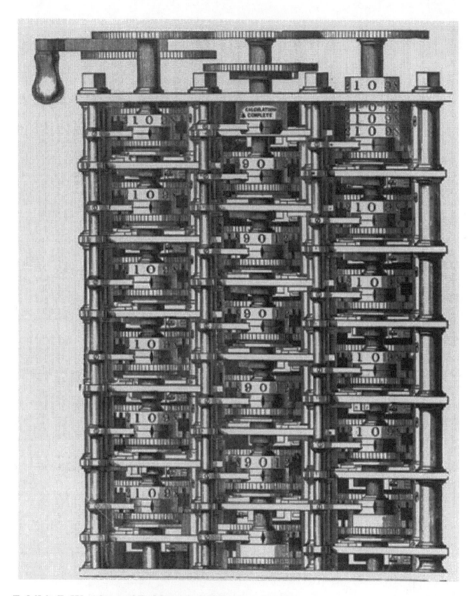

Exhibit 7. Woodcut of Babbage's Difference Engine.

use the information, fueling the creation of more books, containing more information, revolutionized the world in ways that continue to this day.

What the Lascaux cave paintings were to books, Charles Babbage's Difference Engine (see Exhibit 7) was to computers. This 20-decimal-place mechanical device (the equivalent of a 64-bit processor), although never completed, was designed to calculate differences, a kind of finite differential,

214

that can be used to approximate any simple polynomial. The "programming" was mechanical, and involved setting values on dials. The "processing" of the program was effected by turning wheels until the program "termination" event occurred (a dial appeared with the words "calculation complete").[*]

In the broadest sense, any set of instructions given to a machine to control its operation can be thought of as a "program." Babbage's machine shared some similarities with other programmed mechanical machines of the time, such as cotton looms, the key difference being that the purpose of Babbage's machine was the calculation itself. In a cotton loom, the program and the functioning of the machine is entirely secondary to the production of the cotton cloth. With the Difference Engine, the program was the point of the machine. This, more than its capability, was the main distinction between Babbage's machine and other programmed mechanical devices of the late Victorian era.

With the development of ENIAC (Electronic Numerical Integrator and Computer) in 1944–1945 came the initial attempts at programming languages. John Von Neumann is generally credited with the first statement of the concept of a stored computer *program* in June 1945.[**] This puts the earliest software, in today's generally accepted sense, at around 1950. The evolution of the computer and its associated languages from this point forward is a fascinating but very big subject. All computer programs, and by inference the data on which they operate, are forms of stored knowledge. There are many differences in the nature of the five knowledge storage media, but the key characteristic of software is that it is *executable*. Software has the capability of running, of changing its state, of processing inputs and producing outputs, and of interacting with the outside world. It is this characteristic that makes software so valuable and drives much of what we do.

Software is the fifth and most recent knowledge storage medium.

The Characteristics of the Knowledge Storage Media

These five different knowledge media (see Exhibit 8 and Exhibit 9) have significantly different characteristics of storage capability. The characteristics that are of most immediate interest are:

- *Persistency/volatility.* Once knowledge is stored in this medium, how long will it remain without casual (nonintentional) corruption or loss? For the purposes of this comparison, we will not consider normal "aging" of knowledge with respect to some outside standard

*Swade, D., *The Difference Engine: Charles Babbage and the Quest to Build the First Computer,* Viking Press, 2001.
**McRae, Norman, *John Von Neumann,* American Mathematical Society, 1999.

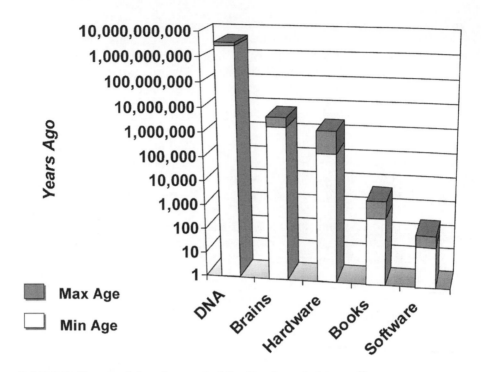

Exhibit 8. Temporal development of the five knowledge media.

Exhibit 9. Comparison of Properties of Knowledge Media

Storage medium	Persistency in medium	Update frequency	Intentionality	Ability to self-modify	Ability to modify the outside world
DNA	Very persistent	Very slow	Low	Moderate	Quite limited
Brain	Very volatile	Very fast	High	High	Quite limited
Hardware design	Very persistent	Slow	High	Low	Limited to specific design
Books	Quite persistent	Quite slow	High	None	None
Software	Quite persistent	Fast	Quite high	High	Relatively unlimited

as being an element of volatility. Knowledge that, at one point in time, was fresh and new in peoples' heads, on paper or in machines at some later point becomes "old." This is not a function of the knowledge, but rather of the world in which the knowledge exists. People can spend their lives learning a skill, which a machine renders worthless or obsolete. A book can become outdated with respect to other sources of knowledge. This is a form of volatility, but because it is more a function of the world than the medium, we will not address it right now. We will consider only the persistency of knowledge with respect to its originally stored structure.

- *Update frequency.* How rapidly can knowledge stored in the medium be modified, either intentionally or otherwise? This "updatability" is generally a function of the physical nature of the medium, the complexity of the knowledge stored in it, the input and output mechanisms, and the coding activity required to frame the knowledge in the medium.

- *Intentionality.* How much the storage and modification of the knowledge in the medium can be done deliberately (this does assume that there is "deliberation" by some party in the change). There are two sides to intentionality: the ease of purposeful adding of knowledge, and the resistance a medium may have to accidental or incorrect updating, which is the persistency or volatility.

- *Ability to self-modify.* How much the knowledge stored in the medium can affect itself (i.e., modify its own knowledge representation). Any capability in this area implies that the medium has some way of adjusting itself. It is usually the case that there exist *two* kinds of knowledge in the medium: the knowledge itself and the knowledge of how to modify that knowledge. These represent some of the most fundamental characteristics of the software medium.

- *Ability to affect the outside world.* How knowledge stored in the medium can modify its surroundings (external to the knowledge storage medium itself). No "pure" form of knowledge, whatever that might mean, can directly and physically affect things in the outside world. It must always act through some kind of physical agent. This characteristic is usually a function of how closely coupled this physical agency is to the knowledge store.

DNA

Persistency. DNA exists for the purpose of creating proteins. We could actually argue that the primary purpose of DNA is to create more DNA, which is true of all autopoietic (self-generating) systems. But at the simplest level, DNA is a set of instructions on how to create proteins. Different sets of instructions create different proteins. The general view of the storage of knowledge in strands of DNA is that they occurred either through interaction between the DNA's host and its environment or through spontaneous mutation. The concept of evolution, at its most basic level, provides that the only changes that are retained over periods of time are those that are advantageous to their own replication (even if sometimes at the expense of the host). Once knowledge has been encoded in DNA it is both quite fragile and remarkably resilient, depending on whether we talk about the instance or the system. Physical stressors such as radiation can eradicate both the medium and its message. The coding can be changed through mutation, either beneficial or otherwise. The DNA carrier can die prematurely and fail to carry on the genetic information. So knowledge-in-DNA tends to be as resilient as its *set* of hosts. While instances of DNA are delicate, the system often is not. We have found DNA in bacteria that seems to have been unchanged for a billion years. Because the coded content, the knowledge, in the DNA can be changed through casual or selective mutation (such as breeding for certain characteristics), its persistency actually varies over a wide range.

Update Frequency. The update frequency of DNA is usually a function of the generation cycle. In *Diptera* (the insect order that includes fruit flies), the generation cycle is about two weeks, and mutations can be readily generated and observed in the laboratory. There is a variety of models of evolutionary change ranging from gradual and incremental to quite sudden, punctuated, large-scale changes.* The sum of this is that, in general, DNA is rather slow to update.

Intentionality. We have recently started to develop capability to intentionally and directly manipulate DNA. Mankind has long tinkered with nature in this regard, selectively breeding horses, flowers, dogs, vegetables, and cattle to bring out favored characteristics. Since Gregor Mendel's work on the combination of genetic components of the pea plant published in 1866, we have gained some significant understanding of the mechanisms of intentionally manipulating the coded instructions in DNA. Nevertheless, from a human perspective, DNA as a knowledge store is of low intentionality. Only recently have we been able to deliberately alter the instructions that govern the details of DNA operation; but even there our successful attempts resulted in intentional changes to the *results* of the DNA coding rather than the coding itself.

Self-Modification. The question of self-modification of DNA is answered with both a yes and a no. In general DNA does not self-modify, most of the function of DNA is dedicated to identical replication. However, DNA does create cells in which certain characteristics may be dominant. This is how, from a single fertilized ovum, the human body ends up containing brain cells, skin cells, and kneecap cells. Therefore DNA's self-modification ability is presumed moderate.

Modify Surroundings. Finally, DNA does have the ability to modify its surroundings. In a very small way through protein synthesis and in a macro way by the creation of a plant or animal that interacts with its surroundings.

*Mayr, Ernest, and Diamond, Jared, *What Evolution Is*, Perseus Book Group, 2002.

This modification tends to be quite limited, restricted to the capabilities of whatever organism the DNA creates.

Brain

Persistency. Thoughts are very transitory. Much of what we classify as "thought" is not only transient, it is inaccessible in that the person thinking the thoughts may be quite unaware of them. Certainly, all brain-resident knowledge stops on the death of the person. And we can easily forget knowledge when it is stored in the brain. It evaporates if not used or consistently refreshed. It may be removed through trauma, old age, illness, and lack of use. The brain is DRAM, not SRAM

Update Frequency. While certain modes of behavior and thought patterns may be firmly ingrained in some people, and acquiring and storing more knowledge — the activity of learning — may occur faster in some people than in others, in general brain-stored knowledge can be very quickly replaced or updated.

Intentionality. Humans do absorb quite a lot of information unconsciously, as an unintentional act, particularly when we are infants or children. However, most of our learning is intentional — we do not usually become accidentally expert in something. In fact, society intentionally sets up entire systems, buildings, and cultures solely for the purpose of learning.

Self-Modification. Human inertia notwithstanding, the human brain has a great deal of capability to reorder itself. In fact, much of our learning process involves this self-modification. Therefore the brain's self-modification capability is high.

Modify Surroundings. Knowledge in the brain does have some ability to modify its surroundings. Not directly through thought, of course, but through the agencies of hands and feet, and through the design of hardware and tools. Usually, this ability is more constrained by the physical nature of the body or tools than by the capability of the brain. Therefore this capability is quite limited.

Hardware Design

Persistency. Depending on the sturdiness of the hardware components, hardware design is quite persistent. We have found stone tools pretty much the way their maker left them, as in the case of the Acheulean hand axe, around 700,000 years ago. While modern hardware does not tend to have quite such long a mean time between failure, it is reasonable to assert that hardware knowledge persistency is high.

Update Frequency. This depends greatly on the particular design and what it is supposed to achieve, but generally, hardware-resident knowledge cannot be "updated" quickly. Having said that, of course, many hardware designs incorporate their own adjustability, often through mechanical dials and level settings and electrical potentiometer settings (see Exhibit 5, for example). These adjustments can only operate over a narrow and predefined range. "Updating" the knowledge outside of this range requires redesigning and rebuilding the hardware device; therefore, hardware typically has a slow update frequency.

Intentionality. While we do sometimes build machines, and through serendipity find other uses for them, it is hard to imagine accidentally constructing a successfully functioning machine. Therefore, hardware usually has high intentionality.

Self-Modification. In a way similar to the update frequency, hardware can be constructed, within a narrowly defined range, to modify its internal state by itself. Outside of that narrow range, any self-modification (for example, due to friction) is usually entropic. Therefore, hardware's self-modification capability is generally low.

Modify Surroundings. The reason hardware exists at all is to allow modification of the surroundings. Hand axes, for instance, were created to overcome the limitations of human hands in cutting things. While we have become very clever at designing even purely mechanical systems to incorporate environmental variability into the machine's operational adjustment, hardware still tends to modify the surroundings only to the extent it was designed. In general the ability of hardware to modify its environment is limited to its specific design.

Books

Persistency. Books share with hardware a persistency that is a function of its substrate. We have stone tablets from several thousand years ago, but paper rarely lasts a few centuries. The knowledge content disappears with the decay of the substrate, so knowledge in books can be considered to be quite persistent. Certainly, we do have the option of creating books out of titanium, which would presumably be very persistent.

Update Frequency. Books are not particularly quick to update. Electronic publishing and book-like electronic media, such as e-mail, can certainly be modified quite quickly, but in general books are slower to update than thought and quicker than hardware. Therefore, the update frequency of book-stored knowledge is on the "quite slow' side.

Intentionality. Books share with hardware the characteristic that it is not easy to "accidentally" create them. Therefore, books have high intentionality.

Self-Modification. Knowledge retained in book form has absolutely no capability of updating itself. Indexing tools that automatically operate on written words (such as LaTeX) are, of course, software.

Modify Surroundings. Knowledge in books has no way of modifying the world outside the book. True, the ideas in a book may be revolutionary, but the knowledge in the book must first be transported into one of the other media before it can take action. Knowledge in books is utterly passive.

Software

Persistency. Software, justifiably, has been accused of having a very short shelf life. However, this is mostly a function of packaging. Certainly, software systems become corrupted through repeated maintenance. The need for the function disappears or changes, or the software is simply lost through negligence. But with halfway effective software configuration management (SCM), the knowledge in software, particularly if kept at a fairly atomic level and actively managed by other software, could be quite persistent.

Update Frequency. People have said that one of the primary advantages of software is that it is easy to update, and one of the primary disadvantages of software is that it is easy to update. Both are true. We are not as good at this as we need to be, for a number of reasons. The main problem is that we are much better at quickly damaging the software knowledge representation than we are at quickly and effectively adding to the knowledge. There are several reasons for this, entropy is one, and peoples' ability to understand complex systems is another. We will address this later. However, it is evident that the update frequency for software is fast.

Intentionality. Software is quite intentional in one respect — it is hard to "accidentally" create an effective system. The other side of the intentionality coin is not so shiny. It is quite easy to accidentally create software that does not work well. Developers' protests that such mistakes are "features" notwithstanding, software's intentionality is quite high, although, for a number of reasons, probably not as high as for books and hardware.

Self-Modification. Software has a considerable capability for self-modification that we are only beginning to explore. Some research indicates we may be able to create software that reprograms itself in such a way that the result is intrinsically nondeterministic. Most software is not this sophisticated at the moment, and the modifiability is more on the lines of typical hardware (although much greater) operating across a well-defined range of "normal operations." The self-modification capability of software is high.

Modify Surroundings. Software shares with thought in the brain that it cannot of itself affect the outside world, but must do so though some physical agency. Once we get over that hurdle, software can do pretty much anything humans can go and a lot more. Software can actually fly a plane, restock shelves, drill for oil, and make drugs. Given the right (hardware) interface, software's ability to modify its surroundings is relatively unlimited.

Building on Knowledge

DNA first made knowledge, of any sort, storable. It also made it applicable and provided the basis, the medium, for knowledge acquisition. Knowledge in DNA is active and persistent, but it is both unintentional and invariable.

Ultimately, the knowledge content of DNA encompassed another medium; DNA "learned" to make a brain. The brain, particularly the human brain, has an apparently limitless ability to learn. Certainly we do not seem to have tapped it out yet. Knowledge in brains does have the capability to affect the outside world but its major limitation is that it is a highly volatile medium. Therefore, knowledge in brains is active and variable but volatile.

One of the kinds of knowledge that the human race learned over millennia was how to construct tools, how to recognize a need, develop a knowledge-in-brain concept that would satisfy that need, and convert it (transpose the knowledge) into another medium — hardware. The combination of brains and hardware knowledge storage is very powerful — the hardware "remembers" the knowledge and provides ways of manifesting it. The brain imagines (creates the knowledge) and fashions the hardware tool to instantiate it.

Another extension of knowledge-in-brains was to find a medium that shared the persistency of hardware but could contain more knowledge. Perhaps the early developers of painting and writing used the knowledge persistency of their tools as a clue to the medium that would provide them with the means to overcome their brains' volatility. Books made knowledge portable. Prior to books, the knowledge of the human race was transported in the brain-to-brain interchange known as talking. The oral tradition of peoples is the best that brains can do to establish permanent knowledge. Books made knowledge portable in two ways: through space and through time. Prior to books, if we needed to transport knowledge from one physical place to another, a person having that knowledge had to physically move between the locations. To transport knowledge through time, we had to tell stories. To ensure the consistent repetition of the stories, we had to tell many people, in a memorable and consistent manner. The establishment of the mythology of the human race represents this attempt at knowledge longevity.* The problem with knowledge-in-books is that it is utterly passive. A book on how to play tennis does not play tennis. To incarnate this knowledge, it must be transferred into one of the other media. Because we do not have the capability of developing tennis-playing DNA (yet), this means the knowledge must be transferred either to brains (teach someone how to play tennis) or hardware (create a tennis playing machine). The advantage of books is that the resident knowledge is at least somewhat persistent. Books, therefore, are persistent but passive knowledge stores.

The advent of books and the associated skill of literacy (the knowledge of how to use books, which, of course, can be resident in books but to be executed, must be transferred into brains), enabled an enormous revolution. Knowledge persistency allowed us to build on each other's ideas, and to build on ideas from earlier generations. One of these ideas led to the creation of the fifth knowledge storage medium. The difference between knowledge in books or book-like media such as inactive Web pages and software is simple. Knowledge in software executes — knowledge in books does not. We are rapidly moving into an era where the line between these two is blurred. The apocryphal *"self documenting code"* is an example of a knowledge store that tries to serve two masters: execution and understanding, software code, and written book. Active server pages straddle the line between being both descriptive and active; between showing a page and executing a function. This blurry boundary notwithstanding, the differentiation of *executability* between knowledge-in-books and knowledge-in-software makes a valuable distinction. If it *executes* the knowledge, it is software; if it *describes* the knowledge, it is a book. Peter Drucker, in *Post Capitalist Society,*** pointed out that pharmaceutical companies do not spend their time and money in making drugs anymore. They spend their efforts *learning* how to make drugs. Where, then, do they put this knowledge? The choices are DNA, Brains, Hardware, Books, and Software. In today's world, most of this knowledge is properly put into software because software is a persistent, active medium for the storage of knowledge.

Brains, Books, and Software

For most purposes and most kinds of knowledge we have only three places in which we can store our knowledge. Except for particular kinds of knowledge, DNA is not a suitable medium, although this will doubtless

---

*Campbell, Joseph, *The Power of Myth,* Anchor Publishers, 1991 (reissue).
**Drucker, Peter, *Post Capitalist Society,* HarperBusiness, New York, 1993.

Exhibit 10. Stages of knowledge media evolution.

The stages of knowledge storage evolution can be characterized as:

DNA	Unintentional knowledge storage, and application
Brain	Intentional knowledge storage
Devices	Intentional knowledge application
Books	Portable intentional knowledge
Software	Intentional knowledge development, storage, transport and application

change in the distant future. The three main repositories of knowledge are Brains, Books, or Software.

What about hardware? Certainly, in order to make drugs at all, we need to have a suitable chemical diffusion machine available for the knowledge-in-software to act on. However, increasingly, the construction and operation of these machines is becoming software-resident, which means that while a representation of the knowledge may exist in book or in hardware form, the *controlling representation* of the knowledge is in software form (see Exhibit 10).

A simple example may illustrate the choices we have of knowledge location: If I happen to (for instance) know the U.S. Tax Code and how it is interpreted, there are three things I can do with that knowledge.

1. I can leave it in my brain and become your accountant. The problem with this is there is only one of me, and there are many people who need their taxes done.

2. I can write a book on how to interpret the Tax Code. This is not likely to be a bestseller, but it does make the knowledge available to a wider audience. However, if you want to use that knowledge, first you have to read the book. Of course, you may not understand it unless you have the *context* in which to interpret the knowledge — you must know something about taxes and accounting, and this is knowledge that is not in the book but in your head, or not. Doing this would require a lot of effort on your part. The result of your efforts would be that you end up knowing what I know, and presumably could then do what I can do.

3. My third option is to put this knowledge into software. If I do this, then you could execute the knowledge — you could actually do what I can do, without having to know what I know. This is very valuable. And this is why, all across the planet, accountants are putting accounting knowledge into software.

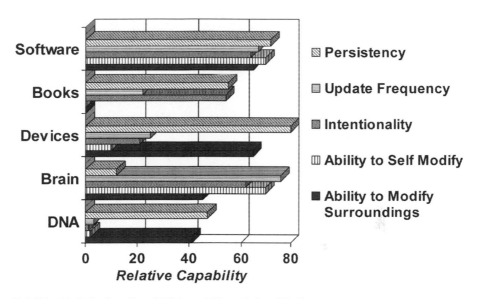

Exhibit 11. Relative Capabilities of Knowledge Media

Summary

Software is the most recent of five knowledge storage media that have existed since the beginning of the world. The knowledge that can be and is stored in each medium is enormously variable. The capabilities of each medium also vary widely. From Exhibit 11 it is easy to see that, of all the knowledge media, software has the widest range of capability. This is the primary reason, at the present moment in time, that we are busy transcribing all of our knowledge into this medium.

An important note: simply because the software medium has significant advantages over knowledge storage in other media does not mean that it invalidates them. When brains developed, DNA did not become obsolete. When we created books, we did not stop thinking. Indeed, of all five media, only the brain truly has the capability to *create* knowledge. Once the knowledge is created, however, it can be instantiated in any of the media.

We are at the beginning of an era in which the medium of choice for the storage of all the knowledge of the human race will be software. Far from limiting the knowledge-in-brains, it will liberate it. And the first place this will start is in the process of developing software.

Appendix B
The Five Orders of Ignorance

He who knows not and knows not that he knows not; he is a fool — shun him!
He who knows not and knows that he knows not; he is simple — teach him!
He who knows and knows not that he knows; he is asleep — wake him!
He who knows and knows that he knows; he is wise — follow him!

— Isabel Lady Burton 1831–1896
Arab Proverb, *"The Life of Captain Sir Richard F. Burton"*

Software is not a product. It is the fifth knowledge storage medium that has existed since the world began. This premise leads us to an interesting question: If software is not a product, then what is the "product" of our efforts to "produce" it? The answer, of course, is that the real product is *the knowledge contained in the software.*

It is rather easy to produce software; dangerously so, in fact. It is much harder to produce software that "works," because before we can produce it, we must understand what "works" means. It is easy to produce software that is simple, because it does not contain much knowledge. It is easier to produce software using an application generator, because the knowledge of how to produce a system (although not necessarily of the system that needs to be produced) is actually stored in the application generation software. It is easy for me to produce software if I have already produced this type of software before, because I must have already obtained the necessary knowledge — assuming I have not forgotten how to create it.

Therefore, the hard part of building systems is not building them, it is in knowing what to build — it is in acquiring the knowledge necessary to build the system.

This leads us to another very important observation:

> If software is not a product, it is a medium for storing knowledge; then software development is not a product-producing activity, it is a knowledge-acquiring activity.

It is quite easy to show this using a (slightly exaggerated) example, as shown in Exhibit 1.

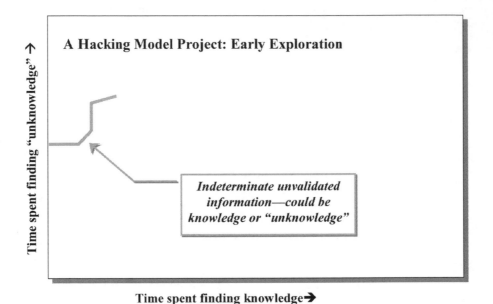

Time spent finding knowledge➜

Exhibit 1. Hacking project early exploration.

The activity of hacking (in the software life cycle sense, rather than the other common usage of illegal entry into someone else's computer system) is the writing of code for the purpose of constructing a system whose function is at least somewhat unknown at the outset. While this kind of hacking has a justifiably bad reputation, it is quite common for programmers to use this approach in the small — for simple problems and for systems where the knowledge-to-be-gained is primarily the program steps or control sequence.

In the earliest stages of hacking, we have little or no basis on which to validate the knowledge content of the code — we just write code. The diagram in Exhibit 1 represents a project using this hacking approach to development. The approach could be summarized as *"we have no idea what we're doing, but we'll do it and somehow it'll work."* In a nonrigorous sense, both the X and Y axes in the diagram represent time. X-time is time spent mostly in developing "correct" knowledge, that is, knowledge that will ultimately find its way into the product shipped to the customer. Y-time is time spent mostly in developing "incorrect" knowledge, which is knowledge that is not immediately relevant to the product at hand and will not be, or rather should not be, incorporated into the product. Because hacking (except in the trivial case where we have already built this exact system before, in which case we might reasonably ask why are we doing it again?) is building a system without knowing what it should do, the fact that the

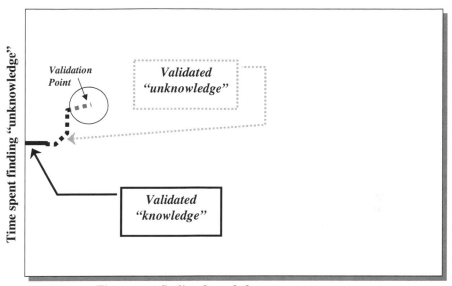

Time spent finding knowledge

Exhibit 2. Hacking project: validating the knowledge.

path deviates from the straight and narrow is simply caused by the fact that we do not know what to begin with, what that path should be, and where it should go.

Using hacking we usually salvage *some* useful knowledge (shown in the solid line in Exhibit 2), from the coding activity. Much of what we learn, however, is not useful knowledge, at least not for this particular system. This *"unknowledge"* is shown as a dotted line. Generally, it is stripped from the code product, leaving only the solid "useful" knowledge. This strategy continues until the complete set of knowledge is obtained (we hope).

At some point, to determine whether what we have done is knowledge or unknowledge, we have to "validate" the knowledge we have gained and incorporate it into the code artifact. In Exhibit 2 it is called the "Validation Point." With hacking, this usually occurs quite frequently. It also means, incidentally, that we must have access to another source of knowledge about what the system should do; otherwise we must end up comparing the knowledge store against itself.

There are two results from this validation process:

1. We determine what works.
2. We determine what does not work (for this particular system).

The "what works" we leave in the code, the "what does not work" we usually remove.

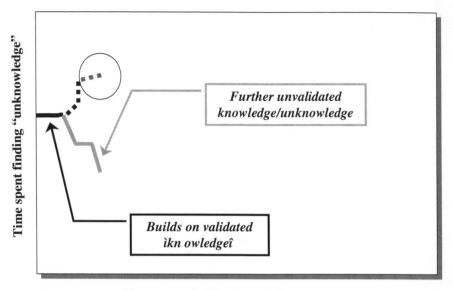

Time spent finding knowledge

Exhibit 3. Hacking project: building on the knowledge.

Using the residual "what works" knowledge, we commence further exploratory coding, as shown in Exhibit 3.

Carrying on in this fashion, we continually add to the system knowledge, backtrack, and purge the "incorrect" knowledge. The final "product" is shown in Exhibit 4.

There are a few observations we can make about this activity:

- *The problem of late discovery.* The approach does not work too well when there is a likelihood of later knowledge invalidating earlier knowledge. On the graph this would mean a very big backtrack and a lot of dotted "unknowledge." In the real world this would mean a large amount of redesign late in the development cycle. This happens often in larger, complex systems where a great deal of information is obtained from the later design and testing phases. It also seems to be a feature of embedded real-time systems and other applications where there is a high degree of design dependence.
- *Two kinds of knowledge.* We are actually acquiring two different kinds of knowledge: solid-line and dotted-line, knowledge and "unknowledge," or in English what works and what does not (for this system). Note that the "solid-line" knowledge is incorporated into the software artifact, while the "dotted-line" unknowledge is simply thrown away. We could argue that knowing what does not work is also

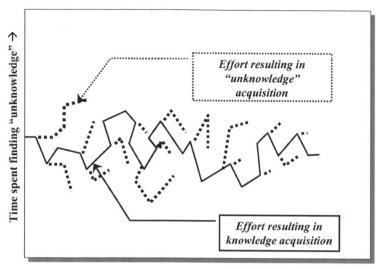

Time spent finding knowledge➜

Exhibit 4. Hacking project: Full build.

Exhibit 5. Edison quote.

Just because something doesn't do what you planned it to do in the first place doesn't mean it's useless…. If I find 10,000 ways something won't work, I haven't failed. I am not discouraged, because every wrong attempt discarded is just one more step forward.

— Thomas Alva Edison

potentially very valuable information but such unknowledge is usually thrown away. Thomas Edison's apt quote in Exhibit 5 does not tell the full story. Not only are missteps eliminating "wrong" paths, the process of "misstepping" may be the only mechanism available to us to illuminate the real path. Sometimes we have to try it to find out what will work by exploring what does not.

- *Corrupted knowledge.* The final delivered product (the wandering solid line) is not usually a good and clean representation of the knowledge necessary for the system. The "kinks" in the line are caused by the activity of acquiring the knowledge or, more correctly, the activities of separating the knowledge from the unknowledge and validating the knowledge in some way. That is, the final code representation of the knowledge does not just contain the knowledge

231

Exhibit 6. A path through the woods.

necessary for the system to function correctly. Unless great effort is made to separate what works from what does not, it also contains the remains of the journey to find that knowledge.

Invariably, the final code product is somewhat contaminated with the legacy of the process used to build it. Usually the developer knows this and understands that the code, while "correct," is not "good code." However, no one else does. And in a year's time, even the original developer will be at a loss to explain just why the code is written the way it is. The reason for this is that the *contextual knowledge* (knowledge of *why* the code was written the way it was) was stored in the most volatile of knowledge stores — the human brain of the developer.

A Walk in the Woods

An analogy may help to explain. Imagine walking through a dense wood through which you have never set foot (see Exhibit 6). Given that you have never walked through this wood before, it would be close to impossible to traverse the wood without taking a "wrong" path. This is intrinsic to the process of discovery. Even if the destination is clearly visible (the requirements are well defined), the path to get there is at least partially obscured.

In fact, we could argue that the only way in which we could flawlessly navigate to the destination is if we had already been there (we have already built this system). In which case, we could argue *"why are we going there again?"* If we had a map available to us to assist us in minimizing our wrong turns, it means that *someone* (the map maker) must have followed this path. This means this product has already been built — so, again, why are we building it? The concept of a process "map" is often held out as the purpose of establishing process in software development. We shall see later how flawed this idea is in practice.

The only way in which we can very quickly and effortlessly navigate to the destination is if someone has built a six-lane highway through the wood. In this case we are, of course, going in the same direction as everyone else. In the systems sense, we are building the same kind of system everyone else is building, in which case we have no competitive advantage.

A Path Less Traveled

We could argue that the only paths we should travel are those that *no one* has taken before. These are the journeys that lead into the unknown, to the novel destinations, that uncover new knowledge, rather than revisit old knowledge. While we rarely if ever develop 100 percent new systems, the entire knowledge content of which is novel, most systems of any worth have at least some of this new discovery. But it is in this *new* knowledge that the real value of the systems lies. What we shall explore is the nature of this knowledge and the processes we use to discover and encapsulate it.

Tracks

As we make our way through the woods, we leave footprints. When we find ourselves backtracking because the path we took turned out to be "wrong" — it led to a different destination than the one we wanted — we leave more footprints. Unless we are very careful to wipe out the footprints heading in the wrong direction, they will still be there when someone else follows us. In the absence of other information, these tracks are likely to lead the other person astray also. In code, these tracks are the legacy of the earlier attempts to write effective code. Unless the author works hard to remove them, there will be extra variables, states, conditional statements, loops, and other code devices that are not necessary for the final solution of the problem. It is the sheer amount of rewriting of code to remove this legacy that makes the hacking model a poor one for larger systems

It is not usually possible to tell immediately if the code is "real path" code or a legacy from a "false path" — unless one has an alternative source of knowledge. For the person writing the code, it may be in his or her brain. For the maintenance programmer several years later, the comments in the code (a form of knowledge-in-books) may explain why the code looks the

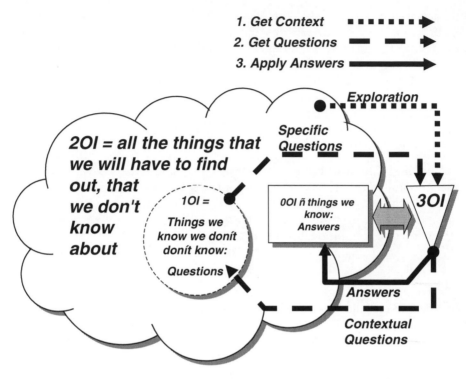

1. Get Context ■ ■ ■ ■ ■ ■ ■ ▶
2. Get Questions ▬ ▬ ▬ ▶
3. Apply Answers ▬▬▬▬▬▶

Exploration

2OI = all the things that we will have to find out, that we don't know about

Specific Questions

1OI =
Things we know we donít donít know:
Questions

0OI ñ things we know:
Answers

3OI

Answers

Contextual Questions

Exhibit 7. Prototyping.

way it does. The difficulty of separating real knowledge from the missteps is one of the reasons that reverse engineering activities have rarely been effective.

Code is, in essence, a *write-only* knowledge store — it is much easier to put knowledge into code than it is to extract it.

Prototyping

From the prototyping example (Exhibit 7) it is evident that the real job is not writing the code or even "building" the system — it is acquiring the necessary knowledge to build the system. In fact, when hacking we use the activity of building the system (or rather attempting to build the system) as the *mechanism* for understanding what the system has to do. Hopefully, the correctly coded system is a by-product of this activity. The problem arises when we think the code *is* the product rather than the knowledge in the code. Then we are tempted to ship the code as it is, however it is, once we get enough of it. If we wished to gain an untainted representation of the code, what we should do with the hacking model, of course, is to rewrite the code so that it cleanly represents the knowledge *after the hacking stage*. If we have done a good job of capturing what we have learned by hacking the code, writing it again should be straightforward and rather quick. The act of doing this intentionally is called *prototyping*.

As a development life cycle model and arguably a business model prototyping actively acknowledges that our job is not to build a system but to acquire knowledge. We do not expect to get a functioning system first time out when we prototype. What we do expect to get is (at least some of) the knowledge we need to build the system. We use prototyping particularly when we do not know in advance what kind of knowledge we might need. We would not consider prototyping in situations where we knew what we had to do in advance.

While we have used the activity of hacking code as a way of explaining this concept, it is actually true of all development and all development stages. We leave tracks and missteps in feasibility studies. We have ambiguities and mistakes in requirements and design documents. We learn things that invalidate what we have put down to date during the creation of test cases and test plans just as much as in code. All software development is predominantly knowledge acquiring rather than product producing.

The Expectation of Product

However, the acquiring of knowledge is neither the business expectation nor the business goal in most companies. Few companies, even those that create and sell software only, count knowledge acquisition and management as their highest priority. Most operate on a modified manufacturing model that views the creation and delivery of the system to the customer as the highest priority. It is not, and this prevailing view has caused considerable problems to both customers and developers for decades.

Kinds of Knowledge

If our job is to acquire knowledge, what kinds of knowledge should we acquire? In a later chapter we will discuss systems knowledge as well as other kinds of essential knowledge that is not coded into the functional artifact. For now, we will talk in more-general terms about what we might know and what we might not know.

For every item of knowledge we possess, we also have a certain amount of ignorance. In fact there is evidence that our "ignorance" *always* exceeds our knowledge. Ignorance is simply the other side of the coin of knowledge. If we view systems development as the acquisition of knowledge, then we can also view it as the reduction or elimination of ignorance. We can also reasonably assume that, at the start of the project, we are more ignorant than we are at the end of the project, although as we shall see, in terms of

THE LAWS OF SOFTWARE PROCESS

known ignorance, this may not be true. So what kinds of ignorance might we exhibit?

Based on what we know and what we do not know, we can classify our ignorance into strata or layers. I call these levels the *"Five Orders of Ignorance."* While the concept is quite general and even somewhat philosophical, quantizing our knowledge and ignorance can be helpful as we try to understand what we need to do to learn and build a system that works. The Five Orders of Ignorance (5OoI) also helps to explain some of the puzzling things that routinely happen in the software development environment, and also some of the behaviors we exhibit trying to create software.

The Five Orders of Ignorance

For very logical, but to noncomputer folk entirely baffling, reasons we in the software business always start counting from zero rather than one. Therefore, the 5OoI start with zero.

Zeroth Order Ignorance (0OI): Lack of Ignorance

I have Zeroth Order Ignorance (0OI) when I know something and can demonstrate my lack of ignorance in some tangible form, such as by building a system that satisfies the user.

0OI is provable and proven knowledge that is deemed "correct" by some qualified agency. In software this means that the knowledge is invariably factored into usable form. In all forms of knowledge there must be some external "proof" element that qualifies the knowledge as being correct.

In a nonsoftware arena and as a personal example, because it has been a hobby of mine for many years, I have 0OI about the activity of sailing, which, given a lake and a boat, is easily verified.

First Order Ignorance (1OI): Lack of Knowledge

I have First Order Ignorance (1OI) when I do not know something and I can readily identify that fact.

1OI is basic ignorance or lack of knowledge. Example: I do not know how to speak the Russian language. I could remedy this deficiency by taking lessons, reading books, listening to the appropriate audiotapes, or moving to Russia for an extended period of time.

Second Order Ignorance (2OI): Lack of Awareness

I have Second Order Ignorance (2OI) when I do not know that I do not know something.

That is to say, not only am I ignorant of something (I have 1OI), I am unaware of what it is I am ignorant about. I do not know enough to know what it is that I do not know. Example: I cannot give a good example of 2OI, of course.

Third Order Ignorance (3OI): Lack of Process

I have Third Order Ignorance (3OI) when I do not know of a suitably efficient way to find out that I do not know that I do not know something, which is lack of a suitable knowledge-gathering process.

This presents me with a major problem: If I have 3OI, I do not know of a way to find out that there are things that I do not know that I do not know. Therefore, I cannot change those things that I do not know that I do not know into either things that I know, or at least things that I know that I do not know, as a step toward converting the things that I know that I do not know into things that I know.

For systems development, the *"suitably efficient"* proviso must be added, because there is always a default 3OI process available. The "default" 3OI process is to go ahead and build the system without knowing what is not known. The code hacking model does this using the coding activity. For very small systems, with certain characteristics that we shall discuss later, this can sometimes be an efficient process. For larger systems, the default 3OI process is usually neither suitable nor efficient

Fourth Order Ignorance (4OI): Meta Ignorance

I have Fourth Order Ignorance (4OI) when I do not know about the Five Orders of Ignorance.

I do not have this kind of ignorance, and now neither do you, dear reader. 4OI is *meta ignorance* — it is rather like being ignorant of the subject of ignorance. However, a version of 4OI is the prevalent attitude that this book attempts to challenge; specifically, that software is a product and that the software development business is the business of building systems rather than acquiring knowledge.

Knowledge is highly and intrinsically recursive — to know about anything, you must first know about other things which define what you know. The Fourth Order of Ignorance for software development purposes could be restated as: *"I have Fourth Order Ignorance when I don't know that software development is the activity of acquiring knowledge, and I don't know what my levels of knowledge are."* It reflects the natural recursion we always encounter when talking about knowledge.

The Five Orders of Ignorance in Systems Development

Each of the Five Orders of Ignorance plays a significant role in building systems.

0OI

0OI is provable, functional, and correct knowledge. In order to qualify for the label "knowledge" it must have been:

- "Known" by someone
- "Validated" against another source of knowledge
- Made into an executable form (if the storage medium of choice is software)

These are the correctly functioning elements of the system that I (obviously) understood, and have successfully incorporated into the system. When I have 0OI, I have the *answer* to the problem.

1OI

These are the things I know I do not know. In a typical system's development project, they are the known variables, where the presence of the variables is known, but not their instance values. When I have 1OI, I have the *question*. In the gamut of systems development effort, we usually find that having a good question makes it fairly easy to find the answer. Of course, we may have a good question but not know how or from whom to obtain an answer. This means our 1OI is incomplete, and incorporates other levels of ignorance. We will tackle more subtle variations of the Orders of Ignorance in a later chapter.

2OI

Second Order Ignorance represents my primary problem in constructing systems. Not only do I not have the answer I need, I do not even have the question. This is, in fact, where we start many projects. Usually, when we start a project, we know from experience that there are many things we will have to learn. The problem is we just do not know what they are. 2OI explains, for instance, most variation in project estimates, and the famous "90-Percent-Complete Program Syndrome."

3OI

Third Order Ignorance operates at the process level. Rather than lacking product knowledge (i.e., of the target system), I am lacking knowledge of how to *acquire* the target knowledge. For the fully qualified 3OI, I am lacking the knowledge of how to acquire the knowledge in a suitably efficient way. This means I do not have a sufficiently effective process that will allow me to build the system (acquire the knowledge) within my budget and time constraints. If this is coupled with 2OI, I have a real danger — I simply do not have a way to resolve my lack of knowledge in the time I have available. In later chapters, I maintain that *all* software development methodologies are actually 3OI processes; their job is to show the areas of the product or process where there is lack of knowledge.

Coupled with 2OI, 3OI represents the true challenge of software development. The reasoning is simple: I have 0OI (the answer), then it is simply a matter of putting the extant knowledge into the product (assuming that I know how to do that, of course). If I have 1OI (the question), it is simply a matter of finding out where the answer to the question exists and obtaining that answer. While resolving 1OI is somewhat more effortful than applying 0OI, both these operations are typically low in effort. It is in the reduction of 2OI and 3OI that the real effort lays.

In the pursuit of process and methodologies, people and organizations sign up for some very "heavyweight" procedures: enormous manuals on how to factor systems, huge checklists, multiple process steps, and repetitive reviews and inspections. Others look for the answer in the methodology — they adopt a set of complex and difficult systems definition and design conventions and languages in the hope that in transcribing their knowledge into these modeling forms, they will acquire the knowledge they need. Both process and methods (and languages) have their places and they are important. But it is important to note that the answer we are looking for *cannot* be in the methodology or the process. A methodology simply gives the syntax in which to frame the question and a discipline for identifying those areas where I might have 2OI. But it cannot know what I am trying to do. A process simply gives a framework in which the discovery activities can take place. The process cannot *perform* the discovery activities.

A movement is afoot in the software business that is leaning toward what are called "Agile" (or "lightweight") methods. These methods attempt to allow for the freedom of discovery while still maintaining the consistency of process necessary to obtain predictable and repeatable results. We will discuss these methods at length in a later chapter.

4OI

Fourth Order Ignorance is probably not too much of an issue at a practical level on projects, although I have found thinking of the process of developing software even in the small does help. At an organizational level, I believe this is the problem that is holding us back from truly capitalizing on the productivity gains we are capable of. The nature of knowledge is recursive, and it is appropriate that the "highest" level of ignorance reflects this recursion.

The 3OI Cycle

The function of process is threefold:

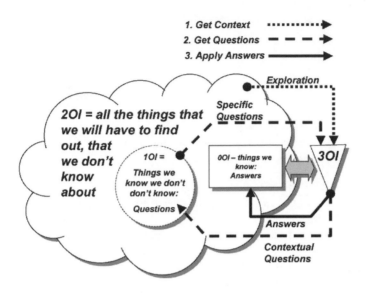

Exhibit 8. Order of Ignorance cycles.

1. To identify whether there are areas where we have ignorance (need to acquire knowledge)
2. To identify what questions we would need to ask to resolve ignorance in these areas
3. To obtain the answers to these questions in a form that we can usefully integrate into the system

The operation of these processes is shown in Exhibit 8.

- The "highest level" 3OI process operates on the "body of *lack of knowledge*" implied by the 2OI cloud. The 3OI process is shown by the small dotted line. The 3OI process somehow acts on both the environment that (presumably) contains the needed knowledge plus the currently available knowledge present in the project team. How the 3OI process actually works depends greatly on the system, the situation, how much knowledge is needed, and what is already known. For situations with high degrees of 2OI, these are extremely exploratory operations, often executed in cycles, with each cycle closing in on the real knowledge source. The output from this phase is a set of contextual questions. Comparing the contextual questions and their answers against the environment allows us to identify where our ignorance lies.
- The next level converts the contextual questions into specific questions. The purpose of the first loop is to identify *where* we might

have ignorance, this second loop is to identify *what* that ignorance might be. Fed through the process, these questions should elicit answers, although commonly each answer generates other questions and sometimes painfully illuminates whole areas that require further investigation.

- The final step is to convert the specific questions into specific answers and apply these answers. At this point we can certify the output as 0OI or extant knowledge.

The steps are:

$$\text{Undifferentiated Lack of Knowledge (2OI)} \rightarrow$$
$$\text{Identified Lack of Knowledge (1OI)} \rightarrow$$
$$\text{Knowledge (0OI)}$$

The fly in the ointment has already been identified — it is that the question-answering process almost invariably generates more questions. Simply put, acquiring knowledge also illuminates more areas of lack of knowledge. For projects tackling systems targets with large quantities of 2OI, this can seem never-ending. For each fact that is found, it seems that an equal number of questions are raised. If a project's or a manager's vision of the goal is a fully factored set of knowledge as exhibited by a working system, simply exposing more and more areas of ignorance is very frustrating. However, if we took the goal to be the acquisition of useful knowledge, we would find the process significantly less frustrating. Here we see one of the functions of changing our business goals, outlook, and expectations away from product and onto knowledge.

The Inability to Measure Knowledge

The view of software as a knowledge medium and software development as a process of acquiring the knowledge necessary to populate this medium leads us directly to a very uncomfortable conclusion concerning what we do. After thinking about the problem for a couple of thousand years, *the human race has not found a way to empirically measure knowledge*. Not only can we not measure it, we do not have a unit for knowledge. We can weigh a book, we can count the number of pages, the quantity of lines and words in it, but we cannot count the quantity of knowledge in it. There is simply no way to do this.

Assessing quantity of knowledge is *always* done using a comparison against another body of knowledge. There are no knowledge measurement axioms on which we can base a quantification system. This is true for books, it is true for humans, and it is true for software. In fact, we assess the quantity of knowledge in a software system in exactly the same way we assess the quantity of knowledge in a human — by examination. In a human, the test results from the completed examination paper (run under controlled conditions) are compared against the professor's answer. If the match is sufficiently close, the person gets a gown, a hat, and a roll of paper. This certifies that the person (at that moment in time) "knows" a quantity of knowledge. For a software system, if the actual observed results of the test (run under controlled conditions) sufficiently match the expected results, it is presumed that the system does, in fact, contain the required knowledge (at that moment in time). The system is certified for use and is released to the world to go and find a real job. Program code inspections closely resemble job interviews for much the same reason — they are both knowledge and capability assessment practices. If a person passes the interview it is presumed that he has either the necessary knowledge or capability or both, and he is offered a job. If a piece of code is deemed by inspection to possess the appropriate knowledge, or is sufficiently well structured that the expected knowledge can be easily added (a measure of knowledge capability), the program is released into the next stage of development.

Our inability to actually measure knowledge means that much of our metric process is built on a foundation of sand. Compounding this is the fact that the critical measure of knowledge in software is not the measure of knowledge in software; it is the measure of the knowledge that is *not* in the software. This is the knowledge we have to *get*, not the knowledge we already have. As described earlier, the key determinant of a software project is the 2OI, which is knowledge we do not know we do not know. So we are in a double bind. Not only can we not measure knowledge we have, what we really want to measure is knowledge we do not have. If we could empirically measure knowledge, we would be able to assess 0OI, and probably we would be able to do a good job at measuring 1OI. We still would not be able to "accurately" measure 2OI, because we would still not know what it is by definition.

This is not a purely philosophical challenge. All project estimation approaches fail to some degree at this point. All project status tracking efforts are compromised by this, and it is the biggest source of recurrent failure in our ability to make commitments we can keep and keep commitments we make.

Summary

At a practical level in developing systems, the critical levels of ignorance on most projects seem to be 2OI and 3OI. It is reasonable to assert that almost all of our work on projects involves the reduction of 2OI into 1OI and finally into 0OI. The rationale is straightforward: if we already have the answer (0OI), it usually does not require much effort to apply it. Even if we do not have the answer, but we do have a specific question (and presumably also the knowledge of how to get an answer), then obtaining the answer does require some effort, but not much. The effort-intensive activity is discovering what it is we do not know. Therefore, it is reasonable to assert that most of our work is the reduction of 2OI. We will also assert that *all* software and systems methodologies are 3OI processes whose job is not to tell us what we know as much as to illuminate our 2OI. The application of a 3OI process to 2OI generates either 1OI or more rarely 0OI. That is, applying an effective development process either gives us the answer (0OI) or, more commonly, it gives us the question (1OI).

Because process and methodologies are often sold on the basis of how much they can structure the knowledge and the activity of acquiring it, it can be quite startling to realize that the primary purpose of process is to show us where we have *lack* of knowledge. Yet if we acknowledge that the true role of the development process is to acquire knowledge, and the most valuable knowledge is knowledge we do not already have, this is the most powerful thing we can do in development.

Index

NOTE: Italicized pages refer to tables and illustrations

A

Accelerating capability, *129*
Accelerating rate of change, *127*
Adaptive Software Development (ASD),
    123–125
Administrator log-in, 30
Agile Alliance, 107
Agile methods, 97–99, 133
    Adaptive Software Development (ASD),
        123–125
    assumptions in, 107–109
    change in, 104
    compatibility with traditional process,
        159
    Crystal Methods, 116–118
    customer centricity in, 106
    defect discovery in, 137
    Dynamic Systems Development Method
        (DSDM), 119–121
    event-driven, 106–107
    Feature-Driven Development (FDD),
        121–122
    feedback in, 104
    and First Order of Ignorance (1OI),
        151–153
    and Fourth Order of Ignorance (4OI),
        157–159
    human factors in, 105–106
    issues in, 130–132
    Lean Development (LD), 122–123
    optimal development time in, 125–130
    and Orders of Ignorance, 159–160
    Scrum, 118–119
    and Second Order of Ignorance (2OI), 153
    stepwide development in, 104–105
    and Third Order of Ignorance (3OI),
        153–157
    XP (Extreme Programming), 113–116
    and Zeroth Order of Ignorance (0OI),
        145–148
Agile Software Development with Scrum, *118*
Amino acids, 208
Ancient Egyptians, record-keeping in, 2

Animal skins, 2
Anthromorphic models, 173–174
Anthropologists, 184–185
Applied generic skills, 190
Architecture stage (waterfall model), 53
Armour's Observation on Software Process,
    14
ASD (Adaptive Software Development),
    123–125
Assembly language, 135, 164, 167
Assembly lines, 51, *52*
Australopithecines, 210
Automated contract, 115
Automatic document generation, 116
Automation, 17
Autopoietic systems, 217
Awareness, lack of, 142–143, *154*

B

Babbage, Charles, 214
Babbage Difference Engine, 214–215
Baking, 55
Basic skills, 190
Beck, Kent, 109
Bertalanffy, Ludwig von, 172
Bombsight, 211–212
Books, 213; *see also* Knowledge storage
        media
    brief history of, 2
    characteristics of, 220–221
    knowledge content of, 222–223
    as one of main repositories of knowledge,
        223–224
    vs. other knowledge media, *4*
    properties of, *3*
    text models in, *86*
Brain, 210; *see also* Knowledge storage media
    characteristics of, 219
    and human evolution, 1
    knowledge content of, 222
    as one of main repositories of knowledge,
        223–224
    vs. other knowledge media, *4*

properties of, *3*
structure of, *2*
Bugs (software), 42
Bulleted lists, 87
Business environment, 103
Business process analysis, 115

C

Calculation, 80
Capability Maturity Model (CMM), *20*
Case-based reasoning, 162
CASE tools, 40
    information retention in, 65
    issues against, 169–172
Cave paintings, *213*
Centers for Disease Control (CDC), 22
Charette, Bob, 122
Chunking, 79–80, 87
Classical models, 74
Clay tablets, 2, 213
CMM (Capability Maturity Model), *20*
COBOL programming language, 135
Codes, 7
    end of, 166–168
    knowledge content of, 228–229
    in meta-process, *29*
    tracks of, 233–234
    in waterfall model, 53
Code Science, 115
Collective ownership, 105, 114
Commercial off-the-shelf (COTS) packages,
    37, 103, 164
Compiler, 135
Complete requirements, 52
Computers, 2
Conformed process flow, *23*
Construct phases, 100–101
Contextual knowledge, 232
Contextual variation, 149–150
Continuous process, 63
Controlled failure, 193–194
Conventional models, 73–75
Corrupted knowledge, 231–232
Cost of process, 102–103
Cotton looms, 215
Counting, 77–78
Creative spaces, 17, 22
Creative teams, 22
Cross-references, 87
Crystal Methods, 116–118
Crystal Reports, 167
Customer and environment models, 83
Customer representatives, 184

Cutting instruments, 2
Cyberspace, 195

D

Data, 91, 205–206
Data collection, 21
Data flow diagrams (DFDs), 46–48, 74
Data structures, 91–92
Debugging, 22, 42
Decimal notation, 80
Defect/development time dependency, *125*
Defect discovery, 136–137
Deliverable product models, 83
Deliverables, 63
Delphi estimation, 115
De Luca, Jeff, 121–122
Design models, *83*
Detailed design stages (waterfall model), 53
Deterministic path, *59*
Development engineers, 34–35
Development environment, 103
DFDs (data flow diagrams), 46–48, 74
Difference Engine, 214–215
Diptera, 218
Directed graphs, *88*, 89
Discipline generic skills, 190
Discrete stages (waterfall model), 52
DNA (deoxyribonucleic acid), 1; *see also*
        Knowledge storage media
    characteristics of, 217–219
    as the first knowledge medium, 208–209
    knowledge content of, 222
    vs. other knowledge media, *4*
    properties of, *3*
    structure of, *2, 209*
Documentation, 131
Domain application learning, 190
Domain context skills, 190
Domain engineer, 166, 184
Domain implementation, 190–191
Domain interdependent systems, 180
Domain knowledge, *165*
Domain modeling life cycle, *178*
Domain-nonspecific tools, 170
Domain-specific methods, 179–180
Domain-specific skills, 190
Domain variable models, 180
Dotted-line knowledge, 230
Dual Hypotheses of Knowledge Discovery,
    84, 136
Dynamic Systems Development Method
    (DSDM), 119–121

E

Effective processes, 11–12
Electronic books, 171
Embedded directed graph, *88*
Embedded life cycles, 99–100
Energy, 91
ENIAC (Electronic Numerical Integrator and Computer), 215
Entity-relationship models, 74
Environment models, *83*
Epistemology, 172, 205
Estimates, inaccuracy of, *8*
Events, 91
Executable tools, 176–177
Explicit process, 28
Extreme Programming Explained, 109
Extrinsic knowledge, 136

F

Factoring, 139–140
Fallacy of identification, 72, 74
Feature-Driven Development (FDD), 121–122
Feedback
    in Agile methods, 104
    in construct phases, 100–101
    corrective cycles, 101–102
Feedback stages (waterfall model), 53
First Law of Software Process, 11–12, 27–28
First Order of Ignorance (1OI), 7–9, 140–141; *see also* Five Orders of Ignorance
    and Agile, 151–153
    in knowledge acquisition, 236
    in problems of process, 27–28
    in problem-solving, 21–22
    in systems development, 238
Five Orders of Ignorance, 7–10
    and Agile, 159–160
    cycles, 239–241
    in knowledge acquisition, 236–237
    mapping of process to, *21*
    and process, *36*
    and process layers, *26*
    subdividing, 138–139
    in systems development, 237–239
Fourth Order of Ignorance (4OI), 7, 144–145; *see also* Five Orders of Ignorance
    and Agile, 157–159
    definition of, 10
    in knowledge acquisition, 237
    in systems development, 239
Fruit flies, 218

Fully overlapped waterfall model, *57*
Functions, 91

G

Gane-Sarson convention, 40
Gantt chart, 116
Gather Requirements process, 9
Generalized directed graph, *88*
General models, 81
Generic skills, 190
Genetics, 218
Granular processes, 9–10
Graphic inserts, 87
Gutenberg, Johann, 163

H

Hacking, 228–229
Hand axes, *3*, *212*
Hardware, 2, 211–212; *see also* Knowledge storage media
    characteristics of, 219–220
    vs. other knowledge media, *4*
    properties of, *3*
Hatley-Pirbhai method, 43
Hierarchical directed graph, *88*
Homo habilis, 1, 211
HTML editors, 168

I

IBM PC team, *22*
Identical repetition, 148
IEEE Standard 1074, 55
Implementation models, 83
Index, 87
Information, 205
Instinctual knowledge, 1
Intentionality, in knowledge media, *3*, 217
Intentional process ignorance, 143–144, *155*
Interdependent models, 180–181
Interfaces, 93
Interrupts, 91, 92
Intrinsic knowledge, 136

J

Jet planes, 60–62
Joint application development (JAD), 54

K

Kirchoff's Laws, 75

Knowledge, 205
  acquisition of, 27
  building on, 222–223
  classification of, 205–208
  contextual, 232
  corrupted, 231–232
  deployment of, 162
  design dependence of, 68–69
  development of, 194
  dotted-line, 230
  execution of, 162–163
  extrinsic, 136
  factoring, 139–140
  hierarchy of, *206*
  history of, 1–3
  intrinsic, 136
  kinds of, 235–236
  late discovery of, 230
  measurement of, 241–242
  in process, 30–32
  solid-line, 230
  spectrum of, *186*
  storage, 147–148
  unknown, 158
  variability with time, 68
Knowledge discovery
  dual hypotheses of, 13–14, 84
  and Five Orders of Ignorance, 236–237
  phases, *67*
  walk-in-the-woods analogy of, 232–234
Knowledge engineer, 166
Knowledge engineering, 172
Knowledge-in-software, 162
Knowledge Management movement, 162
Knowledge repository elements, 63
Knowledge storage media, 1–3
  characteristics of, 3–4, 215–216
  comparison of properties of, *216*
  history of, 208–215
  relative capabilities of, *3, 225*
  stages of evolution of, *224*
  temporal development of, *216*
Kuhn, Thomas, 111

L

Laws of Software Process, 5–7
  applications of, 16–17
  First Law, 11–12
  Second Law, 13–14
  Third Law, 15–16
Leakey, Louis, 1
Lean Development (LD), 122–123
Learning, 191–193

  application gap, 191
  controlled failure in, 193–194
  factors in, 188
  levels of, 190–191
  problems in, 189
  variable rate of, 69–70
Learning systems experts, 186
Learning teams, 22–23
Lemma of Eternal Lateness, 12, 33
Life cycles, 51
  definition of, 62–63
  domain modeling, *178*
  generalized model, *64*
  phases, *64*
  true, *174*
  variables, *70*

M

Major variation, 149
Management models, 72
Manufacturing industries, 51
Massively overlapped waterfall model, *56*
Material, 91
Mendel, Gregor, 218
Meta-ignorance, 144–145, *158*
Meta-languages, 168, 181
Meta-models, 81, *92, 111*, 181
Meta processes, 9, 28–30
Methodologies, 39–43, 48–49
Methodologists, 183–184, 196
Methods, 73
  mapping onto problem and solution
    space, 90–91
  vs. models, 89–90
  non-executable, 170–171
  standards, 39
  in systems development, 93–94
Miller, George A., 76
Miller, Stanley, 208
Minds, 94–95
Minor variations, 148
Model-based software engineering, 172–173
Modeling language, 175–176
Model linguists, 183
Models, 73
  bootstrapping, 84
  of convention, 73–75
  entity-relationship, 74
  environment, *83*
  general, 81
  interdependence of, 180–181
  logical nature of, 88–90
  management, 72

mapping onto problem and solution
space, 90–91
meta, 81, *92, 111*, 181
of numbers, 75–76
object-oriented, 180
physical nature of, 85–88
project, 81
standards and process, 81
in systems development, 93–94
text, *86*
transform, 74
Modified process flow, *24*
Modular architecture, 115
Moveable types, 2
Multi-tasking, 91

N

Natural numbers, 77
Neumann, John von, 2, 215
New knowledge
application to existing structures, *111*
embedding into existing structures, *113*
full integration into existing structures,
113
non-integration into existing structures,
112
partial assimilation to existing structures,
112
90-percent-complete Syndrome, *8*
Noise, 205–206
Non-executable methods, 170–171
Norden Bombsight, 211–212
Notational system, 88
Numbered lists, 87
Numbers, 75–76

O

Object-oriented models, 180
Olduvai Gorge, Tanzania, 1
Ontologists, 183, 196
Operational variation, 149
Optimal development time, 126–128
Optimal termination, 15
Organizational resource coordinator,
182–183
Outsourcing, 128–129
Overlapped waterfall model, 55–56

P

Packages, 129
Pair programming, 105, 113–114

Palmisano, Sam, 163
Papyrus, 2
Persistency, in knowledge media, *3*, 215–217
Personified requirements, 115–116
Phases, 63, *64*
PLAN assembly language, 135
Porting, 9
Post-Sprint (Scrum), 119
*Practical Guide to Feature-Driven
Development, A*, 121
Pre-Print stage (Scrum), 118–119
Problem-solving teams, 21–22
Process
compared with Agile methods, *159*
creating, 32–33
engineers in, 34–35
and Five Orders of Ignorance, *26, 36*
getting, 33–34
granular, 9–10
ignorance of, 143–144
initiatives, 129–130
inventing, 25
knowledge acquisition in, 27, 30–32
lack of, 143, *155*
mapping to Five Orders of Ignorance, *21*
meta, 9, 28–30
vs. meta-process, *29*
Orders of Ignorance, 239–241
problems in, 27, 102–103
purpose of, 26–27, 35–36
Third Order of Ignorance (3OI), 40–41
traditional view of, *173*
Process definition, 5, 16
Process engineers, 34–35, 183
Process flow
conformed, *23*
layers of, *25*
modified, *24*
Process groups, 15, 34–35
Process labs, 17
Process-metaprocess hierarchy, *29*
Process Value Propositions, 30, 32–33
Product and system models, 83
Product backlog, 118–119
Program libraries, 83
Programmable interface, 174–176
Programmable tool sets, components of, *175*
Programming languages, 167–168
Project models, 81
Projects
behavioral domains, *93*
collective ownership of, 105
defect discovery in, 136–137
design dependence of knowledge, 68–69

example of, 194–203
jet plane metaphor in, *62*
knowledge variability in time, 68
Lemma of Eternal Lateness, 33
life cycle variables in, 70–72
models, 81
process discovery in, 24
range of unknown unknowns in, 67–68
unknowns in, 24
variable rate of learning in, 69–70
Zeppelin metaphor in, *61*
Project teams
example of, 194–203
future, *182*
radical setup, 181–187
traditional view of, *181*
types of, 20–23
Prototyping, 234–235
Psychology of Computer Programming, 135

R

Rate of development, 103
Rational Unified Process (RUP), *65*
Real systems, 81
Refactoring, 111
Regression test, 115
Release backlog, 119
Remote Administrator log-in, 30
Repeatability, 19, 131–132
Repository engineers, 184–185
Requirements, 91–93
    domain, 93
    models, *83*
Requirements stages (waterfall model), 52
Research groups, 22–23
Resource and environment models, 81
RNA (ribonucleic acid), 208–209
Rocks, 2, 211
Roman numeral system, 80
Royce, Winston, 51
Rule of Process Bifurcation, 13
RUP (Rational Unified Process), *65*

S

Scalability, 130–131
Schwaber, Ken, 118
Scope, 169–170
Script kiddies, 168
Scripts, 32
Scrum, 118–119
Second Law of Software Process, 13–14, 29

Second Order of Ignorance (2OI), 7–9,
    141–143
and Agile, 153
in knowledge acquisition, 22, 236–237
in systems development, 238
SEI (Software Engineering Institute), 20
Self-generating systems, 217
Self-modification, in knowledge media, *3*, 217
Self-referential statements, 12, 33
Sequencing, 91
Sequential numbers, 77
Skill transfer, spectrum of, *186*
Software, 213–215
    artifacts, 43
    knowledge content of, 223
    as one of main repositories of knowledge,
        223–224
    vs. other knowledge media, *4*
    product in, 227
    properties of, *3*, 221–222
Software development, 4–5
    conventions in, 85
    as an educational activity, 187–189
    future of, 161
    knowledge acquisition in, 27
    life cycles of, 51
Software/domain knowledge, ratio of, *165*
Software engineering, 172
    demise of, 163–166
    domain interdependent, 180
    domain specific, 179–180
    domain variable, 180
    executable, 176–177
    model-based, 172–173
    model interdependent, 180–181
    object-oriented, 180
    programmable interface, 174–176
    variable rule based, 176
Software Engineering Institute (SEI), 20
Software knowledge, *165*
Software process, 19–20; *see also* Process
    anthromorphic models, 173
    armour's observation on, 14
    creating, 32–33
    domains, *82*
    effective, 11–12
    embedded models, *82*
    engineers in, 34–35
    getting, 33–34
    inventing, 25
    knowledge acquisition in, 27, 30–32
    mapping to Five Orders of Ignorance, *21*
    problem of, 27
    purpose of, 26–27, 35–36

translatable, 177–179
twin goals of optimal termination in, 15
Software teams, 23–24
Software testing, 42
Software wizards, *31*
Solid-line knowledge, 230
Spectrum of ignorance, *138*
Sperry, Elmer, 212
Sprint (Scrum), 119
Standardization, 175
Standards and process models, 81
States, 91
Story actors, 115–116
Structured analysis, 40
Structure of Scientific Revolutions, 111
Subordinate chunks, 87
Sumerian clay tablets, 213
Systems development
    effective, 11–12
    and Five Orders of Ignorance, 237–239
    getting processes in, 33–34
    methods and models, 93–94
    modeling activities in, 80–81
    people in, 94–95
    Rule of Process Bifurcation in, 13
Systems models, 81, 83
System test, 53
System test representatives, 185–186

T

Table of contents, 87
Tactical teams, 20–21
Tapscott, Don, 162
Tasks, 62
    dependencies, 63
    and project trends, *71*
Teams, types of, 20–23
Test cell switch DFD, *44, 45, 47*
Testers, 185
Testing, 62–63
    maturity of, 48
    software, 41
    system, 53
Testing languages, 149
Test phases, 99–100
Test system, 43–48, 149–150
Text documents, 85–87
Text models, *86*
Textual lists, 89
Third Law of Software Process, 15–16, 35
Third Order of Ignorance (3OI), 7, 143–144;
    see also Five Orders of Ignorance

and Agile, 153–157
cycles, *41*
definition of, 9–10
in knowledge acquisition, 237
processes, 40–41
in systems development, 238–239
Timing, 91
Tool artifacts, 169
Training, 189
Transform models, 74
Transforms, 91, 92
Translatable models, 177–179
Twin Goals of Optimal Termination, 15

U

Unintentional process ignorance, 143, *155*
Unit test, 53
Universal Modeling Language (UML), 74
Unknown knowledge, 158
Unknown unknowns, 67–68
Update frequency, in knowledge media, *3*,
    217
Useable requirements, 52
Usefulness dilemma, 27–28
Users, 184

V

Validation, 63, 229–230
Value of process, 102
Variable rule based methods, 176
Venus of Willendorf, 213
Verification, 41, 62
Volatility, 215–217

W

Waterfall life cycle model, 51; *see also* Life
    cycles
    embedded, *98*, 99–100
    with external feedback, *100*
    feedback, *99*, 101–102
    highest level of, 10
    overlapped, 55–56
    premise of, 52–53
    structure of, *52, 98*
    V-shaped, 112
Weinberg, Jerry, 135
Windows operating system, 14
Wisdom, 206
Work product dependencies, 63
Work products, 62

X

XP (Extreme Programming), 109; *see also* Agile methods
  Code Science, 115
  coding standards, 115
  collective ownership in, 113–114
  continuous integration in, 114
  limited work-week in, 114
  on-site customer in, 114
  pair programming in, 113–114
  planning game in, 109–110
  refactoring in, 111
  simple design in, 110–111
  small releases in, 110
  testing, 112
  use of metaphor in, 110

Y

Yourdon convention, 40

Z

Zeppelins, 57–59
Zeroth Order of Ignorance (0OI), 7–8, 139–140; *see also* Five Orders of Ignorance
  and Agile, 145–148
  in knowledge acquisition, 236
  in systems development, 238
  in tactical knowledge acquisition, 21

Printed and bound by CPI Group (UK) Ltd, Croydon, CR0 4YY

17/10/2024

01775692-0003